D0906602

HEROES & HERETICS

of the Reformation

HEROES &
HERETICS

of the Reformation

Phillip Campbell

TAN Books
Charlotte, North Carolina

Cover design by Caroline Kiser

Library of Congress Control Number: 2017944220

ISBN: 978-1-5051-0870-5

Published in the United States by
TAN Books
P.O. Box 410487
Charlotte, NC 28241
www.TANBooks.com

Printed and Bound in the United States of America.

To all my students, current and former—especially the history nerds

I would also like to thank Ryan Grant for his help with chapter 8.

Contents

Introduction

Reformation. As soon as the word is uttered, we immediately realize we are dealing with a loaded term. It implies two agents, an active and a passive—one initiating reform, the other the object of reform. What was being reformed? Was it truly in need of reform? What constituted the reform? Who was behind the reform, and what were their motives? These are "big" questions, the answers to which are inextricably linked to other questions, which are difficult to answer without an appeal to principles beyond history.

When historians refer to the Reformation, they are referring to both a series of events as well as a general epoch—or perhaps a general epoch characterized by a certain series of events. The events of the Reformation era brought the Catholic Church into conflict with various sectarian movements that were united essentially by their rejection of the Catholic Church's claims, as well as its prominent role in medieval civilization, but divided on many other critical points. How long this conflict continued depends upon whom you ask. The year 1648 is a common cut-off date for the Reformation, as that year marks the Peace of Westphalia that ended the Thirty Years' War, the last of Europe's religious wars.

Others might draw the era out until 1689, the so-called "Glorious Revolution" in England that saw the overthrow of James II, the last Catholic king of England, by Protestant parliamentarians.

For the sake of this book, I take the Reformation up to about the year 1598, the year King Henry IV of France promulgated the Edict of Nantes ending France's wars of religion. This is not to say nothing of import passed between Catholics and Protestants after this date, but by 1598 the basic contours of post-Reformation Europe have definitively been sketched out. Protestantism was firmly entrenched in those kingdoms where it had taken root, the Catholic Church had reoriented, dare we say reformed, itself in light of the decrees of the Council of Trent, and the theological positions of Catholics and the differing Protestant groups had been worked out.

Though this book makes every attempt at historical objectivity, it is certainly written from a Catholic viewpoint; that is, it presumes that the claims of the Catholic Church to be the Mystical Body of Christ are true, that the Bishop of Rome is the successor of St. Peter and Vicar of Christ. This does not mean the book universally "bashes" Protestants while vindicating Catholics. Every era has its heroes and its villains, and Catholics are certainly numbered on both sides. Rather, I have attempted with this book to understand the theological, social, and political causes of the Reformation through the experiences of some of the most important people of the age.

What lessons can we, both Catholics and others, learn from the history of the Reformation era? In this year, the five hundredth anniversary of the posting of Martin Luther's *95 Theses*, should the events of 1517 and beyond be celebrated or condemned? What practical benefit can we derive from studying this tumultuous period?

It is my hope that the answers to these and other questions will become clear as we journey through the sixteenth century. We will learn about not only the events of the era but the people who shaped those events. We will see how there is nothing more revolutionary or earth-shattering than an idea. We will see how new ideas concerning the nature of faith and the role of the Church in the world caused massive societal upheaval that effectively brought medieval civilization to a close and ushered in modernity. And we will do this through examining the lives of some of the major figures who lived through and influenced that tumultuous era, that age of storms.

CHAPTER I

Saint for the Age: St. Peter Canisius

It is May 1521. We are in the Dutch city of Nijmegen, an ancient, sprawling metropolis nestled beside the Waal River in the eastern reaches of Holland. Nijmegen is a typical Dutch city of the late medieval period. With the gently flowing waters of the Waal providing direct access to the Atlantic, the medieval tradesmen of Nijmegen have grown wealthy as merchants in shipping. Growing from its ancient center on the southern banks of the Waal, by the sixteenth century the city had spilled over onto the northern side of the river. If we were to stroll through the narrow, bustling streets of Nijmegen in 1521, we would see an eclectic blend of older medieval structures and more modern buildings, reflecting the growing wealth of Nijmegen's merchants.

Like most Dutch cities of the age, Nijmegen enjoyed a considerable degree of autonomy. It was governed by a municipal council composed of a cross section of the city's most wealthy and important men. This body in turn elected a *burgomaster*, a kind of mayor. The burgomaster of Nijmegen in 1521 was Jacob Kanis, a notable citizen of considerable wealth. We do not know much about the life of Jacob Kanis, but as the political class throughout Holland was dominated by its financial interests, we may presume Jacob was involved in various shipping ventures, as were most of Nijmegen's elite.

As burgomaster Jacob must have been perpetually engaged with local civic affairs, in addition to mediating the relationship between his city and his temporal lord, Emperor Charles V, the Holy Roman emperor; then, as now, political office was a paradox of privilege and grinding responsibility. And, of course, Jacob still had to attend to his personal business affairs.

In May of 1521, however, Jacob Kanis had other things on his mind besides business and politics. His wife, Aegidia, was about to give birth. We may imagine the scene in the Kanis home when Aegidia went into labor: servants bustling here and there, bringing fresh water and linens; the midwives attending to their mistress as she works to bring forth her child; Jacob pacing anxiously in the drawing room awaiting news of the delivery. Childbirth in the 1500s was fraught with danger; it was not uncommon for women to die in labor.

But such will not be the fate of Aegidia. It is not long before the sound of rejoicing is heard from the bedroom. The servants rush excitedly downstairs and bring the happy news to Jacob; his wife has brought forth a healthy baby boy.

The new parents named their boy Peter, after the prince of the apostles. It was May 8, which in 1521 was commemorated as the feast of the Apparition of St. Michael, in memory of a visitation of St. Michael to a small Italian town in the fifth century.

Catholicism was ubiquitous in the world Peter Kanis was born into. Like all infants, young Peter would soon be baptized into the Catholic faith. The most basic Christian prayers would be taught to him from his earliest years, teaching him to speak to God even as he learned to walk. He would attend Mass with his family at one of the many churches in Nijmegen, all clustered together in the old medieval center south of the Waal. The sight of nuns and religious brothers teaching, praying, and working in Nijmegen would have been as common as the sight of merchants and laborers. From the medieval St. Stephen's Church—the Gothic spire of which dominated the town's skyline—to the liturgical feasts whose annual cycle gave rhythm to daily life, to the private Christian devotions practiced within the tranquility of the home, the world of little Peter Kanis was a world shaped in the image of the Catholic faith.

But in May of 1521, that world was rapidly changing.

In far-off Germany, a young monk named Martin Luther was stirring up trouble. This Luther was a theology professor and Augustinian brother from Wittenberg, in the German kingdom of Saxony. Some years back, Martin Luther had won notoriety by challenging certain aspects of the practice of granting indulgences. Eminent theologians had studied Luther's ideas and found them to be heretical; Luther vehemently protested that his teaching was not heresy but grounded in the Gospels and the Church Fathers.

Several high profile disputations had failed to resolve the matter; in December 1520, Pope Leo X issued a papal bull calling on Luther to recant his teachings. Instead, Luther publicly burned the bull in the square at Wittenberg. Jacob and Aegidia—then around four months pregnant with little Peter—must have heard of these troubling events in distant Saxony. But at the time, Luther's protest was little more than a Saxon squabble. Such things were always happening; there was no reason to suppose it would not be resolved soon.

But, in fact, the situation escalated with frightening rapidity. On January 3, 1521, Pope Leo X excommunicated Martin Luther. The Holy Roman emperor, Charles V, opposed Luther; Luther had even appeared before him in late April, as Aegidia was preparing for her delivery. Throughout the spring, Luther won an increasing number of followers to his side, including the influential elector of Saxony, Frederick. Luther also expanded the scope of his protest. Beginning with indulgences, he had started to challenge the authority of the ecumenical councils and the Roman pontiffs. Deriving his ideas from his own interpretation of the Bible, Luther was now setting the Scriptures up as an authority against the Catholic Church and its traditions.

Thus, even as Aegidia was birthing Peter into the world, Luther was birthing what would become the Protestant movement. Of course, little Peter knew nothing of Luther or Saxony's troubles as he lay quietly nursing at the breast of Aegidia in their spacious home overlooking the Waal. But as Peter's life unfolded, amazing parallels would emerge between himself and the spread of Protestantism. For example, on the very day Peter was born—May 8, 1521—Emperor Charles V issued the Edict of Worms, banning the works of Luther and calling for him to be detained. As Peter grew, he would become intimately familiar with the ideas and personages of the Protestant movement. In fact, his whole life would be defined by it.

But in May of 1521, that was all in the future. The Kanis family had other more immediate worries. Aegidia fell ill and died when Peter was only five years old. Peter thus came under the direct tutelage of his father, Jacob, who no doubt acquainted his son with his trade and the art of politics from a young age. We do not know much about Peter's early years, but they are not difficult to imagine. It was probably a busy sort of childhood, where time with private tutors was combined with accompanying his father about his civic and business affairs. To be a burgomaster, Jacob must have been a practical, hard-nosed sort of man; no doubt young Peter learned from his father the virtue of discipline and the subtle arts of diplomacy. From the circle of merchantmen of which Jacob was a peer—ever keeping meticulous count of the last penny—young Peter must have picked up the sort of precise, calculating exactitude of mind that would serve him so well in his future career.

By the time he was a young man, Peter demonstrated considerable aptitude. He was disciplined, responsible, personable, and trustworthy with the tasks old Jacob entrusted to him. His father deemed it time for Peter to travel abroad to get a more formal education. In the High Middle Ages, a university education was generally reserved for those who intended to serve the Church or go into law. This was still largely true in the early 1500s, but by Peter's time, the universities of Christendom were also catering to a larger segment of the European population. In Peter's day, a youth of a well-to-do family might attend university simply in preparation for a secular career, either as a successful merchant or merely as a well-rounded noble who would be expected to manage his estates intelligently. Thus, in 1536 at the age of fifteen, Peter Kanis bid his father farewell by the banks of the Waal and set off to the University of Cologne in Germany.

Cologne was one of the most important cities in the Holy Roman Empire. Located on the Rhine, Cologne was a city grown wealthy from shipping. In this respect, it must have had a certain familiar feel to young Peter. Merchants were merchants, whether Dutchmen or Germans or English; as Peter strolled along the banks of the Rhine, he must have smiled reminiscently at the haggling, industrious merchants of the river.

But unlike Nijmegen, Cologne was a flourishing center of intellectual and religious life. The University of Cologne was one of the most eminent universities within the Holy Roman Empire. When Peter began his studies in 1536, the University of Cologne had been in operation for almost 150 years, but the city had an intellectual tradition stretching back much further. The cathedral school there had once been graced by the teaching of St. Albert the Great, the famous Dominican, whose relics reposed in Cologne's Gothic cathedral.

In those days, most universities offered a single course of study with very little diversification; Peter studied the liberal arts, civil law, and theology, along with every other student. Courses were all taught in Latin, the official tongue of the Church and the common language of Europe. It was here that Peter Kanis began going by the latinized version of his name, Peter Canisius, by which he would be known for the rest of his life.

It was also in Cologne that Peter first began to develop the interest in theology and spirituality that would eventually draw him away from the secular career his father envisioned and lead him into the bosom of the Church. Like all medieval universities, Cologne was essentially a religious institution. Chartered by Pope Urban VI in 1388, clerics destined for ecclesiastical careers had traditionally made up the bulk of its students. In fact, all university students, whether destined for the Church or not, wore the clerical tonsure and were admitted to minor orders. As noted, this was beginning to change in Peter's day, but it was still an education soaked in the intellectual tradition of late medieval Catholicism.

Religion was inescapable in Cologne; the city itself was a kind of German pilgrimage site. It was known as the German Rome; its cathedral as one of the marvels of Christendom. Built during the height of the Gothic era, Cologne Cathedral's double spires were the highest in northern Europe. To this day, the cathedral boasts the largest façade of any church in the entire world and is the most visited landmark in Germany. Absolutely dwarfing the other structures in the city, the imposing cathedral contained not only the relics of St. Albert but more famously those of the three wise men. The bones of the Magi were encased in a magnificent golden casket kept above the high altar. No doubt, young Peter must have spent time here in prayer before the altar of this magnificent edifice, gazing with wonder at the reliquary of the Magi and contemplating the mystery of Our Lord's Incarnation.

But it was not only contact with the monuments of Christendom that turned Peter Canisius to the Church. As the German Rome, Cologne was filled with eminent ecclesiastical figures who were to play a decisive role in his formation. Peter's discipline and devotion brought him to the attention of Johann Gropper, the influential canon of Cologne Cathedral. Presumably through the influence of Gropper, Peter was introduced to many other important clerics. Among Peter's Cologne friends were Georg of Skodborg, the archbishop of Lund in Sweden (who had been violently expelled from his diocese by Lutherans), the Carmelite monk Eberhard Billik, and the Carthusian Justus Lanspergius. The Carthusians were particularly prominent in Cologne and had a grand monastery there known as the Cologne Charterhouse. Peter knew many of the Cologne Carthusians, including the two successive priors Peter Blommeveen and Gerhard Kalckbrenner. Blommeveen (a Dutchman like Peter) had established a printing press and bookbindery at the monastery and turned the Charterhouse into a noted producer of Catholic apologetical works. It was Blommeveen's successor Gerhard Kalckbrenner, however, who would have a much greater influence on Peter, for it was Kalckbrenner who first supported the Society of Jesus (Jesuits) when they came to Cologne seeking to establish their first German chapter.

These eminent men of the Church no doubt exercised an influence on Peter, drawing his intellect more keenly to the truths of the Catholic faith and providing a balanced example of Christian virtue. But even more influential was Nicolaus von Esch, the theologian Peter took for his spiritual director while at Cologne. Von Esch was a theologian and canonist from Louvain, who gave up a promising educational career to seek Christian perfection living as a solitary in Cologne. Von Esch was close to the Carthusians of the Charterhouse; it was probably through Prior Blommeveen that Peter made his acquaintance, as von Esch, like Blommeveen, was a Dutchman.

Fourteen years Peter's elder, von Esch would be a decisive influence on Peter's spirituality. We do not know the precise manner of von Esch's direction of his promising young pupil, but we can imagine the mystic and his student wandering the streets of Cologne, their excited conversation moving seamlessly from theology to spirituality to apologetics and the turmoil in the world. We can envision von Esch passing on his most treasured spiritual books to Peter for his edification, or the two sharing secrets of the soul by the light of a fire on the cold German winter nights. Under von Esch's tutelage, Peter Canisius began to make real progress on the path to Christian perfection.

As a kind of urban hermit, von Esch was part intellectual, part mystic; he embodied the best of late medieval Dutch mysticism, but was also an exemplar of the rigorous analytical and literary theology known as "Second Scholasticism" that was common in Catholic universities of the age. The spiritual teaching of the mystic-scholar was quite similar to the spirituality of the fledgling Jesuit order. No doubt, von Esch's teaching helped dispose young Peter to be attracted to the Jesuits.

The Society of Jesus was truly a new foundation when Peter came to Cologne. The Spaniard Ignatius Loyola, along with Peter Faber, Francis Xavier, and three other young men, had made their religious profession in 1534, only two years before Peter first walked the streets of Cologne. Indeed, the Jesuits did not receive papal approval until 1540, the year Peter graduated from Cologne. Thus, he was in Cologne during the formative period in the history of the Jesuits.

At the time of Peter's second year at Cologne, St. Ignatius Loyola was in Rome awaiting the approval of the draft of the Jesuits' Constitution by Pope Paul III. Originally a military man from the nobility, Ignatius had experienced a profound conversion after being wounded by a cannonball that shattered his leg. Ignatius subsequently went on to organize the Society of Jesus as a way of bringing an almost military precision to the spiritual life. The introductory words of Ignatius's famous "Formula for the Institute of the Society of Jesus" stated that the Jesuits were to "serve as a soldier of God beneath the banner of the Cross in our Society," a company whose goals were "the defense and propagation of the faith and for the progress of souls in Christian life and doctrine." The formal approval of the Society's Constitution would not come until 1540. The Jesuits would become the intellectual and spiritual answer of the Catholic Church to the threat posed by Protestantism.

And threat it was; the Protestant movement was growing. The same year Peter Canisius came to Cologne, King Henry VIII of England had begun dissolving certain monasteries throughout England and seizing their wealth. By 1540—the same year Peter left Cologne and the Jesuit Constitutions were approved—King Henry had systematically shut down every English monastery and doled out their lands to court sycophants.

King Henry had initially been hostile to Luther's movement; he even wrote a treatise defending the sacraments against Luther's attacks. It was over marriage that Henry came into conflict with the Catholic Church, however. King Henry had petitioned Pope Clement VII for several years to annul his marriage to Catherine of Aragon. Clement had consistently refused to grant Henry his request, for reasons canonical and political. Eventually, Henry severed England's ties with the Church of Rome, proclaiming himself supreme head of the Church of England in 1534. English Chancellor Thomas More and Bishop John Fisher were both put to death in 1535 for refusing to be creatures of Henry's new state-church. After the break with Rome came the dissolution of the monasteries and the seizure of their wealth.

The events in England must have occupied the conversation of Peter and his companions throughout his time in Cologne. How his pious heart must have been stirred at the stories of the English martyrs More and Fisher, and of the many more humble monks who would die at the hands of King Henry's henchmen! Peter must have brooded with concern over the events unfolding across Europe. It must have become clear that for the Catholic Church to survive, she needed heroic, disciplined souls, both knowledgeable and pious. Perhaps this is what ultimately drew him to the Jesuits.

We do not know how well Peter knew the first Jesuits as a student, but we do know that he made the acquaintance of Jesuit cofounder Peter Faber in Cologne around the time he graduated university and that he was profoundly impressed by their manner of living. It was a time of decision for Peter.

Upon his graduation in 1540, his father, Jacob, wanted him to return to Holland and marry a wealthy girl he had hand-picked. No doubt, he hoped his son would continue the family trade and bolster the Kanis patrimony by an advantageous marriage. Peter disappointed his father, however, revealing that in February of that year, he had made a vow of celibacy. Thus, at age nineteen, Peter had committed himself irrevocably to the service of God.

After some time of discernment, Peter traveled to Mainz where his Jesuit friend Peter Faber was then residing. He made the spiritual exercises under Faber's direction and thereafter made the decision to join the Society of Jesus. He was received into the Society on May 8, 1543. His Jesuit superiors thought the talents of young Peter Canisius could best be used in Cologne, the city where he had spent his formative years and made so many contacts. Accordingly, Peter was sent back to Cologne to found the first German chapter of the Society of Jesus. The Society in Germany at the time was minuscule, but Peter Canisius would change that. He spent his time preaching in public and debating at the university, where it became evident that he was gifted as a preacher and theologian. He was ordained to the priesthood in 1546.

Peter Canisius would quickly earn a reputation across Europe, and his apostolic labors would bring him into contact with some of the most important figures of the mid-sixteenth century. He attended and spoke at the first sessions of the Council of Trent, spent time in Rome under the personal tutelage of St. Ignatius Loyola, and was personally selected by Pope Paul III to teach theology at the

University of Ingolstadt. Peter had a character that suited the Jesuits well: a combination of mental precision and personal affability, no doubt inherited from his merchant family and perfected under the hands of his spiritual mentors. St. Ignatius grew fond of Peter and personally entrusted him with missionary work in Austria. The region was then being rent asunder by Protestantism, causing many parishes to fall into neglect. Peter labored there with unceasing zeal, bringing whole parishes back to the Catholic faith. He was present at the famous 1555 Diet of Augsburg with Emperor Charles V, where the famous Peace of Augsburg that ended a generation of religious strife was negotiated. He would go on to found Jesuit colleges in Ingolstadt and Prague and became the Society's provincial superior in Upper Germany.

Who can enumerate all the accomplishments of Peter Canisius? He would return to subsequent sessions of Trent as a papal theologian, become a fierce opponent of the Protestants, and win a reputation for sanctity such that crowds surrounded his confessional and the altar where he said Mass. Further educational endeavors followed. He would become the confessor to kings and queens. He wrote a catechism of Catholic doctrine that went through two hundred editions and was translated into twelve languages during his lifetime. Even his Protestant opponents recognized his moral integrity.

It seemed that God had raised up Peter solely for the purpose of defending the Catholic Church against the errors of the day. Peter, like generations of Catholics before and since, believed that the Catholic Church, in union with the pope, the successor of St. Peter the Apostle, was the one and only

Church founded by Jesus—the Bride of Christ. On behalf of that bride, Peter Canisius spent his life in writing, disputation, and apostolic labors, seasoning all his efforts with heartfelt prayer that his toil for souls might not be in vain. As wrinkles creased his face and his hair grayed, Peter grew into a true saint, pure and precise in his knowledge and perfected in charity.

In 1580, Peter came to the Swiss city of Fribourg to found a Jesuit college. Little did he know this Swiss city would be his final home. In 1584, while traveling to a meeting of the Society in Augsburg, Peter made a pilgrimage to the famous image of the Blessed Virgin at Einsiedeln. While rapt in prayer before the image, he was visited by an apparition of St. Nicholas, the patron saint of Fribourg. The saint told Peter that he was to remain in Fribourg for the rest of his life. Peter obeyed the vision; once, when the Society wanted to transfer him, the citizens, city council, and even the papal nuncio intervened to keep Peter in Fribourg. Peter was eventually left alone and spent the remainder of his days writing, instructing converts, and edifying the brethren of his order who came to visit him.

By the 1590's, Peter was renowned as a living saint, shrouded in the aura of legend, one of the earliest Jesuits and a companion of Peter Faber who had personally studied under St. Ignatius. Young Jesuits came from across Europe to speak with the venerable old man, hear stories of the Society's founders, and receive his blessing. He was by then noted as one of the most eminent theologians in Christendom.

Peter was debilitated by a stroke in 1591. He lived on in simple retirement until his death on November 21, 1597.

Peter Canisius was entombed before the high altar of Fribourg's church of St. Nicholas, at the request of the local bishop. The Jesuits pushed for his immediate beatification, but his cause lingered until 1864 when he was finally beatified by Blessed Pius IX. The beatification led to a renewed interest in the life and works of Peter Canisius, and his reputation continued to grow. St. Peter Canisius was eventually canonized in 1925 and proclaimed a Doctor of the Church, a title so eminent it is shared with only thirty-five other men and women to date.

There is much more that could be said, but it is beyond the scope of this chapter to enumerate all the achievements of St. Peter Canisius. The point of our little sketch is not to provide an exhaustive biography of Canisius but to use his life as a template against which to view the drama of the Reformation and Counter-Reformation, the epic ideological struggle that rent the unity of Christendom in the sixteenth century. In this book, we will examine the most eminent persons, events, and ideas of the Reformation era—both those Protestants who rejected the perennial claims of the Catholic Church and the zealous Catholic men and women who defended them. St. Peter Canisius's life epitomizes the struggles of the age; born the year Luther was excommunicated, Peter came of age during the religious wars in Europe and later, as a college student, watched with consternation while England detached itself from Rome. As a Jesuit, he labored tirelessly in schools and parishes combating Protestant errors and modeling Catholic piety even as the Council of Trent undertook the same tasks universally. As a theologian, he became intimately familiar with the theories of

Luther, Melanchthon, Calvin, and the other reformers and combated them with an erudition that won even the admiration of his opponents. He built up the Society of Jesus throughout Germany even as the Counter-Reformation undertook to reform the Catholic Church in a spirit of austerity. Toward the end of his life, he finally found peace in retirement at Fribourg in the 1590s; when he died in 1597, the religious strife that had torn France apart for a generation was coming to a close. Peter Canisius found rest from his struggles even as the age of the religious wars was coming to an end.

We will continue to reference the life of St. Peter occasionally throughout this book, his holy life forming the golden thread that will tie the narrative of the Reformation together. But before we can begin to examine the complex historical phenomenon known as the Protestant Reformation (or the Protestant Revolt depending on one's point of view), it will be useful to take a step back and consider the world of early sixteenth-century Christendom, the world into which St. Peter was born. Before we can understand the brokenness of that century, we must first grasp just what exactly had been broken.

CHAPTER 2

The Exhaustion of Christendom

Traditionally, the outbreak of the Protestant movement has been taken as the beginning of the "modern age." This has been standard fare for most western historians. The twentieth-century French cultural historian Jacques Barzun traced all the essential elements of the modern world back to the ideological and political climate of the Reformation, in which he saw, in seed form, all the core characteristics of modernity.[1] What those core characteristics are exactly and what "modern" means could certainly be debated. Nevertheless, it is certainly true that the appearance of Protestantism signaled the end of the medieval age.

In this chapter, we shall examine the precise nature of that age, focusing on the political and religious landscape of Europe in the late Middle Ages. We must necessarily paint with broad strokes, as the medieval world was very complex. It is beyond the scope of this work to treat medieval history comprehensively, and after all, this is a book about

---

[1]   This is one of the premises of Barzun's magnum opus, *From Dawn to Decadence: 500 Years of Western Cultural Life.*

the Reformation, not the Middle Ages as such. Still, the Reformation did not happen in a vacuum. It was the culmination of an entire epoch of conflict that characterized the late medieval period. To understand the conflict of the Reformation period, we need to acquaint ourselves with some of the conflicts that contributed to it.

No epoch of human civilization idealized harmony as much as the Middle Ages. This may come as a surprise to those who view the medieval world solely in terms of its incessant wars and disorders. It cannot be denied that the medieval world was one of extreme turbulence. Medieval people were constantly at the mercy of warring nobles whose armies tromped across the land with impunity. Though agricultural knowledge was increasing through the late Middle Ages, a goodly portion of the medieval peasantry was only one bad harvest away from destitution. Roads were poorly maintained and infested with robbers. Around the Mediterranean coast, no one was ever completely secure from the raids of Muslim pirates and slavers, those corsairs who would continue to plague the Mediterranean into the eighteenth century. Plague and disease meant life was always an uncertain thing, and a common man who reached sixty was counted very old.

Yes, medieval life was chaotic. Is it not then a laughable contradiction to say that no people ever strove more ardently for harmony than the medievals?

No, for we do not mean that medieval life itself was always harmonious, but rather that it was ingrained in medieval thought that the world and all its disparate pieces were all parts of a single, harmonious whole. The medieval mind adored harmony and order; even if that order was not always realized in the chaotic lives of men, that was no reason not to enshrine it as the ideal. Medieval people did not let the dirty reality of how things are distract them from how they should be.

Following Christian tradition, the medievals believed all things were governed by God's eternal law. All-powerful and all-knowing, God created the world out of his own goodness and established it according to the rational principles inherent in his own nature. God's wisdom was manifest in the orderliness of the world—the way the rain nourishes the plants of the earth, the symbiosis between the bee and the flower, the circle of life and the chain of predator and prey, the beauty and mathematic precision of the cosmos, the manner in which the earth provides all things necessary for the life of man, the very complexity of the human body—all of these beautiful and orderly systems were reflections of the wisdom of God embodied in the very natures of the things he created.

Everything had its place in the universe. God created nothing superfluous. Every contradiction in the world was only apparent; everything was capable of being harmonized into God's order. This was eminently true of human beings, who alone among the creatures of the world were made in God's image. All the creatures of the world manifest God's order in their nature, but man alone, being endowed with reason, has the capacity to conform to God's law voluntarily. The works of man should thus mirror the laws of God. Insofar as any act of man is rational, it participates in God's divine law. St. Thomas Aquinas, the greatest of all medieval theologians, had written, "All laws, in so far as they partake of right reason, are derived from the eternal law."[2]

This may sound awfully heady, philosophical, and not entirely relevant to man's daily grind. To think thus betrays our modern prejudices. The practicalities of daily life were not divorced from philosophy in medieval thought. Philosophical truth and practical truth were both realities of the world, and hence could, in fact had to, be harmonized. For medieval thinkers, there was no political or social problem that could not be brought into harmony with God's law. Every contrary could be reconciled, and all people, even those ostensibly at odds with each other, could find their place in God's masterpiece. Nothing was more practical than philosophy.

This is a very ambitious idea when we think about what it implies. Imagine all the different disputes people can get themselves into! And the medieval world certainly had its share of disputes. Theologians versus philosophers. Towns versus country. Nobility versus king. Nobility versus nobility. Religious orders versus diocesan clergy. Pope versus emperor. Yet, despite the struggles endemic in medieval life, men kept faith that they could be reconciled. If people would simply bend their minds and hearts to the will of God, there did not need to be any losers; everybody could win. This was the ideal of the just society, where everything was in its proper place and everyone received their due.

How different this way of thinking is from our own day! The modern mind, following Hegel but especially Marx, has tended to view the world not as a harmonious whole but as a

---

2   St. Thomas Aquinas, *STh*, I-II, Q. 93 art. 3.

series of power struggles. For one group to advance, another must lose ground. In the modern age, we prefer to view the animosity between the haves and the have-nots as irreconcilable; it is inherent in the way of the world. Unlike the medieval system that mirrored the eternal law of God, modern man has tended to view the world as a brutal struggle to the top, full of winners and losers. "Red in tooth and claw," to quote Alfred Lord Tennyson, there is nothing harmonious about the world. Rather than seeing contradictions as only apparent, modernity sees essential contradiction at the very heart of society, with order being the special prerogative of the powerful. Modernity has inverted the medieval ideal. Indeed, when we get to the Reformation, we shall see the enshrinement of this inversion.

The medieval world was full of struggle, but the two greatest conflicts of the late medieval world were those between church and state, and between faith and reason. The former was the great conflict of socio-political life, the latter of intellectual life. It was in the heat of these battles that the foundations for the Protestant revolt were laid. Let us look at them in greater detail.

In the Gospels, Jesus Christ had taught, "Render therefore to Caesar the things that are Caesar's, and to God the things that are God's" (Mt 22:21). This was very easy to understand in the pagan Roman Empire, when Caesar and God were in two opposing camps. What, however, were Christians to do when Caesar and God were on the same team? In a Christian society, what should the relationship between the Church and the political power look like?

Traditionally, Christians thought of this problem in terms of the relationship between two types of authority, the spiritual authority (*sacerdotium*) and the political authority (*imperium*). It was a very tidy concept in the late Christian Roman Empire, where all political authority was derived from the will of the Roman emperor, and all spiritual authority was derived from the successor of St. Peter, the pope. Thus, the *sacerdotium* and *imperium* both had their respective representatives in pope and Christian emperor.

Of the two powers, which was supreme? Where did the authority of one begin and the other end? Pope St. Gelasius I (492–496) told the Christian emperor Anastasius that the authority of the Church was greater insofar as the Church's supernatural ends were greater than the merely temporal ends of the state. "There are two powers," he told Anastasius, "by which this world is chiefly ruled, namely, the sacred authority of the priests and the royal power. Of these that of the priests is the more weighty, since they have to render an account for even the kings of men in the divine judgment. You are also aware, dear son, that while you are permitted honorably to rule over human kind, yet in things divine you bow your head humbly before the leaders of the clergy and await from their hands the means of your salvation."[3]

The Christian empire and the Church both contribute to building up the kingdom of God, but each in accordance with the means proper to them. The *imperium* uses temporal means, and the *sacerdotium* the teachings and spiritual treasures entrusted to the Church by Christ; the state works with temporal things, the Church with eternal things.

---

[3]   Pope Gelasius to Anastasius, 1.

One is natural, the other supernatural. Each is supreme in its own sphere. That does not mean they are equal, however. As Pope Gelasius taught, the sacred authority is greater, since the Church bears responsibility for the soul of the emperor as well. Thus, the Church can pass judgment on the deeds of the state when they come into conflict with God's law, but the state has no authority over the Church.

In the Middle Ages, this arrangement was symbolized by an episode in the Gospels where Jesus tells the disciples to buy swords. St. Peter presents two swords to Jesus and says, "Look, here are two swords!" to which Jesus replies, "It is enough" (Lk 22:36–38). The allegorical reading the medievals gave this passage was that the two swords represented the *sacerdotium* and *imperium*, the two sources of authority in the world. In allowing St. Peter to wield these swords, Christ committed supreme authority to the Church; the second sword is lent to the state to help bring about God's justice in the temporal sphere.

One of the greatest medieval popes, Innocent III (r. 1198–1216), compared the Church and state to the sun and the moon. He wrote, "Just as the founder of the universe established two great lights in the firmament of heaven, the greater light to rule the day and the lesser light to rule the night, so too He set two great dignities in the firmament of the universal church . . . the greater one to rule the day, that is, souls, and the lesser to rule the night, that is, bodies. These dignities are the papal authority and the royal power."[4]

---

4   Pope Innocent III to Acerbius and the Nobles of Tuscany
     (1198).

From the medieval Church's perspective, the relationship between *sacerdotium* and *imperium* was very clear. The fullness of power was committed to the Church by Christ and was exercised personally by the pope. The state had a true and proper authority that also came from God but was subordinate to the Church insofar as merely temporal goods are subordinate to eternal goods. The state and the Church both work together to further the kingdom of God, but if the state should begin to act outside the realm of its natural authority—say, by suppressing the rights of the Church, promoting heresy, or corrupting morals—the Church stood in the place of God to exercise judgment over the state and its ministers.

This view, however, more often represented the dreams of canonists and papal apologists than the actual situation on the ground. The reality was quite a bit messier. The *imperium* did not necessarily like being subordinate to the *sacerdotium*. The fact was, for most of Christian history, the political powers generally never missed an opportunity to keep the Church ground down into submission. Bishops were usually selected by the king or local noble, not the pope. Monasteries were founded on the patronage of wealthy lay people and their monks expected not only to pray for their patrons but to heed their wishes when it came to the management of the monastery. In Germany, Holy Roman Emperor Otto I (r. 962–973) turned the entire episcopacy into a state apparatus by appointing bishops to the most important political positions. For over a century, the Holy Roman emperors claimed the prerogative of choosing the pope. In many realms, the king dominated the local church, often with the complicit approval of the clergy.

Thus, while theologians waxed eloquent about the Church's superiority, in practice the Church often found herself dominated by the whims of laymen. This humiliation was best exemplified by the practice of lay investiture. Lay investiture was a very common practice throughout the High Middle Ages, whereby a newly appointed bishop, before entering into his office, had to pledge fealty to his temporal lord. The lord would typically present him with the signs of his spiritual office, his episcopal crozier and ring. Many in the Church bitterly resented this practice because it seemed to signify that the bishop was obtaining his office from his temporal lord, not from the Church. Powerful lay people desperately wanted to retain the practice, however, for it gave them a strong degree of control over their local episcopacy.

This dispute boiled over into a conflict history remembers as the Investiture Controversy, which lasted roughly from the 1050s to the middle of the twelfth century. Under the leadership of the reforming Pope St. Gregory VII (r. 1073–1075), the papacy fought tenaciously against Holy Roman Emperor Henry IV to end lay investiture. Before it was all over, Henry IV would find himself excommunicated and his kingdom in rebellion; shortly thereafter, he could be found kneeling in the snow for three days before Pope Gregory agreed to absolve him. Eventually, the papacy and the Holy Roman emperor agreed to a compromise whereby bishops would no longer receive their staff and ring from their temporal lord but still swear loyalty to him for their temporal lands. It was not a perfect victory, but most historians agree that the Church ultimately got the better of the emperor in the controversy over lay investiture.

For a brief time in the twelfth and thirteenth centuries the Church seemed to have realized the order envisioned by Pope Gelasius. But that moment was fleeting. By the late Middle Ages, the landscape was changing. The old feudal kingdoms were consolidating; the nation-state was emerging, with its powerful central government and autocratic king. With their increasing control over the state, and with greater amounts of wealth and coercive power at their disposal, the monarchs of the late Middle Ages were more willing to challenge the Church's claims to supremacy.

The flash point for the church-state conflicts of the latter Middle Ages would be the taxation of the Church. From the time of Emperor Constantine, the Church had been exempt from taxation. By and large the political authorities had grudgingly respected this arrangement, although from time to time unscrupulous kings might pressure the Church for "donations" to the royal coffers. But for the most part, the Church was left alone in this respect, and those who tried too hard to secure the resources of Christ for the services of Caesar were threatened with excommunication.

Things began to change in the late Middle Ages. Professional armies were replacing the older, private armies of the feudal age. Most Christian kingdoms had expanded their civil service into a true bureaucracy. Then, as now, the demands of the nation-state were expensive and Christendom's kings were perennially short on cash. The churches and monasteries became temptations too lucrative to pass up. The vast majority of medieval Catholic parishes were not wealthy, but cathedrals or popular pilgrimage churches might hold vast sums of precious metals from generations of donations. Golden candlesticks, chalices, patens, and statues gilded with gold or studded with jewels all aroused the covetousness of some royals, who wished to put the ornaments of divine worship to use funding the wars of men.

One of the longest conflicts of the late Middle Ages was the running war between the English and the French over control of several French territories. The origins of this conflict are buried back in dynastic squabbles we need not review here; suffice to say that the English and French spent well over a century and a half in bitter war over the question. King Philip IV of France (r. 1285–1314), looking to fund his expensive wars against Edward I of England, began taxing the churches in his realm to raise the money. The clergy naturally protested, and the dispute came before the pope.

The pope at the time was Boniface VIII (r. 1294–1303). Pope Boniface strongly reaffirmed the Church's teaching that churches could absolutely not be compelled to pay taxes to the king against their will. He threatened King Philip and his henchmen with the strictest censures and clerics with excommunication if they helped the king. Philip didn't budge, however; he responded by cutting off the trade routes between France and Italy, thus putting financial pressure on the pope.

In 1302, Pope Boniface issued *Unam Sanctam*, undoubtedly the most famous expression of papal supremacy in Christian history. In forcibly taxing the Church, King Philip had asserted that kings had a special authority over the churches in their realm. In response to this, Pope Boniface invoked the teaching of Pope Gelasius and the imagery of the two swords to remind King Philip that it is the *sacerdotium* that judges the *imperium,* not vice versa. The pope went on to state, "We declare, we proclaim, we define that it is absolutely necessary for salvation that every human creature be subject to the Roman Pontiff." Kings are not above the spiritual authority of the pope; their very salvation depends on their submission to the Church's lawful authority.

When Pope St. Gregory VII had similarly threatened Emperor Henry IV, the latter did penance in the snow for three days. But at the beginning of the fourteenth century, times were different, and King Philip responded by sending a band of thugs to kidnap Pope Boniface and beat him. The elderly pope escaped the ordeal but was severely shaken and died three weeks after. Following his death, King Philip pressured the cardinals into electing a French pope, and the papal court was soon after relocated from Rome to Avignon in France. There it would remain for seventy years, a pawn of the French monarchy.

Seventy years of the popes residing in France would be followed by almost forty years of confusion during which there would be more than one claimant to the papal throne—the Great Western Schism. This period, from 1378 to 1417, was a time of bitter confusion for Christendom. At first two, and then three, rival men all claimed to be pope simultaneously. Each claimant had his own curia, his own papal court, issued his own edicts and his own excommunications. They all had their own political supporters among the different kings of Christendom, whom they courted for support. And when those claimants died, each curia elected new claimants who perpetuated the confusion.

The Great Western Schism was finally resolved at the Council of Constance in 1417, but it had done irreparable harm to the Church. The moral authority the popes had contended for throughout the early Middle Ages was squandered as the rival claimants all jostled for recognition. The schism also exacerbated nationalist tensions already flaring up throughout Europe, as rival papal claimants courted support from different kingdoms, which typically fell along nationalist lines. France and England were political rivals; therefore it stood to reason they would support rival papal claimants as well. The spiritual power of the Church had ceased being something that united Christendom and became instead another tool of division. The prestige of the Church was grievously wounded. The dreams of the harmonious relation between *sacerdotium* and *imperium* seemed less like an attainable ideal and more like a fantasy.

In short, though the Church had always taught her own supremacy and independence from the state, by the eve of the Reformation the rulers of Christendom increasingly felt themselves empowered to challenge this supremacy with impunity. And the Church was increasingly impotent to resist.

The conflict between faith and reason was the other great dispute of the late medieval world. Throughout the early Middle Ages, theology was the undisputed queen of the sciences. To be sure, classical logic and philosophy were preserved, but philosophy held a secondary place to theology. The medieval tradition had never been dismissive of reason;

following St. Augustine, the medieval attitude was summed up by the phrase *Credo ut intelligam*, "I believe so that I may understand." Reason had its place, but because man was fallen and his intellect darkened, it stood in need of being enlightened by faith. Faith did not contradict reason, but went beyond it, enabled it to ascend to heights it could not reach unaided by grace. Thus faith and reason were harmonized, working together to bring man to God

This all began to change with the re-introduction of the writings of Aristotle into the West in the twelfth and thirteenth centuries. There is certainly nothing contrary to faith in studying the works of Aristotle—the best Christian thinkers of the Middle Ages were steeped in his writings—rather, it was the new intellectual climate occasioned by the study of his works which led some medieval thinkers to begin detaching philosophy from theology. Instead of seeing each discipline as contributing to the comprehension of truth, some began to view them as two distinct or even opposing sources of truth.

The emergence of philosophy as a distinct discipline during this time provoked bitter debates on its place within the Christian intellectual edifice. Some, like the thirteenth-century philosopher Siger of Brabant (d. 1280), argued for a position known as the double truth theory—since faith and reason are two separate sources of knowledge, they might arrive at contradictory truths without detriment to either. Others remained faithful to the Church's traditional principles but profoundly mistrusted the exaltation of rationalism fostered by the new learning. St. Bernard of Clairvaux (1090–1153) was famously skeptical of the intrusion of philosophy into Catholic thought, and many conservative theologians of the day shared his skepticism. Scholars at the emerging European universities hotly debated the extent to which the writings of Aristotle and other non-Christian philosophers could be integrated into Catholic thought.

St. Thomas Aquinas (1225–1274) exemplified the best of medieval thought in his answer to the problem. The right relationship between philosophy and theology lies in understanding that since truth is a statement about reality, there can only be one truth just as there is only one reality. Philosophy and theology cannot come to contradictory truths; this, however, does not mean they do not have important distinctions between them. Faith and reason arrive at the same truths, but they consider them under different aspects. Theology is based on what has been revealed by God; as such, it considers truth as it relates to divine revelation. Philosophy is based on what can be known by reason unaided by faith; it considers truth as it relates to what men can naturally deduce about the world. The two disciplines mutually enrich each other. Theology still has pride of place because its truths are revealed directly by God and, hence, more certain, but philosophy can also make true and independent contributions to our knowledge about the world. By working towards an understanding of the truth from different principles, a more comprehensive knowledge of the truth is possible than either faith or reason could provide unaided.

Unfortunately, the harmony that St. Thomas envisioned was not maintained. As philosophy developed throughout the late Middle Ages, many thinkers became skeptical that the true nature of things could even be known. Some taught that there was no such thing as "natures" at all; human nature, animal nature, divine nature—these were not independently existing realities, only names invented by men to describe the various distinct things we encounter in the world. This was the school of William of Ockham, the Nominalists, from the Latin *nomen* ("name"), because of their belief that there really were no independently existing natures, only names made up by men to categorize things. It was ultimately a denial of the traditional Christian teaching that God created all things "according to their kinds" (Gn 1:25); a denial of faith in God's orderliness and rationality in creation. As the Middle Ages wore on, this kind of rationalism became more and more common. Nominalism would be implicit in much of the thought of the Protestant reformers.

The rationalism of the late Middle Ages was best characterized by the Humanist movement. The Humanist movement emerged with the Renaissance and flourished as the Middle Ages waned. As a movement, Humanism was broad and is difficult to define; it spanned literature, philosophy, politics, architecture, and more. But the core of the Humanist creed was the exaltation of the natural virtues above the supernatural virtues. Humanists such as Petrarch (d. 1374) and Erasmus (d. 1536) popularized Humanism throughout Europe. We shall revisit the Humanists in our next chapter, but for now we ought to note that Humanism, with its focus on the centrality of the natural virtues and secular learning, was another pivot toward rationalism and away from the medieval synthesis represented by Aquinas.

Though the Catholic Church and the Christian faith still retained a central place in European culture, by 1500 the harmonious vision of the Middle Ages had been grievously wounded. The medieval world was coming to an end, not because Christendom had been conquered by foreign armies or suffered from some cataclysmic natural disaster, but simply because people had gotten tired, weary from the intellectual precision it took to keep the medieval world in harmony. Men tired of having to balance church *and* state, faith *and* reason; it was so much easier to just choose between church *or* state, to cast one's lot with faith *or* reason. The harmony was distorted, and the outbreak of the Protestant Revolt would be the expression of this distortion, as we shall see.

In our last chapter, we introduced the character of St. Peter Canisius as a biographical backdrop against which to examine the events of the sixteenth century. We have surveyed the ideals and struggles of the medieval world that was coming to an end with St. Peter's generation. In our next chapter, we shall begin this journey by examining the intellectual climate in Europe on the eve of the Protestant Revolt in the person of Christendom's most famous Humanist— Erasmus of Rotterdam.

Chapter 3

Laying the Egg:
Erasmus of Rotterdam

In 1498, the troubles of the Protestant Reform were still a generation away. Martin Luther was still a teenager laboring through his studies in the trivium. Jacob Kanis was a young boy learning numbers and accounting in Nijmegen. Leonardo da Vinci was at the height of his fame, and Michelangelo was putting the finishing touches on his famous *Pieta*. The Renaissance was in full bloom, an age of artists and scholars and passionate exuberance. In London, a seven-year-old Henry Tudor, the future Henry VIII, was being tutored in Latin and French. And that year, 1498, the celebrated literary figure Erasmus of Rotterdam was arriving in England to mingle in the intellectual circles of the kingdom.

In this chapter, we shall consider the cultural movement known as Humanism through the life of Erasmus, one of its most famed scholars. But first, we must say a few words about the epoch that gave Christendom the Humanist moment—the Italian Renaissance.

The Italian Renaissance was one of the most singular episodes in Western history. Nothing quite like it has happened before or since. It was also paradoxical; we can immediately recognize the artistic and architectural styles of the Renaissance on sight, but if pressed to explain exactly what the Renaissance was, the sheer vastness of the whole movement leaves us groping for answers. Whether we discuss it as an artistic movement, or as something literary, architectural, or political, we immediately feel like we have not said enough.

The truth is that the Renaissance was all of these things and more. Yes, it was characterized by certain methodological advancements in paintings and perspective, and like other epochs, the Renaissance had its own architectural style proper to it. Certainly it had its own literati and intellectuals, its own political theory, its unique fashions, and its own civic spirit. Yet the Renaissance was more than any of its characteristics, considered alone or cumulatively. The Renaissance was ultimately a *zeitgeist*—a spirit of the times. It was a broad, overarching intellectual mood that colored everything it touched. The Renaissance was an ideal to which the men of that age bent all their aspirations.

And what was this ideal? More than anything else, the spirit of the Renaissance was an exaltation of the human spirit in the tradition of classical Greece and Rome but transfigured in the image of late medieval Christian piety. From whence did this extraordinary movement arise?

The invention of the movable type printing press around 1440 had accelerated the growth of literacy. With the advent of the printed book, literacy became more attainable to the common man and less a special prerogative of the clerical class. Fledgling publishing houses, mostly in Germany and Italy, churned out new editions of the Greco-Roman classics. Knowledge of the ancient Greco-Roman authors had never been totally lost in the West, but their works had been confined to a very small literary circle. With the spread of printed books in the fifteenth century, these works found a new and expanded audience. Playwrights, historians, philosophers, poets—the whole treasure trove of antiquity was laid open before a literature-hungry public.

The word *renaissance* means "rebirth," and throughout the Renaissance, we see a rebirth of classical culture and mores. Still, the Italian Renaissance was not the first renaissance in Europe; Christendom had experienced similar cultural movements in the twelfth and ninth centuries, both of which drew inspiration from the Greco-Roman tradition and integrated them into the Christian civilization of Europe. Yes, the Italian Renaissance was nourished by a renewed appreciation of the classical heritage, but we should not follow the modern tendency to see the period in fundamental discontinuity with what came before it. Most of the major figures of the Renaissance were devoted Catholics whose thinking was deeply molded by the medieval tradition. "Test everything; hold fast what is good," St. Paul says (1 Thes 5:21). The thinkers of the Renaissance diligently sorted through the gems of antiquity, holding onto those that could adorn the temple of Christendom. Thus, the Italian Renaissance ought to be seen as the final, greatest flowering of the medieval world, both new and old, as every renaissance is.

In our last chapter, we briefly mentioned Humanism as a development of late medieval rationalism. Humanism was the literary-philosophical school of thought that emerged simultaneously with the Renaissance. Humanism as a movement idealized a literate, virtuous public capable of engaging in the civic life of their communities. Though not essentially antithetical to Christianity, Humanism tended to emphasize the civic virtues: eloquence in the spoken and written word, public service, a well-rounded education, and everything pertaining to the formation of a virtuous, engaged citizenry. In many ways, it was a reaction against late medieval Scholasticism, which the Humanists rightly or wrongly tended to view with derision as too theoretical and rigidly formalistic. Their conception of the most important aspects of the Christian faith was much more personal: What does it mean to be a human? What is my ultimate purpose in life? What does it mean to love?

Thus, Humanism can be viewed as both a development of and reaction against what preceded it. In its search for wisdom, love of literature, Christian sensibilities, and pursuit of the beautiful, Humanism was very much within the late medieval tradition. But in its dismissal of Scholasticism, its emphasis on the civic and practical over the religious and theoretical, and its view of the classical world as superior to the medieval, Humanism was also a reaction against the late Middle Ages. It was a movement caught between two worlds, both affirming the glory and power of the human person and admitting man's dependence on the grace of God.

Many of the most famous literary figures in western history were noted Humanists. Florentine poet Dante Alighieri (d. 1321) blended the Scholastic tradition with the burgeoning ideals of the Humanist movement to create the *Divine*

Comedy, the most exquisite example of late medieval poetry. Another son of Florence, Petrarch (d. 1374), was a failed lawyer who turned his considerable talents to the study of the Latin classics. Boasting that Virgil and Cicero were his teachers, Petrarch developed a command of Latin that was second to none. Petrarch was a renowned poet; his love sonnets in Italian vernacular were widely read in his own day and continued to win praise long after his death; in fact, his name is used to refer to the style of sonnet he perfected and popularized.

Petrarch was a deeply religious man; in his book *Secretum,* he examines his own faith and the state of his soul in an imaginary dialogue with St. Augustine. The *Secretum* reveals Petrarch as a man torn between the call of God and the love of secular learning. He desires the goods of the spiritual life and the pursuit of holiness, but the glory of civic life calls to him deeply. The modern Catholic may scratch his head and wonder why a man might not be both a pious Christian and be animated with a lively civic zeal. But it should be remembered that, like every cultural reaction, Humanism tended to define itself in contradistinction to what came before. It would take time for Humanism to become integrated into Christendom and for the leveling power of time and reflection to moderate some of its excesses. One of the true tragedies of the Reformation is that it interrupted this process, depriving us of knowing what a well-integrated Humanism might have been.

Despite his deep religiosity, Petrarch looked with derision upon the religion and culture of the late Middle Ages. Like many Humanists, he saw medieval piety as superstitious, its people wrapped in ignorance. In fact, it was Petrarch who coined the phrase "Dark Ages" to refer to the medieval period. The world of classical Greece and Rome was the pinnacle of human achievement; the medieval Christian era was one of darkness. Petrarch hoped that a better world would come, that the medieval world would eventually pass and yield to a new age of the human spirit. In the epic poem *Africa*, he wrote, "My fate is to live among varied and confusing storms. But for you perhaps, if as I hope and wish you will live long after me, there will follow a better age. This sleep of forgetfulness will not last for ever. When the darkness has been dispersed, our descendants can come again in the former pure radiance."

The "better age" to come, and the classical age of the past, were like two eras of glory, between which were sandwiched the medieval age of darkness. Incidentally, this is why the medieval era is commonly called the "Middle Ages," a term which reveals the historical bias of the Humanists. The whole epoch of Christendom was like a dreary "middle age" that one regretfully had to pass through on one's way from classical antiquity to the glorious "better age" to come.

There were too many renowned Humanist authors to elaborate upon them all; Boccaccio and Machiavelli deserve special mention. But the quintessential Humanist of the age was not an Italian, but a Dutchman, Desiderius Erasmus (1466–1536). Like Petrarch, Erasmus was characterized by the contradictions of his age. However, unlike Petrarch, providence compelled Erasmus to sort out his own views against the backdrop of the Protestant Reformation.

In an age when one's parentage could largely determine social mobility, Erasmus was not dealt an easy hand. He was the illegitimate son of a priest and his common-law wife. Despite the unorthodox nature of his parents' union, they both doted on the boy and cared for him as best they could. The unconventional family resided at Gouda, a town a few miles from Rotterdam in Holland.

At age nine, his parents sent Erasmus to the school of the famous Humanist Hegius at Deventer in central Netherlands. There, the talented scholar awakened in the young boy a love for the humanities. Erasmus blossomed as a student, demonstrating a very strong memory and a broad comprehension. He developed a love for the classics and mastered Latin early on. However, his idyllic days at Deventer were cut short by the death of his parents from the plague. Erasmus passed under the guardianship of some distant relatives, who possessed neither affection for the boy nor deep concern for his studies. He was summarily packed up and shipped off to the monastery school at Hertogenbosch in Brabant in 1483, the same year Martin Luther was born.

Monastic education at the time was still centered on the late medieval Scholasticism the Humanists despised. Erasmus loathed his life at Hertogenbosch and considered his time there as lost. By the time of his maturity, Erasmus found himself a young man with considerable intellectual prowess but no worldly means. His status as a bastard, the death of his parents, the indifference of his guardians, and his own poverty all severely limited his options. Eager to be rid of the lad, Erasmus's guardians insisted he take up the religious life. Nothing was more repugnant to the young scholar than the secluded life of a monastery. Erasmus had been awakened to the world of letters and desired more than anything to be a man of the world in the Humanist mold. Nevertheless, the biting hunger of necessity finally compelled him to abandon his literary aspirations. Erasmus returned to Gouda and entered the monastery of the Augustinian Canons in 1486.

Erasmus would later view his entry into the monastery as the worst mistake of his life. He was not suited by temperament for the life of a monk. He thrived on engagement with the affairs and ideas of the world. He wished his service to God to be spent in the spread of knowledge, not in contemplation. His time in the monastery was joyless, and perhaps to his time there we can attribute his distaste for the contemporary state of Catholicism in general and monasticism in particular. It was some consolation that his superiors at least recognized his discontent and left him considerable free time to pursue his studies. The young monk spent hours alone in his cell studying the Greco-Roman classics and the Church Fathers. Erasmus was ordained a priest in 1492, by which time he had begun to develop a reputation locally as a talented Latinist and man of letters.

This was fortunate, for the bishop of Cambrai had heard of the young monk's reputation and asked Erasmus to accompany him as secretary on a visit to Italy. The trip never happened, but it got Erasmus out of the monastery. The bishop was so impressed with his companion that he retained him in his service for several years. Recognizing his thirst for intellectual engagement, in 1496 the bishop sent Erasmus to the University of Paris to immerse himself in the academic milieu of the age.

It was at Paris that Erasmus came into definitive conflict with the state of contemporary Christianity. Though
Humanist mores had begun to penetrate Paris throughout
the Renaissance, the University of Paris was still a center
of Scholasticism. The Scholastic method of instruction—
popularized during the thirteenth century by such master
theologians as St. Albert the Great, St. Thomas Aquinas, and
St. Bonaventure—had by Erasmus's day begun to grow stale.
A rigid formalism had long since replaced the robust search
for truth that had characterized the university in Aquinas's
day. For Erasmus, Scholasticism epitomized everything that
was wrong with contemporary Catholicism. He was so exasperated by what he perceived to be the stifling academic
climate that he abandoned his studies to travel abroad. He
supported himself by tutoring the sons of English noble-
men, which brought him into the circles of the English literary classes.

We began our chapter with the year 1498. In that year,
Erasmus received an invitation by William Blount, Baron
Mountjoy, to return with him to England. The coming of
Erasmus to England would be a pivotal turning point in
the life of the young scholar. Erasmus was inducted into the
society of the English Humanists, centered at Oxford and
Cambridge. Of particular importance in that milieu were
the young law student Thomas More, Fr. John Fisher, chap-
lain and confessor to the Queen Mother, and celebrated
Humanist and biblical scholar John Colet.

We have noted that from his time at the monastery and his
studies at Paris, Erasmus had developed a virulent dislike of
the current state of Catholicism. Like many other Humanists,

he had joined his voice to those of many others calling for reform. The objections of Erasmus to contemporary Catholicism were legion. What escaped the scathing satire of his pen? Like all good Christians, he despised worldliness in the clergy, but his biting wit attacked more than worldliness. He castigated the medieval allegorical tradition of scriptural interpretation as ignorance; Scholasticism was seen as the greatest perversion of Christian theology. He regretted that Christianity had become enamored with what he deemed hair-splitting philosophy, which Erasmus traced back to the Christological controversies of the fourth and fifth centuries. For monasticism he had the harshest critiques; the monkishness of Catholicism had wrapped a thick cloak of ignorance and superstition over the Christian people. Fasting, pilgrimages, the cult of the saints and veneration of their relics, the Divine Office, and the crudity of popular piety he ridiculed sharply, attributing them all to the perverting influence of Scholastic tendencies within medieval Christianity.

In some aspects, Erasmus's thought anticipated Protestantism. He appears to have rejected the divine origin of the primacy of Peter, as well as the sacrament of confession. Never one for the intricacies of theological debate, Erasmus's view on the Eucharist is difficult to discern, but he seems to have believed in a sort of real spiritual presence of Christ, similar to what the Protestant Zwingli would later propose. Like Luther, he would deny the indissolubility of marriage. In other respects, he seemed to anticipate the Enlightenment of the eighteenth century. For example, the purpose of the Bible, according to Erasmus, was not to record the story of God's supernatural interventions in the affairs of man, but merely to present a model of moral life. In this, he was positively Jeffersonian; Christ's teaching is not the Gospel of salvation but a kind of philosophical ethic about living a good life. Of course, such a naturalistic ethos obscures the distinction between Christian and pagan morality, but this did not seem to bother Erasmus.

These positions had necessarily put Erasmus in opposition to Christianity as it was practiced in his day. To a modern well-informed observer, it seems odd that an intellectual such as Erasmus was unable to sort out the distinction between a legitimate custom (pilgrimages) and an abuse (simony or nepotism). It is always, however, easier in hindsight. In Erasmus's day, pious customs and abuses often were so intermingled that it was easy to condemn not only the abuse but also the use. As such, the early writings of Erasmus tend to see Humanism as antagonistic to the ancient Faith.

It was perhaps providential that Erasmus came to England, for Humanism in England was much more moderated than on the continent. It retained a deeper grounding in the Christian worldview, embracing the best ideas of the Renaissance without rejecting the spiritual orientation of the Middle Ages. It was the English scholar John Colet who consoled Erasmus. Colet told Erasmus that his real difficulty was due to his equation of Scholasticism with Catholicism. Colet encouraged Erasmus to reconcile the Catholic faith with Humanism by abandoning the Scholastic framework and devoting himself to the study of the Scriptures.

This advice was balm to the troubled soul of Erasmus. He could never praise Colet enough; he later wrote, "When I listen to Colet it seems to me that I am listening to Plato himself."[5] Nourished by the advice of Colet and the encouraging example of scholars such as More and Fisher, Erasmus returned to the continent in 1500 to begin the most prolific period of his writing.

He published several works on various subjects throughout the first decade of the 1500s. He was a relentless voice for reform, and though he asserted that his critiques of decadent Catholicism were in no way meant to undermine the authority of the Church itself, his criticisms strike too close to the heart for any devout Catholic to be comfortable with. For example, in his 1503 work *Handbook of the Christian Knight*, meant to be a treatise on Christian morality, we find the following biting attack on the veneration of the saints:

> Now there are not a few who are given over to the veneration of saints, with elaborate ceremonies. Some, for example, have a great devotion to St. Christopher. Provided his statue is in sight, they pray to him almost every day. Why do they do this? It is because they wish to be preserved from a sudden and unprovided-for death that day. There are others who have a great devotion to St. Roch. . . . This has gone to the extent that each nation has its own. Among the French St. Paul is esteemed, among us Germans St. Jerome has a special place. . . . This kind of piety, since it does not refer

---

5   Erasmus to John Fisher, December 5, 1499. Erasmus, *The Correspondence*, 1: 235. Ed. Beatrice Corrigan et al. (Toronto: The University of Toronto Press, 1974), as cited in https://en.wikipedia.org/wiki/John_Colet#A_Christian_humanist. Last updated Dec. 12, 2016.

either our fears or our desires to Christ, is hardly a Christian practice.

Erasmus's other works contain similar barbs. While in Italy in 1509, he composed his most famous work, *The Praise of Folly*. Dedicated to his friend St. Thomas More, the work presents us with the figure of an anthropomorphized Folly speaking on the condition of society. From the highest classes to the lowest, all men prefer folly over wisdom. Folly's harshest critiques are for the pastors of the Church who forsake their spiritual call for worldly ambition.

Years before, Colet had admonished Erasmus to turn to the Scriptures. Erasmus's magnum opus was, no doubt, his Greek New Testament of 1516. Humanism as a scholarly movement advocated a return *ad fontis*, to the founts or sources of divine revelation. Thus, wherever Humanism spread, there also flourished an intense interest in Scripture study in the original language. Erasmus's New Testament was bilingual, featuring the Greek text in one column and the Latin Vulgate opposite. The work was an intense labor, for which Erasmus studied ceaselessly. The text was accompanied by his own commentaries, often featuring his by now trademark criticisms of contemporary ecclesiastical affairs. Erasmus wrote of this tremendous work:

> I perceived that that teaching which is our salvation was to be had in a much purer and more lively form if sought at the fountain-head and drawn from the actual sources than from pools and runnels. And so I have revised the whole New Testament (as they call it) against the standard of the Greek original. . . . I have

added annotations of my own, in order in the first place to show the reader what changes I have made, and why; second, to disentangle and explain anything that may be complicated, ambiguous, or obscure.[6]

Erasmus's commentaries on the Scripture depart sharply from the conventional methods used since the High Middle Ages. He elaborates on the moral implications of Christ's teachings and, of course, takes potshots at ecclesiastical corruption; he also takes extreme liberties with his assertions about the text, hinting that the Epistle of St. James is not apostolic, that Ephesians may not have been written by St. Paul, or that Hebrews may have been by St. Clement of Rome, for example.

The year after the first edition of Erasmus's New Testament, the German Augustinian monk Martin Luther posted his *95 Theses*, setting in motion a chain of events that would lead to the rending of Christendom. By 1517, Erasmus was at the height of his fame. He had been dispensed from his monastic and priestly vows by Pope Leo X (himself a Humanist) so he could pursue his work unhindered; he was on familiar terms with all the monarchs of Europe and was a scholar of international repute. The academics of Europe thus wondered what Erasmus would make of the events unfolding in Germany. Certainly he would support this fiery monk, who was motivated by the same reforming zeal

---

[6]   Erasmus, Letter 384. *Collected Works of Erasmus*. Vol. 3: Letters 222 to 223, 1516 (tr. R.A.B. Mynors and D.F.S. Thomson; annotated by James K. McConica; Toronto: University of Toronto Press, 1976). As cited in https://en.wikipedia.org/wiki/Novum_Instrumentum_omne. Last updated Sept. 25, 2016.

that burned in Erasmus? Had not Luther also spoken against the corruption of ecclesiastical governance? Would Erasmus lend his voice—and his pen—to the cause of Luther?

Erasmus seems to have initially supported the reforms proposed by Luther. Bear in mind, of course, in the very early days of Luther's protest it was not clear that a total rupture from the Catholic Church was imminent. Luther initially represented himself as a reforming presence within Catholicism, not a force hostile to it. Luther, too, initially praised Erasmus's fame and erudition and invited him to join the Lutheran movement. Erasmus, however, was not interested in lending his pen to Luther, being naturally disposed to eschew overtly partisan conflicts. He preferred a life of pure scholarship and intellectual achievement.

This was the beginning of the rift between Luther and Erasmus. Luther was deeply offended by Erasmus's refusal to support his movement and attributed Erasmus's position to cowardice. He soon wearied of the scholar. "My liking for Erasmus declines from day to day," Luther wrote. "The human is of more value to him than the Divine. . . . The times are now dangerous, and I see that a man is not a more sincere or a wiser Christian for all that he is a good Greek or Hebrew scholar."[7]

Erasmus, on the other hand, was shocked by the mounting violence Lutheranism was causing in Germany. As the situation rapidly spiraled out of control, it became clear to Erasmus that Luther's movement represented not a reform

---

[7]   Cited in Joseph Sauer, "Desiderius Erasmus," *The Catholic Encyclopedia*, Vol. 5 (New York: Robert Appleton Company, 1909).

of the Catholic Church but a rupture from it. This was intolerable to Erasmus, who had always protested that his criticisms were never leveled against the Church herself, only against the follies and abuses of contemporary churchmen. "I know nothing of your church," he wrote to Luther's companion Melanchthon in 1524, "At the very least it contains people who will, I fear, overturn the whole system and drive the princes into using force to restrain good men and bad alike."[8] Though he refused to join Luther, however, Erasmus advocated against his suppression and continued to affirm the need for a reform.

Erasmus's refusal either to overtly support Luther or condemn his movement drew ire from both sides. He had the misfortune to be a man who disliked partisan disputes in an age in which all of Christendom was being divided into two rival camps. Some Catholics blamed Erasmus indirectly for contributing to the moral climate that made Luther's breach possible. Had not Luther and Erasmus leveled similar criticisms of ecclesiastical abuses? Had not some of Erasmus's ideas anticipated aspects of Luther's thought? Had not the sarcasm and stinging jabs that flowed relentlessly from his pen over the past two decades subtly poisoned the minds of his readers against the Church? During Erasmus's own life, there was a saying going about that "Erasmus laid the egg that Luther hatched."

---

8   Erasmus to Melanchthon, Sept. 6, 1524, Collected Works of Erasmus. 10. (Toronto, University of Toronto Press, 1992). p. 380. As cited in https://en.wikipedia.org/wiki/Erasmus#Disagreement_with_Luther. Last updated June 8, 2017.

Erasmus vehemently denied his responsibility for the Lutheran movement. Perhaps he had laid an egg, but whatever Luther hatched was a different bird entirely. Though both Luther and Erasmus opposed certain elements of contemporary Catholicism, their orientations were fundamentally different. Erasmus, as a Humanist, leveled his critiques from a worldview steeped in the fundamental glory and dignity of the human person. Luther's view was that Catholic theology tended to attribute *too much* importance to the role of man. Thus, the former wanted man exalted higher, the latter to put him in his place.

Nowhere was this more evident than in their dispute on free will. Luther had argued that fallen man no longer possessed free will in any meaningful sense. Sin so obstructed man's capabilities that his will is fixed on evil continually. Only a unilateral act of God can change the orientation of man's heart and turn it to good. For Luther, this was a necessary consequence of God's sovereignty.

Erasmus bitterly contended with this position, authoring the scholarly treatise *The Freedom of the Will* in 1524. The work drew on a wide array of patristic and medieval theologians to establish the classical Catholic position that, while salvation is truly a work of God's grace, nevertheless human will is not irrelevant. Humans truly are free and must take responsibility for responding to the grace of God to work out their own salvation. In many ways, this work was ahead of its time and anticipated some of the deeper theological controversies about will and grace that would come in the seventeenth century.

It is a shame Erasmus's scholarly foray into theology did not get the response it merited. Luther retorted with *On the Bondage of the Will* the following year, a bitterly emotional diatribe in which Luther denied Erasmus was even a Christian. He reiterated his position that sin absolutely incapacitates the will of man and that to deny this was an insult to the glory of God. Later in life, Luther boasted that he considered *On the Bondage of the Will* to be among his greatest works.[9]

Erasmus responded with his *Hyperaspites* the following year, but the work was too long and scholarly for most to follow and did not win a wide circle of adherents. This fact demonstrates the fundamental difference between the appeal of Luther and Erasmus. Erasmus was primarily a scholar; writing in pristine Latin or Greek, his works were addressed to a very small circle of intellectuals. Luther, on the other hand, was a popularizer who wrote impassioned works in the vernacular to appeal to broader audiences. As time wore on, the persistent, scholarly voice of Erasmus was drowned out in the cacophony of popular diatribe that poured out of the Lutheran movement.

The outbreak of Protestantism forced Erasmus into a very uncomfortable position, but perhaps it was a blessing in disguise. It compelled him to take sides. His later works are more pious and defensive of Catholicism. In light of the

---

[9]   Luther to Wolfgang Capito, July 9, 1537, *LW* 50:172-173, *Career of the Reformer III. Luther's Works*, Vol. 33 of 55. Watson, Philip S. and Benjamin Drewery, trans. (Philadelphia: Fortress Press, 1972), as cited in https://en.wikipedia.org/wiki/On_the_Bondage_of_the_Will#Luther.27s_later_views_on_his_writings. Last updated May 13, 2017.

disruptions and confusion Protestantism ushered in, Erasmus seems to have come to see and appreciate the divine element of the Church much more profoundly. Though he was
always somewhat suspect to the ardent Catholic apologists of
the Counter-Reformation, he remained loyal to the Catholic
faith and the authority of the pope. By 1536, the year of his
death, the Humanist moment was passing. This was aptly
symbolized in the execution of Sts. Thomas More and John
Fisher the year prior. How Erasmus, by then approaching
seventy years, must have mourned with frustrated anguish
at the news of the execution of his two old friends. Erasmus
himself died suddenly from an attack of dysentery that came
upon him during a visit to Basel on July 12, 1536, a year and
six days after the beheading of his old friend More. His last
words were "Dear God."

Given Erasmus's ambiguous relationship to the Protestant
Reformation, we must ask whether the Reformation was a
logical outgrowth of Humanism or an interruption of it.
The answer is complex. Of course, the Humanist movement
immediately preceded the Reformation chronologically,
but we must not therefore assume causation. The worldly,
civic-minded leaders of the Humanist movement had very
little in common with the intense theological, sometimes
apocalyptic, vision of the reformers who cared only for the
glory of God, as they understood it. The academic appeal of
the Humanists contrasted sharply with the populism of the
reformers, and the wistful nostalgia for pagan Greece and
Rome was incomprehensible to men like Luther and Calvin.
The piety of the Humanists, especially in northern Europe,
was in solid continuity with the late medieval tradition.

Humanist exaltation of the human spirit was in diametric opposition to the depraved view of humanity advocated by most reformers. In this respect, the Reformation represents a rupture with the developments of Humanism. What would the intellectual climate of Europe have looked like had the Humanist movement had more time to absorb the medieval tradition and produce a balanced synthesis? The Reformation deprived us of ever knowing that answer.

On the other hand, the Humanist insistence on a return to the study of antique languages was adopted eagerly by the reformers, who advocated a broad study of Scripture in the original Greek and Hebrew. Humanist critiques of the corruption of the contemporary Church were sometimes echoed verbatim by the early Protestants; we have seen Erasmus even anticipated some of their doctrines with regards to the papacy, confession, and matrimony.

We must also consider the attitude of the early reformers, who, upon the breach with Rome, naturally assumed the Humanists would be among their allies. Luther and his associates instinctively thought Erasmus would be a natural ally of the Protestant movement. Why would the founders of Protestantism assume this if there were not some strong affinity between the aims of the two movements?

Erasmus was brilliant in many ways. He had a voluminous memory, a wit second to none, and was undoubtedly one of the most talented writers Europe has ever produced. Yet he was not a theologian, and he had little patience for the precise distinctions theology requires; such necessary distinctions were viewed as perverse Scholastic hair-splitting. In the fire of a reforming zeal, it is tempting to want to hack through distinctions and counterarguments in pursuit of simplification. And yet distinctions exist for a reason, and we discard them at our own peril.

Erasmus conceived of Christianity as a fundamental core of truth that had unfortunately been obscured by a layer of abuses. Christianity could only be restored to its natural, pristine simplicity if these centuries of un-Christian accretions were scraped away. Essentially, the Church of Erasmus was like a ship encrusted with barnacles. But this view was fundamentally too simplistic; like many others before and since, Erasmus presumed there was a very clear, easily discernible dividing line between the essential "core" of the Christian message and the various traditions and customs that had accumulated over the centuries. He assumed restoring the Faith was as simple as pruning an overgrown bush or scraping off a layer of paint to reveal the original wall beneath.

The truth is much more complex. Not only the Church's essential core, but the broad strands of its historical and cultural development are attributable to Divine Providence as well. For example, Erasmus assumed the primacy of the pope was a historical development due primarily to political factors. Yet centuries after Erasmus, Pope St. Pius X taught that the Roman Church became the head of all the churches, not through political considerations, but from Divine Providence.[10] Yes, there are many human traditions in the Church, but even the human traditions develop in light of divine doctrine, such that to simply hack away all

---

10   Pope St. Pius X, *Lamentabile Sane*, 56 (1907). See http://papalencyclicals.net/Pius10/p10lamen.htm.

custom simultaneously attacks the divine teaching at the root of these customs. The Church is not like a ship covered in barnacles; rather, it is more like a mature tree with a complex root system. One root might look insignificant or disposable, but to what other roots is it attached? If this root dies, how does it affect the whole organism? Not all roots are equally important, but every root nourishes the tree to some degree, such that to chop it off is to inevitably wound the tree. Whether Erasmus himself realized this by the end of his life is known only to God.

In the summer of 1536, when Erasmus died, Peter Canisius was preparing to depart Nijmegen for his studies in Cologne. Henry VIII of England was beginning the dissolution of the monasteries. St. Ignatius Loyola was tarrying in Spain after poor health compelled him to leave the University of Paris. Martin Luther was desperately trying to hold his movement together amidst growing disputes about the nature of Christ's presence in the Eucharist.

We shall examine each of these individuals in turn, but let us now turn to Martin Luther, the man forever associated with the outbreak of the Protestant Revolution.

CHAPTER 4

The Gloomy World
of Martin Luther

The loose collection of ideas that coalesced in the Protestant Reformation did not begin with Martin Luther.
Some of the theological positions advocated by Luther were
actually first taught by the English theologian John Wycliffe
and his Czech disciple Jan Hus in the late fourteenth and
early fifteenth centuries. As we have seen, many of the Protestant criticisms leveled at the Church were anticipated
in Humanist thought and writing. Nationalist rumblings
against the authority of Rome went back to the Avignon
papacy and further. As for ecclesiastical abuses and corruption, such have been detested by pious Christians of all ages.
The novelty of Martin Luther was not so much in what he
said, but in the dynamic personality of Luther himself and
the unfortunate timing with which he burst forth onto the
European stage.

Yes, though the seeds of the Reformation go back prior
to Luther, and though the Protestant movement itself was

much bigger than Luther, the name of Martin Luther will always be firmly anchored to the emergence of Protestantism. He is so intimately bound up with the events of 1517 that, rightly or wrongly, the Reformation will always be remembered as the drama of Luther. Regardless of who laid the egg, it is undeniable that Luther hatched it.

Before examining the fateful events of 1517 and beyond, let us take a step back and learn about Martin Luther the man, his religious formation, and the teachings that set the world on fire.

In the heart of medieval Germany there is a little town called Eisleben. Stacked neatly with stately late medieval timber frame buildings, its central district today looks much as it did in the fifteenth century when it was the home to Hans and Margarethe Luther. Hans came from peasant stock but had managed to become leaseholder of some copper mines in the region; his wife, Margarethe, was a hardworking townswoman. From their humble origins, the Luthers had managed to scrape their way into the middle class, though they retained a degree of rusticity. Martin Luther would later recall his father as a stern, inflexible man; he once whipped Martin so severely the boy ran away from home. His mother, too, could be cruel and demanding.

It was a hard life that Luther was born into on November 10, 1483. He was baptized the very next day on the feast of St. Martin of Tours and given the name of that saint. The baptismal font still exists, preserved in Eisleben's church of Sts. Peter and Paul, a late Gothic structure a few steps from the Luther home.

Luther would be the eldest of several siblings. As Luther was the oldest, his father Hans was insistent that the boy help the family climb the social ladder. Having worked himself up from the peasant class to become a financially secure townsman, Hans believed a career in law for Martin would help the Luthers take the next step. The family soon relocated to Mansfeld, where young Martin would attend school studying the trivium (grammar, rhetoric, and logic).

Martin Luther's experience in school was similar to that of Erasmus. He found the curriculum tedious and the manner of instruction devoid of spirit. Still, the boy showed great intellectual prowess and was received into the University of Erfurt in 1501 at age nineteen. Like Erasmus, Luther was disappointed in the rigidity of the instruction—the rote memorization and strict adherence to the forms of a decaying Scholasticism long bereft of its original intellectual vigor. Besides his academic complaints, Luther was also sensitive to the poor spiritual state of the university, which he likened to a whorehouse or a beer hall. Unlike Erasmus who left college to become an itinerant scholar, Luther suppressed his discontent and muddled through, receiving his master's degree in 1505 when he was twenty-two years old.

Luther began the study of law that same year at Erfurt but immediately entered into a kind of spiritual crisis. During his undergraduate studies, the loose morals of the university had upset him. Now it was the fluid nature of law that troubled the young man. Lawyers, by profession, flourish on arguing a particular interpretation of law depending on the needs of their clients. The lawyer presents one side of a case

here, another side of it there, stressing or suppressing different aspects of law from case to case.

But the mind of Martin Luther was not interested in
interpretations of things and sides of an argument, nor
mere aspects of the truth. Law thrived on uncertainty and
obfuscation. Martin wanted clarity. He wanted to know the
fullness of truth, to have surety about life and the world.
His dissatisfaction led him to abandon the study of law and
plunge headlong into the world of late medieval philosophy.

What philosophers nourished the mind of Luther? He
studied Aristotle, as did most intellectuals of the day, but
he was also drawn to the writings of the Nominalists, men
such as William of Ockham (d. 1347) and Gabriel Biel (d.
1495). For a time, Luther studied with notable Humanists
Bartholomaeus Arnoldi von Usingen and Jodocus Trut-
fetter. Humanism, however, was not palatable to Luther.
He imbibed from his Humanist tutors a skeptical attitude
toward authority—a trait that would have disastrous consequences later in his life—but the very "man-centeredness"
of the Humanist ethos irked Luther, whose view of human
nature was too pessimistic to assent to the Humanist glorification of man.

It was not just Humanism but philosophy itself that ultimately proved dissatisfying. What good was it appealing to
the use of human reason when the human intellect itself is so
darkened by sin, so mired in error, so captive to the powers
of the evil one? Luther sought a deeper ground of truth, a
certitude at the source of all other certainties, that greater
than which nothing can be conceived. He sought the living
God, and what could human reason say in the face of such

a reality? All the reason of Aristotle was dumb before the burning reality behind all created things. It was this reality, the Lord of Hosts, whom Luther sought to lay hold of.

Thus, philosophy drove him to the study of theology, especially the Sacred Scriptures. The sixteenth century had brought with it a renewal of Scripture scholarship. Biblical commentaries were ubiquitous in Luther's age. Luther threw himself into the study of God's word with zeal, seeking the solace that had hitherto eluded him. The study of theology both consoled and tormented Luther, just as the figure of God both fascinated and terrified him.

On July 2, 1505, something happened that would change the course of Luther's life. Martin had gone home for a visit and was returning to Erfurt. Passing on horseback through a deserted area, he was caught in a violent thunderstorm and was terrified; he took the storm to be a portent of God's anger at him for his sins. When a bolt of lightning struck a nearby tree, Luther cried out, "Help, St. Anne! I will become a monk!"

An essential part of any vow is deliberated freedom; no vow uttered so rashly and impulsively without the least discernment could possibly be considered binding. Yet Luther took his words as an unbreakable oath. He sold all his possessions and entered the Augustinian monastery at Erfurt on July 17, 1505, a mere two weeks after the incident. Hans Luther was understandably furious at his son's sudden vocation. For Luther's father, his son's decision was putting his education to waste; he might as well have taken all the wealth Hans had scraped for and dumped it into the Rhine. Tremble as he might at Hans's wrath, in the cloister Luther was beyond the reach of his father. Now he had only God to contend with.

Unfortunately for Luther, religious life did not bring him peace. Not that he did not throw himself into his vocation with admirable zeal; he fasted, prayed, made frequent confessions, and even made a pilgrimage to Rome in 1511. Despite all this, Luther was haunted by a looming sense of his own sinfulness. His superior, the eminent theologian and Augustinian vicar Johannes von Staupitz, counseled Luther to turn his mind away from his own sins and toward the merits of Christ, whose grace could change even the most hardened heart. Nevertheless, Luther began to fall into despair. The omnipotence of God was not a consolation to him, but a terror; whereas his superior saw in God's power the potential to make any man a saint, Luther saw it as the power to throw any man into hell.

Of course, it is both. The same God is both savior and judge; God's justice and mercy are not opposed to one another. True, between the creature and the Creator there was no similarity that did not imply an even greater dissimilarity, as the Fourth Lateran Council had taught, but that was not the end of the story. Through the Incarnation, God had bridged the gap between divinity and humanity in the flesh of Christ, such that St. Paul could say, "Let us then with confidence draw near to the throne of grace, that we may receive mercy and find grace to help in time of need" (Heb 4:16).

To Luther, however, the thought of God's immensity was so terrifying that it practically obliterated the bridge between God and man established in the flesh of Christ. He found it hard to accept God's mercy when preoccupied with his own inadequacies. He was unable to interiorize the advice of Staupitz—focus on the grace of Christ—and instead developed a crippling scrupulosity about his own sins. This scrupulosity colored the way he viewed himself and eventually how he perceived God. He was an insignificant, sinful worm in a gloomy world under the glowering eye of a vengeful God. This is an essential point in the development of Luther's thinking: the doctrines that would become the cornerstone of the Lutheran revolt were essentially born out of the anguish of Luther's tormented soul.

Luther was ordained to the priesthood in 1507. Staupitz sent him to teach theology at the new University of Wittenberg, where he would eventually become chair of the theology department. He was a popular professor, with his talks on the Sacred Scriptures drawing pupils from all over Europe. The focus of Luther's theological studies was the New Testament, specifically the epistles to the Romans, Galatians, and Hebrews. As he studied and preached on these books, he began to piece together the fragments of what would become his doctrine of justification by faith alone.

By 1510, Martin Luther had become morbidly scrupulous. As his duties increased as a teacher and a religious—in 1515 his order promoted him to provincial vicar of Saxony and Thuringia—his spiritual life became more erratic. He neglected the prayers of the breviary for weeks, only to return to them in a paroxysm of despair and exaggerated penance. He waxed and waned between unhealthily severe asceticism and appalling laxity. The very instability of Luther's religious devotion convinced him ever more firmly of his inadequacy.

How could a perfect, infinite God find any pleasure in his tainted works? Luther saw in himself only laziness, cupidity, and pride—the results of his slavery to sin. How could all the prayers and Masses and pilgrimages his wretched soul offered ever contribute one bit to his salvation?

Ironically, Luther's despair was a kind of pride. Catholic tradition teaches there are two ways to sin against hope: presumption and despair. Both are forms of pride; a presumptuous man is so prideful that he assumes he does not need God's grace, while a despairing man is so prideful he does not think God's grace is sufficient. He who despairs places his own sins outside the realm of God's healing power, thus telling God that the blood of Christ is not good enough for him. It is a most destructive delusion.

Luther was ultimately unable to break outside his own despair and see it for what it was. He alternated between ecstatic zeal and brooding depression, sometimes unable to feel anything but hatred for a God who would put man in such a dilemma. As he struggled through his scruples in his early years as a professor, he continued to study and lecture on the New Testament, which was his only solace. It was in this state of spiritual despondency that he first began to read into the works of St. Paul a meaning other than what Christianity had always taught.

The pivotal passage for Luther was Romans, chapter 3. There, St. Paul had written:

> But now the righteousness of God has been manifested apart from law, although the law and the prophets bear witness to it, the righteousness of God through

faith in Jesus Christ for all who believe. For there is no distinction; since all have sinned and fall short of the glory of God, they are justified by his grace as a gift, through the redemption which is in Christ Jesus, whom God put forward as an expiation by his blood, to be received by faith. This was to show God's righteousness, because in his divine forbearance he had passed over former sins; it was to prove at the present time that he himself is righteous and that he justifies him who has faith in Jesus. Then what becomes of our boasting? It is excluded. On what principle? On the principle of works? No, but on the principle of faith. For we hold that a man is justified by faith apart from works of law. (Rom 3:21–28)

In this passage, St. Paul emphasizes that the sacrifice of Christ renders the observation of the ritual laws of the Jews superfluous; Christ had shed his precious blood for all mankind, and therefore there was no sense in boasting of the observation of the Mosaic Law. Because all men have been redeemed by the blood of the Lamb, there is no more distinction between the Jew who keeps the Law of Moses and the Gentile who does not, for in Christ's universal salvation the power of God was manifest apart from the law. Circumcision, ritual washing, kosher dietary prescriptions, and such Jewish works of the law were no longer needed. Thus had the Church traditionally interpreted the passage.

Luther, however, read different meaning into it. For Luther, St. Paul was not speaking of the superfluity of the ritualistic law of the Jews, but the moral precepts of the Church. When St. Paul said, "A man is justified by faith apart from works of the law," the Church understood it to say that the virtue of faith opened the door of salvation to man without recourse to the Jewish ritual law; when Luther read the passage, he understood it to mean that a man's salvation depends solely upon an act of faith in God without any participation on the part of man whatsoever. The Church said men no longer had to do certain, specific things; Luther said they did not have to do *anything*. Essentially, Luther's reading destroyed any part for the free will of man to cooperate in God's salvific acts.

Luther thus began to establish an antithesis between faith and works. Faith, for Luther, was not assent to the truth revealed by God, but rather the sinner's total act of trust in him despite his sinfulness. The Catholic Church had traditionally viewed God's grace as operative through pious works. Luther saw God's grace in opposition to man's pious works. Projecting his own personal inadequacies onto the human condition as such, Luther concluded that sin had so blinded man as to orient his nature fundamentally toward evil. This orientation necessarily destroyed man's freedom, which meant that all man's deeds, even pious ones, were merely extensions of his own corrupt nature and held no value in God's sight whatsoever. For a person to think their good deeds could have any merit in God's eyes was actually a grave sin.

With human nature completely in bondage to sin, man's will enslaved, and even the best of his works no better than filthy rags, how could man possibly be saved? Here, Luther placed faith as an antidote to the false reliance on works. By an act of faith in Christ, the perfect merits of Christ become our own—not in the sense that Christ enables us to truly become righteous, but that his righteousness covers us like a cloak given to a beggar. It was a completely gratuitous act of God to which the sinner could not contribute in any way, neither by prayer nor by any pious deed whatsoever. All he could do was merely consent, and on that act of consent, all salvation depended.

Thus was the doctrine of justification by faith alone first conceived; it was conceived in opposition to what Luther believed was a slavish dependence on our own good deeds. The saddest thing about the story of Martin Luther is that he attributed his scrupulous condition to the Church's teaching on good works, although ironically he was living in direct opposition to everything the Catholic tradition taught and his confessors advised. Never had Catholic tradition taught that a man is saved by his own works; such was the heresy of Pelagianism, which the Church had soundly condemned in the fifth century. Neither Luther's spiritual director nor any Catholic saint or authority had counseled any person to make their own sinfulness the fundamental reality in one's relationship with God apart from the grace of Christ to remedy that sinfulness. "I can do all things in him who strengthens me" (Phil 4:13); this has been the dynamic truth in the heart of every Catholic saint since time immemorial. What Luther was rebelling against was not Catholic doctrine, but a convoluted caricature of Catholicism created by a tragic conflux of his own insecurities and his faulty view of God.

Luther may have continued struggling with his scruples and working out his doctrine of justification by faith alone in the privacy of his cell at Wittenberg had he not been living and teaching while a notable scandal was unfolding in the German church.

Pope Leo X was a portly man of the famous house of Medici. The Medicis were the dominant family in Florence and renowned for their Humanist sensibilities and patronage of the arts. As a Medici, Pope Leo followed in the footsteps of his family by using the wealth and influence of the papacy to beautify Rome in the style of the Italian Renaissance. Consequently, Rome in the time of Pope Leo was abuzz with artistic projects. The pope had appointed none other than the great Raphael as custodian of the classical antiquities of the city. Everywhere throughout the city, beautiful works were being created. Throughout the fifteenth century, Florence had been the artistic and intellectual capital of Italy, but beginning in the time of Pope Leo, that distinction was in danger of being usurped by Rome.

The crowning jewel of Leo's work was to be the renovation of the ancient Basilica of St. Peter's in Rome. The contemporary structure dated from the time of Constantine and was in dire need of repair. Of course, Leo's great vision did not come cheaply. Historians have debated the merits of Pope Leo's character, but all agree that thriftiness was not one of his strengths. The man spent lavishly on public and private endeavors alike, leaving precious little for the work at St. Peter's. The pope thought that perhaps the Christian faithful would be disposed to contribute to so worthy an endeavor, and consequently, he authorized the preaching of an indulgence throughout Christendom for the purpose of raising the necessary funds to renovate St. Peter's.

Enter the character of Albert of Brandenburg, archbishop of Mainz. That many ecclesiastics in the early sixteenth century were not living up to the apostolic ideal was common knowledge; much of the criticism leveled by Erasmus and the Humanists centered in on this very point. Archbishop Albert could be a case study in the problems of that era's German episcopate. Hailing from a wealthy family and nursing political ambitions, Albert used his influence to get himself appointed bishop at age twenty-three; in 1514, at age twenty-eight, he used bribery to obtain a cardinal's hat and the lucrative see of Mainz, which was also an important political post in the Holy Roman Empire that made Albert one of the seven prince-electors who chose the Holy Roman emperor. By all accounts, he was a man driven by the acquisition of mammon and political influence, only nominally attached to the honor of the Church of which he was a cardinal. After the Reformation had broken out, he was somewhat lax in combating the spread of Lutheranism in his diocese, especially after the Protestants of Magdeburg paid him 500,000 florins to leave them alone. It should also be mentioned that Wittenberg was within Albert's diocese; Albert was Luther's bishop.

The bribe that gained Albert his office had cost him a considerable sum, which he had obtained on a loan. Albert, however, had an enterprising mind. He knew the new Medici pope was looking for funds to restore St. Peter's and had recently promulgated an indulgence to raise money for the project. Albert approached Pope Leo and asked permission to supervise the collection of funds in Mainz. Albert proposed that he and the pope split the collection, with half of all funds going to Pope Leo's renovation and the other half into the pocket of Albert for the payment of his creditors. Pope Leo agreed to the arrangement and sent the Dominican preacher Johann Tetzel to Mainz to preach the indulgence.

What is an indulgence exactly? Most Catholics are confused about indulgences; Protestants and non-Christians tend to misunderstand them entirely. The *Catechism of the Catholic Church* says, "An indulgence is a remission before God of the temporal punishment due to sins whose guilt has already been forgiven, which the faithful Christian who is duly disposed gains under certain prescribed conditions through the action of the Church which, as the minister of redemption, dispenses and applies with authority the treasury of the satisfactions of Christ and the saints" (CCC 1478).

All sin brings consequences in its wake. The consequence for grave sin is the destruction of charity in the soul, which, if not repaired, leads to eternal separation from God. Because of the redemption merited by Christ, all sin, even serious sin, can be forgiven. However, the fact that we have been forgiven does not mean the effects of our sin somehow no longer exist. If a man breaks his neighbor's window, the neighbor may forgive him, but at the end of the day, the window is still broken. Contrition and forgiveness repair the relationship, but they do not repair the damage. Something further is needed; the window itself must be replaced.

Similarly, sin damages the soul. It weakens our will, disorders our passions, and prevents us from seeing things the way God sees them. It withers or destroys charity and makes it harder for us to persevere in virtue. This damage remains even if the sin is absolved. There are many ways to illustrate this truth: a patient who has recovered from a dangerous surgery is still weak from the rigors of his ordeal; a nail pounded into a board may be removed, but the hole made by the nail remains.

It is to rectify sin's disorders in the soul that the Church from time immemorial has prescribed penance. A man may be absolved of his sin, but if he is to regain his spiritual vitality and undo the damage caused by sin, he must do penance. St. Paul compares penance to the training a boxer goes through to discipline his body and bring it into submission (see 1 Cor 9:27). The various traditional penances the Church has always recommended—fasting, prayer, pilgrimage, almsgiving—are all meant to bring the passions under the firm control of reason, undoing the disordered effects of sin and, by God's grace, rendering the soul fit for union with God.

The problem, however, was that in the past penances were generally more challenging and some sins carried very lengthy penances. A notorious sinner returning to the faith or a person struggling with habitual sin might amass a discouraging amount of penance. For this reason, the Church instituted indulgences, from the Latin word *indulgentiam* meaning "pardon" or "forbearance."

When a penitent received an indulgence, he was essentially "swapping out" a greater penance or suffering due to already forgiven sin—either on earth or in purgatory—for a lesser one in return for some other good act. Indulgences are acts of mercy that the Church has the power to bestow; ideally, they should inspire a return to sound Christian habits and lead to greater devotion in the recipient. For example, a

sinner who might be obligated to years of penance is permitted instead to make a single pilgrimage to a shrine, or one
who was given a severe penance like fasting on bread and
water for a year might receive an indulgence that allowed
him to merely participate in a public devotion on a particular feast day to fulfill his obligation.

It is beyond the scope of this work to go into the history of indulgences; they are documented in the Church
as early as the time of Tertullian (c. AD 200) and are mentioned extensively in the writings of St. Cyprian of Carthage
(d. 257). (As an aside, indulgences are still part and parcel of
the Catholic faith, and for many people, they are important
parts of their devotional lives.) By the Middle Ages, they
were ubiquitous. When Tetzel came to Germany to preach
the papal indulgence, it was already a very well-established
custom that a voluntary contribution of money to a charitable cause could be an indulgenced work.

Tetzel has suffered grievously at the hands of Protestant
historians, who have portrayed him as an unscrupulous ped-
dler of indulgences who would recklessly promise anything
to a gullible public if he could get them to cough up a coin
or two. Tetzel was only an amateur theologian during his
German assignment; he had not yet obtained his doctorate
in theology, and it is certainly possible that his preaching
lacked a certain finesse that comes with experience. The historical documents seem to suggest that Johann Tetzel was
no better or worse than any other late medieval preacher
of indulgences. He traveled the cities of Germany dutifully, preaching the Church's doctrine of indulgences and

soliciting contributions for the pious work of the rebuilding of St. Peter's.

Unfortunately, the arrangement between Archbishop Albert and Pope Leo was the worst-kept secret in Germany. The gossip spread amongst the alehouses, university students, and monasteries that half the money from the indulgence was going not to St. Peter's, but to pay off the personal debts of the archbishop. The reform minded among the German church grumbled at this scandal.

But even more unfortunate was that Tetzel had to preach the indulgence in 1516, at the very moment Martin Luther was developing his doctrine of justification by faith alone. The doctrine of indulgences struck at the heart of everything Luther had been struggling with, for at its core, an indulgence presumes that man is an active agent in his own salvation—that, through his pious works, he can really and truly cooperate with the grace of God. This fundamental concept was in itself deeply troubling to Luther, but the added scandal of the arrangement between Albert and Pope Leo aroused his burning indignation.

He sat down and penned a work entitled *Disputation on the Power and Efficacy of Indulgences* containing ninety-five points for debate, a document which history has come to refer to as Luther's *95 Theses*. Luther's document was written according to a very common template when a professor wanted to propose a topic for public disputation. On October 31, 1517, Luther sent a copy of this document, along with a letter, to Archbishop Albert, as well as to Bishop Hieronymous of Brandenburg. He also circulated the document to a few of his colleagues in the theological faculty at the university, as well as posted a copy of it on the door of the castle-church of Wittenberg. None of this was particularly novel; it was a standard means of inaugurating an academic discussion. But what Luther unleashed would be anything but academic.

CHAPTER 5

A House Divided: Emperor Charles V

At the time of Martin Luther, Germany did not exist as we know it today. Germany was not a kingdom; it was a geographical-cultural expression, the way someone today might talk about New England or Creole country. Central Europe in the sixteenth century was the dominion of the Holy Roman Empire, one of the most important but least understood political powers in medieval Christendom, at least to the modern mind.

What was the Holy Roman Empire? The Holy Roman Empire was the creation of one of the most interesting figures of the Middle Ages, Otto the Great (912–973). In the tenth century, Germany was divided up into several independent duchies. Otto's father, Henry the Fowler, the Duke of Saxony, had more or less united the German duchies into a single kingdom. Otto continued his father's work and built a stable, powerful Germanic kingdom in central Europe, taking the title "King of Germany." After pacifying Italy, Otto was crowned emperor by Pope John XXII.

It is too much here to go into the history of the imperial title in the west. It is enough to note that through marriage, diplomacy, and warfare, Otto forged an empire comprising the wealthy cities of northern Italy, the fertile regions of Burgundy, and the various duchies that covered Germany from the Alps to the North Sea. Otto was a powerful ruler who unscrupulously dominated the Church. In Germany, he controlled episcopal appointments and successfully used the Church to bolster his power; in Italy, he took advantage of civil unrest and a weak papacy to extort the privilege of choosing the pope, a right which Otto and his successors jealously guarded for over a century.

The popes later freed themselves from the oppression of the Holy Roman emperors; in fact, the College of Cardinals was created in the eleventh century as a mechanism for the Church to retake control of its own papal elections. Throughout the Middle Ages, the popes and the Holy Roman emperors came into frequent disagreement over the control of Italy. From the eighth century onward, the popes had exercised power over central Italy through the Papal States, a smattering of territories that they ruled as political sovereigns; an arrangement that ensured the Church's independence from any foreign political influence. The Holy Roman emperors traditionally regarded Italy as within their sphere of influence and worked ceaselessly to break the power of the popes in central Italy.

By the thirteenth century, the popes had largely won this conflict. A more centralized Church prospered from better administration and the leadership of strong popes, such as Innocent III (1198–1216). The Holy Roman Empire, on the other hand, began to lose its cohesion and revert back to a loose union of principalities with varying degrees of autonomy. The Holy Roman Empire in Martin Luther's day was more or less a federation of states. Some of these states could be quite large and powerful, such as Saxony (where Luther lived) and Hanover; Bohemia was so large it was considered a kingdom in its own right, and its princes had the right to style themselves kings within the empire. Other member states could be quite small, no more than a few square miles under the control of some petty noble. The most important cities of the empire also had their own unique standing. Hamburg, Augsburg, Cologne (where Peter Canisius studied), and many others were designated "Imperial Free Cities," meaning they had a high degree of autonomy and functioned as city-states within the imperial structure. The republics and city-states of northern Italy had similar status.

The Holy Roman emperor was selected by an electoral college composed of seven of the most important nobles in the empire: three of them ecclesiastical, four secular. Upon election, the emperor-elect would be styled "King of the Romans" until he could be crowned by the pope, at which point he would take the title "Holy Roman Emperor." The imperial office carried a great dignity; throughout the Middle Ages, the emperors were considered the chief monarchs of Christendom, in theory at least. The reality was much more complex. The imperial powers were broad, but restricted. He could promulgate laws, but he could not levy taxes directly. He was the ultimate judge throughout his dominions, but could only exercise his influence through the mediation of imperial courts. He represented the empire internationally, but his power to wage wars or make treaties was very limited. In practice, much of the government of the empire was administered by three assemblies, representing the imperial electors, the imperial princes, and the imperial free cities.

Since the fifteenth century, the imperial crown had resided in the Hapsburg family, the imperial election becoming nothing more than the ratification of the Hapsburg succession. The Hapsburg emperor at the time of Luther was Charles V. Charles was born to immense power, as multiple royal lines converged in his blood. Charles's grandfather Maximilian was Holy Roman emperor; Charles's father, Philip, had been heir to all the Hapsburg dominions in the Netherlands but had become king of Castile in Spain through his marriage to Joanna, queen of Castile, heiress to the kingdom of Aragon. When Philip died in 1506, little Charles, then only six years old and already heir to Hapsburg Netherlands, inherited the kingdom of Castile, which he began ruling directly upon his majority in 1516. When his grandfather Maximilian passed away three years later, Charles became the Hapsburg heir-presumptive to the Holy Roman Empire.

This nineteen-year-old boy thus found himself in charge of much of the European world. By his succession to the imperial throne, Charles was master of northern Italy, Bohemia, and all of the various principalities and cities of Germany. By virtue of being a Hapsburg, he controlled his family's hereditary holdings in Austria, Switzerland, Burgundy, and the Netherlands—Nijmegen, where Peter Canisius was born, was under Charles's lordship. By virtue of his

Spanish heritage, Charles was king of Spain and not only of continental Spain but of all the land and wealth of the vast Spanish Empire, which in 1519 included the Caribbean, Florida, and all of western South America, with its millions of subjects. Only one month after Charles succeeded to his grandfather's inheritance, the Spanish conquistador Hernando Cortez would invade the Aztec Empire, eventually bringing Mexico, Central America, California, and all of what is now the southwestern United States under Charles's control. The scope of Charles's power and influence was truly immense; who knows what he could have accomplished had he not had the misfortune to have a scrupulous Augustinian monk named Luther as one of his subjects.

Indeed, Charles seemed well suited to the burdens his heritage placed upon him. Raised from birth to rule, he was intelligent, moral, and decisive. He spoke multiple languages and had a sharp wit; a phrase sometimes attributed to him has him say, "I speak Spanish to God, Italian to women, French to men and German to my horse." He was given a thorough education suitable to a prince and was equally at home debating fiscal problems, poring over matters of military strategy, or following an intricate theological argument. A true cosmopolitan, his attention would frequently be focused on Germany; his closest advisors were Spaniards; his heart was always with his home in the Netherlands.

Physically, Charles was peculiar. He had the long face, protruding chin, and vacant stare that generations of royal inbreeding had made a trademark of the Hapsburgs; in later years, he wore a thick beard to conceal his abnormally large chin. Nevertheless, he was active and possessed of a refined manner that made him pleasant to deal with but also capable of forcefully insisting on his demands when compelled.

Charles V thus had at his disposal all the wealth, power, and skills to become a truly great monarch. But political power is not a closed system; it is subject to violent intrusion from external forces and events that suddenly alter the fortune of nations and test even the most capable rulers. Like many rulers before and since, Charles would find his energy perpetually tangled up in crises he never anticipated.

In the early sixteenth century, one unknown variable was a rising sense of nationalism. Charles V presided over a grand empire, but one that was a polyglot mess of ethnic and language groups. Such had been very common throughout the Middle Ages, where a kingdom was not always defined by language or ethnicity. National and ethnic identities existed, to be sure, but it was much less common to define political loyalty by them. A single kingdom might comprise multiple linguistic and ethnic groups bound together under the power of some hereditary dynasty. If we were to travel back to the eleventh century, we would see that a man's political identity depended upon the feudal lord to whom he owed fealty, rather than the nation-state to which he belonged, for the practical reason that the nation-state, as such, did not exist.

But by the time of Charles V, the entity we now know as the nation-state had begun to form. Enterprising kings of the late Middle Ages had consolidated their power and territories at the expense of the nobility. Royal bureaucracies began to emerge that made governing more efficient, further increasing the royal power. As the boundaries of modern Europe began to take shape, a nascent national identity was also rising. Thus, if we were to leap ahead to 1500 and examine the question of political identity, the nation-state would be much more prominent.

In October 1517, when Luther penned his famous *95 Theses*, Charles was just assuming power as king of Castile and Aragon. Luther's treatise had raised fundamental questions about the Church's teaching on indulgences. He questioned the nature of repentance, its intrinsic connection with works of penance, the limit of the pope's power in remitting the penalties due to sin, and what was the nature of the Church's treasury of merits. The document aroused a great deal of interest; versions of it were immediately copied and circulated, making it as far as Switzerland and the farthest reaches of Germany by year end.

Archbishop Albert of Mainz, one of the original recipients of the theses, sent them on to the theological faculty at the University of Mainz. Though Luther intended to start a debate about the merits of indulgences, the theologians at the university immediately perceived that beneath Luther's inquiries was an implicit challenge to the authority of the pope and the Church. The theologians of Mainz did not approve or condemn Luther's theses, but recommended Archbishop Albert prohibit Luther from preaching against them until the questions he raised could be addressed. Albert was still uncertain and sent a copy of Luther's theses on to the Roman Curia for their opinion.

The theologians of the curia spent that winter poring over Luther's theses. Like the scholars of Mainz, they found in Luther's work an implicit denial of the authority of the pope. For example, Luther's fifth thesis states, "The pope does not intend to remit, and cannot remit any penalties other than those which he has imposed either by his own authority or by that of the canons." Indulgences are a remission of penance necessary to atone for the temporal consequences of sin whose guilt has already been forgiven, usually given for the performance of some meritorious act. Canonical penances can be imposed on a penitent by any priest or bishop, but the pope, as the supreme judge of the Church's canon law, has the authority to bind or loose any Christian from any penance whatsoever. This naturally flows from the pope's *plenitudo potestatis*, that is, his supreme juridical power within the Church. Yet Luther had opined that the pope had no authority to dispense a Christian from any penance except those which he had personally imposed, which, if true, would have signified a drastic denial of the juridical power the popes had exercised since antiquity. It constituted a serious revision of the traditional understanding of the pope's role in governing the Church.

Other theses were veiled—or not so veiled—critiques of the pope's prudential decisions. For example, thesis eighty-six asks, "Why does not the pope, whose wealth is to-day greater than the riches of the richest, build just this one church of St. Peter with his own money, rather than with the money of poor believers?" Here, Luther strikes at the indulgence being preached by Tetzel in Germany, essentially chastising the pope for seeking the collaboration of Christians in restoring St. Peter's.

The Roman Curia was sufficiently threatened by the tenor of Luther's theses to make Pope Leo aware of them. In February 1518, Pope Leo X asked Luther's religious superiors in the Augustinians to pressure him to refrain from preaching against indulgences. By that time, however, copies of the theses had worked their way into the various universities scattered throughout the empire. Though Wittenberg apparently never held the disputation Luther was hoping for, the monk had become something of a celebrity amongst other theologians who resented the St. Peter's indulgence. He had continued to preach and speak about the ideas in his theses throughout the period of papal inquiry. Luther believed he was defending the very Gospel itself, and attempts to silence him were fruitless.

In the meantime, Pope Leo asked the Dominican theologian Sylvester Mazzolini to prepare an answer to Luther's theses. The result was the work *A Dialogue against Martin Luther's Presumptuous Theses concerning the Power of the Pope*. This cumbersomely named document centered in on the idea at the core of Luther's thought: a denial of the juridical power of the successor of St. Peter. Upon reading Mazzolini's work, Luther apparently began to realize that his opinions had put him further outside the pale of orthodoxy than he had at first realized. He penned a response to Mazzolini, attempting to refocus the debate on indulgences and deny any attempt to challenge the pope's authority. By then, however, Luther had received a summons to Rome.

By summer of 1518, the controversy had come to the attention of the elector Frederick of Saxony. Frederick was a very pious Catholic (he allegedly had a collection of over seventeen thousand relics); he was also a friend of Pope Leo. Even as Luther was being summoned to Rome, Pope Leo had given Elector Frederick a rose fashioned of gold as a symbol of his affection for the Saxon lord. Frederick preferred to keep the Luther case a Saxon affair and petitioned Leo to allow Luther to answer any inquiries at home in Saxony. Leo agreed.

This was convenient, as there was an Imperial Diet being convened at Augsburg in October. An Imperial Diet was an assembly of the highest estates of the empire. A prominent ecclesiastic, the Dominican theologian Cardinal Cajetan, would be present to petition the princes of the Holy Roman Empire to join in a crusade against the Turks. Luther would be able to attend and present his case before the emperor and the eminent theologian Cajetan. Elector Frederick granted Luther safe conduct to make the arduous three-hundred-mile journey from Wittenberg down to Augsburg in Bavaria.

Luther was brought before Cardinal Cajetan on October 12. He prostrated himself on the floor and professed his loyalty to the Catholic Church, but when Cajetan began questioning Luther's teaching, the two began to argue. Cajetan was no lightweight; an astute theologian and skilled diplomat, Cajetan had founded the religious order of the Theatines and was known for founding hospitals in Viacenza and Venice. He was one of the most studied and formidable minds of the Church.

Cajetan focused on two points at the heart of Luther's teaching: the authority of the pope and the Christian's standing before God. In his fifty-eighth thesis, Luther denied that the pope had the authority to remit the temporal punishments due to sin through the Church's treasury of merit. Cajetan demonstrated that this was in formal contradiction to the teaching of the Church, which had affirmed that very point in the 1343 bull *Unigenitus* of Clement VI. In his seventh thesis, Luther asserted that a Christian who had received absolution for his sins had absolute certainty that he was in God's grace and need have no anxiety about his salvation. Cajetan responded that though absolution gave Christians a sort of moral confidence, it did not imply any sort of absolute certainty. No Christian could presume upon his standing before God in an absolute sense. "I am not aware of anything against myself, but I am not thereby acquitted. It is the Lord who judges me," St. Paul had taught (1 Cor 4:4).

The meetings went on for three days and eventually deteriorated into a shouting match. When confronted with papal bulls and the teachings of St. Thomas Aquinas, Luther rejected the authority of both, stating that the pope had no authority to institute any dogma teaching justification through any means other than Christ alone. Here we see Luther stumbling to further formulate the doctrine of justification by faith alone. Luther was willing to tolerate indulgences, sacramental absolution, papal dispensations, penance, and all manner of external works if it were merely admitted that these things were signs of a forgiveness already accomplished—declarations that a sinner *had* been forgiven, not the means through which grace itself was mediated. For Luther, any insinuation that grace could be merited through any pious work of penitent or pope was unthinkable.

Such, however, was not the teaching of the Church, which had always believed that men were truly cooperators in their salvation. True, sanctifying grace is ultimately merited by Christ in the absolute sense, but men, through penance and works of charity, can merit actual graces that render their salvation more secure, or as St. Paul said, "In my flesh I complete what is lacking in Christ's afflictions" (Col 1:24). When confronted with this teaching from the ecumenical councils and popes, Luther asserted that council and popes could err.

Exasperated, Cajetan demanded Luther recant or face the consequences. His authority as a papal legate allowed Cajetan to arrest Luther if he wished, but he refrained from doing so and Luther departed. He did, however, instruct Luther's immediate superior Johannes von Staupitz to exercise his authority over Luther to get him to recant. Staupitz had borne with Luther for years and tried to help him overcome his scruples, but when he perceived Luther's resolve, instead of pressuring him, he dispensed him from his vow of obedience. This signified Staupitz was effectively washing his hands of Martin Luther and absolving himself of any responsibility for the troublesome monk's teachings.

A truce seemed to have been reached by January 1519, when Luther promised a papal nuncio to keep silent about his teachings so long as he was not attacked. This was a concession to the elector Frederick, who was growing concerned about the attention the controversy was bringing to Saxony. That summer, however, the German theologian Johann Eck challenged Luther to a public debate. Luther could not refuse, and in the ensuing disputation, Luther pushed his position even further, denying that Matthew 16 conferred infallibility upon the popes. Hence, popes and councils could be and had been in error.

By now the situation was rapidly spiraling out of control. Elector Frederick remained in good standing with the

Church, but continued to shelter and defend Luther. Frederick resented any outside influence in his domain and wanted to keep papal power at arm's length. Meanwhile, other theologians had gathered around Luther, making him an informal leader of a burgeoning movement. Two of Luther's earliest supporters were Andreas Karlstadt, chancellor of the University of Wittenberg, and Philip Melanchthon, also a theologian of Wittenberg. Both men had participated in the debate against Eck and were vocally committed to the cause of Luther.

But the real danger was that the disruption was becoming political. Not only theologians, but now secular characters, too, began to see in Luther a luminary for their own ambitions. In 1519, Luther was joined by poet and publisher Ulrich von Hutten. Von Hutten was a bitter opponent of the Church in Germany. A Humanist intellectually but rabid nationalist politically, von Hutten advocated a general crusade of German Christians against the corrupt German bishops, and especially against Italian intervention in German affairs. In von Hutten's view, bishops, through their loyalty to the pope, were essentially agents of a foreign power, and hence they were all complicit in the suppression of freedoms of the German people.

Along with von Hutten came Franz von Sickingen, a renegade knight and imperial power broker. With several castles and a small fortune at his disposal, von Sickingen had variously fought for whatever prince would pay him best. Von Sickingen's interest in Luther's ideas was more crassly materialistic. If bishops could be dispossessed of their holdings, these vast estates could be taken over by secular princes. Von

Sickingen's castles would become places of hiding for the early reformers.

Another military supporter of Luther was Florian Geyer, who in 1519 was a commander in the Swabian *Landsknecht*, a powerful mercenary unit within the Holy Roman Empire. Geyer was won over to the Lutheran cause only gradually, but within a few years, was an ardent devotee of Luther and saw within Luther's teaching the opportunity for radical political reform of the empire.

We do not know how much Charles V initially knew about what was going on in Saxony. Tied up in his own wrangling with the Spanish parliament, the *cortes*, some time probably elapsed before Charles was made aware of Luther. By the summer of 1520, the situation had rapidly escalated. Various disputations had failed to convince Luther to recant; if anything, he had become more obdurate in his errors, and the crystallization of his thought was leading him to even more heretical opinions. Pope Leo X promulgated the bull *Exsurge Domine* in June 1520, offering Luther sixty days to recant various propositions from his writings.

The bull was published in many German cities, but Luther held it in derision; he even sent the pope a copy of his latest work, *On the Freedom of the Christian*, reaffirming his teachings. Luther let the allotted time expire and publicly burned the bull in Wittenberg in December to throngs of cheering crowds. Since 1517, Wittenberg had become a flashpoint for Lutheran sympathizers and anti-Roman sentiment. Upon hearing of Luther's stubbornness, Leo excommunicated him on January 3, 1521.

Charles V had recently arrived in Germany and had convened an Imperial Diet at the imperial free city of Worms in the Rhineland-Palatinate. This was the first time the new monarch had met with the estates of the empire, and the occasion was the Lutheran affair. Per medieval custom, an excommunication rendered a person a heretic ipso facto. As a heretic, it fell to the secular arm to see to the enforcement of all legal penalties against heretics, which could include confiscation and destruction of written works, confiscation of property, imprisonment, or in some cases, death. Charles was thus called upon to examine Luther and execute judgment upon him.

Luther appeared before Charles humbly, apologizing for his rustic manners and lack of court etiquette. The presiding officer of the Diet was Johann Eck, Luther's old opponent. Eck read before Luther a list of works and asked if he was ready to recant them. Although Luther apologized for the tone of his works and some personal attacks, he refused to recant the substance of what he taught. He made an appeal to the Scriptures, saying, "Unless I am convinced by the testimony of the Scriptures or by clear reason (for I do not trust either in the pope or in councils alone, since it is well known that they have often erred and contradicted themselves), I am bound by the Scriptures I have quoted and my conscience is captive to the Word of God. I cannot and will not recant anything, since it is neither safe nor right to go against conscience."[11]

---

[11]   Martin Brecht. *Martin Luther* (tr. James L. Schaaf), (Philadelphia: Fortress Press, 1985–93), 1:460, as cited in https://en.wikipedia.org/wiki/Diet_of_Worms#. Last updated June 6, 2017.

Eck made the very astute observation that "there is no one of the heresies which have torn the bosom of the church, which has not derived its origin from the various interpretations of the Scripture. The Bible itself is the arsenal whence each innovator has drawn his deceptive arguments." He went on to note that "it was with biblical texts that Pelagius and Arius maintained their doctrines." The Church, as the custodian of the truth, can never go against the Scriptures. When heretics promulgate errors in the name of the Scriptures, the Church does not pass judgment on the Word of God, but on faulty interpretations of it.

Luther was dismissed while Charles and his counselors debated his sentence. Charles, who had mainly kept silent during the proceedings, was deeply offended by the conduct of Luther. He declared:

> I am descended from a long line of Christian emperors of this noble German nation, and of the Catholic kings of Spain, the archdukes of Austria, and the dukes of Burgundy. They were all faithful to the death to the Church of Rome and they defended the Catholic faith and the honor of God. I have resolved to follow in their steps. A single monk who goes counter to all Christianity for a thousand years must be wrong. . . . After hearing Luther's obstinate defense yesterday, I regret that I have delayed proceeding against him and his false teachings for so long.[12]

---

[12] C. Kahn and K. Osborne, *World Society: Histories of the Past* (Winnipeg: Portage and Main Press, 2005), p. 291.

Charles was a monarch, not a theologian, but like every ruler of the day, he had been given a sound theological formation. His appeal to a thousand years of tradition against the novelties of a single innovator was a very Catholic impulse.

Before a decision was reached on Luther's punishment, he fled Worms for Wittenberg but was intercepted en route by masked horsemen in the pay of Elector Frederick, who had sent them to retrieve Luther and conduct him safely to Frederick's castle of Wartburg in Eisenach. Luther would spend the next ten months there in hiding.

Meanwhile, Charles and his councilors drafted a document known as the Edict of Worms. It was promulgated on May 25, 1521. The edict proclaimed Luther a heretic and an outlaw. It forbade all subjects of the empire from sheltering him or rendering him any aid whatsoever, declaring that anyone could kill him with impunity. The reading or possession of his writings was banned, and secular and ecclesiastical authorities were called upon to see to the destruction of his works. Several very precise theological points were called out and condemned as well.

Charles was only twenty-one years old when he had his famous encounter with Luther. He had only recently come into the Holy Roman Empire and was still a stranger to most of his nobles there. He was still emperor-elect, awaiting his coronation at the hands of the pope. The vast majority of his reign was still before him—and yet, the events that unfolded in 1521 would have consequences that would plague the young emperor until his dying day.

CHAPTER 6

Angel of the Apocalypse: Thomas Müntzer

In the summer of 1521, Luther was in hiding at Wartburg under the protection of the elector Frederick. He would spend the majority of the next year there writing a German translation of the New Testament (working from Erasmus's text), dictating letters to a growing base of support, and formalizing his disparate theological principles into a more coherent system of thought. By the end of 1521, the essential components of classical Lutheranism were all in place, worked out in the solitude of Frederick's Wartburg.

Given that Elector Frederick was a pious Catholic and would remain formally in union with the Catholic Church until his death, what accounted for his steadfast support and protection of Luther? The answer is a combination of political and personal factors. Charles V had only come into the empire for the first time that year. Having been raised in the Netherlands and reigning the past several years from Spain, Charles was not yet familiar with the intricacies of imperial politics. The young emperor-elect had no substantial base of support other than the kind of nominal hereditary loyalty that came with the Hapsburg name. Not only Frederick, but many nobles understandably desired to take advantage of the situation to accumulate as much power as they could before the emperor-elect began to establish himself. Luther had made an enemy of Charles V, and by protecting Luther, the elector Frederick retained a valuable bargaining chip in future encounters with the emperor-elect. As one of the nobles who elected the Holy Roman emperor, and duke of one of the most powerful German dominions, Frederick's leverage was not inconsiderable.

But we must not underestimate the power of nationalism. Though Charles was the legitimate heir to the house of Hapsburg, as one raised in the Netherlands and surrounded by a Spanish court, he was essentially a foreigner in Germany. Just like the Florentine Medici pope who had recently excommunicated Luther, he was a foreigner there. Just like Cardinal Cajetan was a foreigner. German dislike of Italians, especially Italian churchmen, was very raw in the late Middle Ages and was an inheritance from the earlier struggles between the popes and the Holy Roman emperors in the twelfth and thirteenth centuries. For many Germans, regardless of their religious opinions, something rubbed them the wrong way about this cadre of Italians in Rome meddling in the ecclesiastical affairs of Germany with the backing of a foreign prince. Luther did not originally intend his protest to be grounded in German nationalism, but it would increasingly become so as political interests began to coalesce around the Saxon Augustinian. This no doubt also accounted for Frederick's protection of Luther, as well as the esteem many German princes held for Luther.

For Luther, he viewed his protest as only about the sovereignty of God and the purity of the Gospel—though, as Erasmus and other critics would point out, this inevitably meant the gospel according to Martin Luther. And what was Luther's gospel?

Throughout 1520, Luther published three works that were to become the pillars of his ecclesiology: *Address to the Christian Nobility of the German Nation*, *On the Babylonian Captivity of the Church*, and *On the Freedom of a Christian*. In these three works, we see a crystallization of Luther's thought and evidence of a definitive break from Catholic tradition.

The first of these three works, *Address to the Christian Nobility of the German Nation*, is a plea to the nobles of the empire to exercise a greater role in the temporal affairs of the Church throughout Germany. Catholic ecclesiology since the High Middle Ages had idealized a strong, autonomous Church centered around the papacy and independent from the meddling of temporal rulers. Recalling the two sword theory from chapter 2, medieval theologians viewed the pope's spiritual prerogatives, the *sacerdotium*, as prior to and superior to those of temporal rulers, the *imperium*. It was the *imperium* that was called to put itself at the disposal of the *sacerdotium*, not vice versa. Since their triumph in the Investiture Controversy, the popes had not ceased to propose this ideal, and the political apologists of the Holy Roman Empire had not ceased to repudiate it.

Luther had nothing but contempt for this arrangement, which he thought emasculated the rights of German Christians to govern their own affairs. He pleaded with the German nobles to take up the mantle of authority the popes had unjustly seized. For Luther, this was necessary, as he saw the Church so rife with abuses that there was no other remedy but for the temporal power to use force to correct the Church's errors. Luther says:

> Therefore I say, forasmuch as the temporal power has been ordained by God for the punishment of the bad and the protection of the good, therefore we must let it do its duty throughout the whole Christian body, without respect of persons, whether it strikes popes, bishops, priests, monks, nuns, or whoever it may be. . . . Therefore the temporal Christian power must exercise its office without let or hindrance, without considering whom it may strike, whether pope, or bishop, or priest: whoever is guilty, let him suffer for it.

He goes on to rail against the "Romanists," who by their greed and perversion of the Scriptures have oppressed the German people and prevented them from effecting any meaningful resistance to papal tyranny. How have the Romanists done this? By erecting three "walls" of protection which Luther associates with Catholic doctrines that prevent the Church from being reformed against its will by external agents, such as the temporal power: the first wall being the teaching that the temporal power has no jurisdiction over the Church but that the spiritual is above the temporal; the second wall being the Catholic tradition that the Church is the authoritative interpreter of the Scriptures; the third wall being papal supremacy as reflected in the canonical principles that no ecumenical council may be summoned but by a pope, no council can be valid unless ratified by a pope, and that no Christian may disobey the pope by making an appeal to a future council. By means of these teachings, the Romanists have encircled themselves as in a fortress that prevents their reform. Only force can break down these walls.

He concludes his nationalist screed with an appeal to the patriotism of the German nobility to rise up and resist a Church hierarchy that had bilked German Christians out of their wealth and robbed them of their dignity: "What has brought us Germans to such a pass that we have to suffer this robbery and this destruction of our property by the Pope? If the kingdom of France has resisted it, why do we Germans suffer ourselves to be fooled and deceived? It would be more endurable if they did nothing but rob us of our property; but they destroy the Church and deprive Christ's flock of their good shepherds."

Luther's second treatise of 1520 was *On the Babylonian Captivity of the Church*. In this work, Luther first lays out his sacramental theology. His view of the seven sacraments is informed by his interpretation of the Bible; his doctrine of faith alone is the linchpin upon which the whole sacramental system turns. The Catholic Church had always taught that sacraments are efficacious signs; they are physical signs that actually produce the effects they signify. Baptism utilizes water, which signifies cleansing, and in fact the sacrament of Baptism does cleanse the soul as its spiritual effect.

For Luther, however, no sacrament could actually produce any spiritual effect. Baptism merely signifies the justification that is obtained by faith; sacramental absolution does not actually absolve from sin, but merely proclaims that God has already forgiven one's sins. Luther rejects transubstantiation (though continues to affirm a spiritual presence of Christ in the Eucharist in what will become known as "consubstantiation") and flatly denies that Holy Orders, Matrimony, Confirmation, and Extreme Unction are sacraments at all. He goes on to bluntly accuse the pope of being the Antichrist and keeping the Church in captivity by these superstitious errors of Catholic tradition.

Many of Luther's positions were not novel. His theory of Christ's spiritual presence in the Eucharist was very similar to what the eleventh-century heretic Berengar of Tours had professed. He also recycled some principles found in the Bohemian Hussite movement of the fifteenth century, as well as the writings of John Wycliffe, the fourteenth-century Oxford theologian who anticipated Luther's sacramental theology. But what these late medieval heretics lacked was the principle of justification by faith alone, which unified these various doctrines and gave them a certain internal cohesion, making them into a functional system of thought. The late medieval heretics also lacked the printing press, which allowed Luther a much wider audience than Berengar ever could have imagined.

It was Luther's third treatise of 1520 that would prove to be most pivotal to the events unfolding in Germany. *On the Freedom of a Christian* was published in November 1520. The theme of this work was the freedom of Christians from the need to perform good works as part of their salvation. For the most part, it is fleshing out the doctrine of justification by faith alone in its relation to good works. For Luther, good works are merely a product of faith and done for the purpose of pleasing God. They do not contribute to our salvation in any sense nor can they be the occasion of growth in holiness. "[A] Christian, being consecrated by his faith, does good works; but he is not by these works made a more sacred person, or more a Christian. That is the effect of faith alone," said Luther.

Because of this freedom, the entire traditional Catholic concept of penitential and charitable works done for the sake of one's salvation becomes obsolete, as well as the institutional Church which administers and oversees these works. The freedom Luther proposes is thus very individualistic, doing away with the communitarian aspect of salvation—that we are saved in and through the Church and the communion of saints, which is nothing other than the Body of Christ. For this reason, Luther wrote, "A Christian man is the most free, lord of all, and subject to none," at the introduction to his treatise.

Thus, "freedom" for Martin Luther means an interior freedom, a freedom from having to rely on our own good works to save us. A freedom from fear of punishment by a terrifying God. It is freedom from what Luther saw as a cringing servility to the antichrist sitting in Rome and his regime of works-based righteousness. Luther sees it essentially as a twofold freedom, from our own anxiety and from the demands of the Catholic Church. In fact, the very existence of the institutional Church is a tyranny in Luther's mind. He says:

> Here you will ask: "If all who are in the Church are priests by what character are those, whom we now call priests, to be distinguished from the laity?" I reply: By the use of these words, "priest," "clergy," "spiritual person," "ecclesiastic," an injustice has been done, since they have been transferred from the remaining body of Christians to those few, who are now, by a hurtful custom, called ecclesiastics. For Holy Scripture makes no distinction between them, except that those, who are now boastfully called popes, bishops, and lords, it calls ministers, servants, and stewards, who are to serve the rest in the ministry of the Word, for teaching the faith of Christ and the liberty of believers. . . .
>
> This bad system has now issued in such a pompous display of power, and such a terrible tyranny, that no earthly government can be compared to it, as if the laity were something else than Christians. Through this perversion of things it has happened that the knowledge of Christian grace, of faith, of liberty, and altogether of Christ, has utterly perished, and has been succeeded by an intolerable bondage to human works and laws; and, according to the Lamentations of Jeremiah, we have become the slaves of the vilest men on earth, who abuse our misery to all the disgraceful and ignominious purposes of their own will.

We have mentioned in a previous chapter that the real tragedy about Luther was that he railed against a system that the Catholic Church never actually taught. His superior Johann von Staupitz had tried to correct him, and all of Catholic tradition from the earliest days of Christendom testified that a man cannot merit salvation by his own works. Luther's broadsides against a works-based salvation were ultimately attacks leveled against a straw man.

Of course, the truth could easily be misunderstood by the simple or ignored by the spiritually apathetic. The nuances of the relationship between grace and will could certainly be lost on the illiterate rural peasant; the worldly socialite who was bored by spiritual truths certainly found it easier to arrange their affairs with God by purchasing an indulgence than taking any real spiritual initiative. The truth is always liable to misunderstanding, and it is certainly plausible that the abuses surrounding indulgences in Saxony at the time made it difficult for Luther to see them any other way.

This made no difference to Luther; the whole thing was a "bad system" and a "terrible tyranny" that had to be destroyed root and branch. Luther, however, was about to get his own painful lesson in how one's teachings can be misinterpreted.

By the early 1520s, the Lutheran reform had taken hold of many German churches. Sympathetic princes were allowing parish churches and whole dioceses to be reformed along Lutheran lines. Bishops opposed to Luther were driven from their sees. The traditional Mass with its focus on sacrifice was abolished in favor of a "Lord's Supper" reflecting Luther's sacramental theology. Latin chant was replaced by German vernacular hymns. Images of saints and angels were removed and Lutheran theology was preached from the pulpits.

Luther and his followers did not consider themselves heretics or cut off from the Catholic Church. In the early 1520s, they still considered themselves part of the Catholic Church, but promoters of an aggressive reform. Not everyone saw it this way, however. We have mentioned in chapter 3 how the Lutherans aggressively sought to win the great scholar Erasmus to their cause. Erasmus was of a different mind than Luther. Though a younger Erasmus had sometimes straddled the line between condemning abuses and attacking Catholic dogma, by the 1520s he had come out solidly in defense of traditional Catholic belief, much to Luther's chagrin. Erasmus saw the Lutheran movement as splitting Christianity in two and warned Luther and his associates about the sorts of men who were attaching themselves to Luther's name. In 1524, he wrote of his anxieties that the movement would turn violent in a letter to another reformer which we saw in an earlier chapter: "I know nothing of your church; at the very least it contains people who will, I fear, overturn the whole system and drive the princes into using force to restrain good men and bad alike."[13]

In 1522, Charles V returned to Spain. The absence of the emperor-elect provided the opportunity for some of the most discontented of the lower nobility to cause mischief. A "Brotherly Convention of Knights" was convened by Franz von Sickingen and Ulrich von Hutten, two of the renegade knights who had attached themselves to Luther's cause. The

---

[13]   Collected Works of Erasmus. University of Toronto Press. 1992.
        p. 380.

assembly proposed a radical nationalist revolution, which entailed unifying all German-speaking lands under a single government, the seizure of all Church property by the state, the forcible implementation of the Lutheran reforms throughout Germany, and the establishment of a kind of aristocratic democracy.

Von Sickingen was elected to head the revolution. It was hoped that a bold, decisive action on the part of the knights would rouse the peasantry to support the revolt. Von Sickingen and his gang settled on the city of Trier as their first target, selecting it because its archbishop was a determined foe of Luther.

Von Sickingen led his ragtag force of knights against Trier in early 1522, calling upon the commoners to revolt against the archbishop and establish a new godly society there in the vision of Luther. The people of Trier were loyal to the archbishop, however, and the campaign was an abysmal failure. Von Hutten became sick with one of his recurring bouts of syphilis. Von Sickingen's men lacked supplies and coordination. They attacked the city for seven days before running out of gunpowder and retreating. On their withdrawal through the countryside, they violently plundered Catholic parishes and monasteries.

The archbishop of Trier and some other nobles pursued von Sickingen to his castle in Landstuhl. Von Sickingen hoped to wait out a siege there until help could arrive, but artillery demolished his defenses in a week. The bombardment was so severe that von Sickingen himself was grievously wounded. He surrendered to the nobles on May 7, but died the same day. Von Hutten managed to escape to

Switzerland, but not for long. Wasting away from syphilis, he dragged himself to a monastery on Lake Zurich where he died that summer.

The rash plan of the lower nobility to bring a violent reform to Germany had failed, but danger was not averted. Back in 1517–1518, when events were first unfolding in Wittenberg, Luther had made the acquaintance of a young man named Thomas Müntzer. Müntzer admired Luther, and Luther thought he had talent as a preacher and teacher. Luther helped Müntzer to obtain a teaching position in the town of Zwickau, near the Bohemian border, where he used his influence to peddle the Lutheran reform.

Like Luther, Müntzer was a tireless critic of the Catholic Church. But while Luther viewed his primary end as freeing souls from the bondage of a works-based theology, Müntzer could not help but apply Luther's ideas of freedom to the socio-political realm. Müntzer was an amateur theologian and schooled Humanist, as at home lecturing on the epistles of St. Paul as ruminating on what constitutes a just society. In his diverse interests, he was no different than many other Humanist luminaries. Müntzer, however, was also deeply interested in the works of visionaries and pseudo-seers, which, over time, tended to tinge his thought with a lively strain of apocalypticism. He was also a powerful preacher, capable of drawing large crowds who were moved by his charisma and fiery vision. He eventually left Zwickau and traveled about Europe for a time, preaching wherever his wanderings took him.

Müntzer came from a comfortable middle-class back-ground, but his itinerancy brought him into contact with the rural poor, the peasantry who formed the backbone of medieval society. The peasants of Germany in the early sixteenth century were subject to a variety of economic and political pressures. Their grievances were legion: they were hampered in their economic activity by restrictions on hunting and fishing; their wealth was continually pilfered by a variety of taxes (some of them levied by the Church); they had seen exorbitant increases in rents over the past generation, as well as obligations imposed upon them by the nobility, many of which could be outright insulting, like when the peasants of Mühlhausen were ordered by their lady to collect snail shells upon which she could wind her thread.

This discontent had been brewing for some time. The advent of Luther and his message of the freedom of every Christian energized the peasantry and lent a kind of theological dimension to their cause. "A Christian man is the most free, lord of all, and subject to none," Luther had said. For the peasants, this was not only a theological concept, but a political one. Luther certainly did not create the unrest stirring among the peasantry, but he gave it a degree of fervor it might otherwise have lacked.

Müntzer shared the political aspirations of the peasants he had come to respect. In spring of 1523, he was in the Saxon town of Allstedt, preaching his particular version of reformed doctrine to overflowing churches. Luther got wind of Müntzer's teaching and asked him to return to Wittenberg to explain himself. Luther was alarmed at the revolutionary tone in Müntzer's doctrine; after all, Luther's doctrine was primarily concerned with the freedom of the soul. Luther sympathized with the plight of the German peasants and had spoken on their behalf before, but political revolution was repulsive to Luther. It was nothing other than the very sin of Lucifer himself. He would not have any of his preachers inciting Christians to violent revolt against their lawful sovereigns.

Müntzer, however, rebuffed Luther, opening a breach between the two that would only grow worse as time went by. Luther, whom Müntzer derisively called Brother Fatted Pig and Brother Soft Life, was betraying the Gospel by refusing to put his influence behind the cause of the peasants. Luther grew increasingly alarmed at Müntzer's rhetoric and wrote a tract to the princes of Saxony recommending his apprehension. Müntzer, in turn, published a scathing tract against Luther, humorously titled *A Highly Provoked Vindication and Refutation of the unspiritual soft-living flesh in Wittenberg*. He spent the latter months of 1524 traveling about Germany and Switzerland, meeting both with leaders of various peasant bands as well as other reformers outside the Lutheran pale, who were growing in number daily.

A few months later, in February 1525, the peasants of Memmingen in Bavaria revolted. Peasant bands from the Black Forest, Constance, Bavaria, and the Tyrol also began revolting. The imperial troops of Swabia tried to crush the revolt, but with only twelve hundred men, they were insufficient to deal with the throngs of peasants who were coalescing throughout southern Germany.

It is difficult to pinpoint the exact nature of the peasant revolt, other than that it was an outburst of rage against the existing system. Reformed doctrines spread through the peasant hordes who, urged on by charismatic leaders such as Müntzer, saw their struggle in terms of a kind of crusade against an ungodly order. But it is wrong to think of the revolt as a purely religious thing. How many peasants were part of Luther's movement is uncertain; in fact, as late as 1524, the distinction between Lutheran and Catholic was still a fluid thing in the minds of many. Still, what we know of the peasants from their demands seems to suggest that they were influenced by the reform: twelve articles proposed by the peasant associations demanded, among other things, the right for congregations to choose their own pastors and a general reduction in tithes, both talking points of the reformers.

The peasants soon awoke to the strength of their own numbers. Various bands moved throughout southern Germany during the summer of 1525, plundering abbeys and towns and violently uprooting any vestiges of the existing social order. Nobles who had the misfortune to fall into their hands suffered cruel fates. At Weinsberg Castle, a count and seventy nobles who were captured were forced to run a gauntlet of peasant pikes and daggers, perishing slowly from innumerable wounds.

Müntzer, meanwhile, was in Mühlhausen, where he hijacked the local parish and installed himself as preacher without permission of the town council. He began organizing the commoners of Mühlhausen into a militia, called The Eternal League of God. The League was meant not only as a line of military defense for Mühlhausen but also as a kind of corps of godly Christians preparing for the apocalypse. The town's city council was replaced with an "Eternal Council" whose duties were both spiritual and temporal. Mühlhausen thus fell under a kind of theocratic dictatorship whose visionary leaders were Müntzer and his associates, angels of the coming apocalypse.

The nobles of southern Germany were taken off guard by the revolt, but they were not slack in their response. Throughout the spring of 1525, knights and imperial troops were marshaled from all over southern Germany to crush the revolt. Luther sided strongly with the nobles. He was mortified that peasants would use his spiritual teaching as an excuse for base plunder. For Luther, Müntzer had misunderstood the reformed Gospel in a profound way that was repugnant to God. Luther lent his pen to the cause of the nobles with his work *Against the Robbing and Murdering Hordes of Peasants*, published in May of 1525. He accused the peasants of blasphemy, murder, and treason for rebelling against their lawful superiors. There was nothing left for them but the swiftest retribution for their treachery. "Therefore let everyone who can, smite, slay and stab, secretly or openly, remembering that nothing can be more poisonous, hurtful or devilish than a rebel," Luther admonished the princes of southern Germany. "It is just as when one must kill a mad dog; if you do not strike him, he will strike you, and a whole land with you."[14] Luther even went on a speaking tour throughout southern Saxony urging the princes of the realm to resistance.

---

[14]   E.G. Rupp and Benjamin Drewery, *Martin Luther, Documents of Modern History* (London: Edward Arnold, 1970), pp. 121-6. As cited in http://zimmer.csufresno.edu/~mariterel/against_the_robbing_and_murderin.htm.

The imperial princes of the realm were mobilized by early summer and began confronting the peasants throughout Thuringia and the south. The poorly equipped peasant militias were no match for the knights and professional soldiery of the nobility. Everywhere the peasants and imperial armies collided, the peasants were either routed or massacred. In some encounters, thousands of peasants were slaughtered without the imperial armies sustaining a single casualty.

Müntzer and his Eternal League of God arrived at the city of Frankenhausen on May 11, responding to a call for aid from the peasant army of that region who were about to come under attack from the imperial army. Müntzer had barely arrived when the imperial armies of Philip of Hesse and Duke George of Saxony arrived. Müntzer went to and fro amongst his men trying to build their morale, but the situation was daunting. The imperial armies of Philip and George had already slaughtered the peasant bands of Thuringia and were eager for more.

Battle ensued on May 15 when Müntzer's peasant militia engaged the imperial armies on the hill outside Frankenhausen. The peasants were decimated; the slaughter was appalling. Upwards of six thousand peasants were butchered on the hill with almost no casualties in the armies of Philip and Duke George. It was a total collapse of the peasant force.

Müntzer fled into the town and hid himself in a private home. Meanwhile, the imperial armies rounded up survivors of the battle and began summary executions. The killing went on for days. Philip of Hesse and Duke George knew Müntzer was still alive and made a diligent search of the town. He was eventually discovered and identified by a bundle of letters he was carrying. The princes knew how influential Müntzer was in motivating the peasant bands and decided to make a spectacle of him. He was tortured for several days until he recanted his positions. On May 27, after days of torture, he was beheaded.

There would be a few more engagements in the peasant revolt; most of the fighting was over by September, though bloody reprisals continued into 1526. By the time peace returned, between seventy thousand and one hundred thousand peasants had been killed.

Martin Luther had been extremely frustrated that Müntzer had made the reformed message into a call for political revolution. Yes, Luther had said, "A Christian man is the most free lord of all, and subject to none," but he had also written that a "Christian man is the most dutiful servant of all, and subject to everyone." To make of his teaching a political doctrine was abhorrent to Luther, at least when that political vision was too tinged with apocalypticism and antithetical to Luther's own view. Even though Luther was frustrated with what he viewed as a misapplication of his teaching, it cannot be denied that Luther's thought is pregnant with such revolutionary ideals against the social order.

Müntzer had castigated Luther for refusing to take his reform to the next level, just as Luther had insulted Erasmus. Moving in to the 1520s, it was becoming apparent that Luther was not the only representative of the protest against Rome. Other leaders were cropping up all over Europe advocating "reform" of the Church, but on lines different than those proposed by the ex-monk from Saxony. Most of these men Luther considered upstarts and perverters of the

Gospel. Why was that which was so self-evident to him not equally so to every person? Such is the dilemma one faces when arguing private interpretation of Scripture; Luther had established his own principles by appealing to private interpretation, but now there was nothing preventing any other theologian or slack-jawed, ignorant peasant with a Bible from coming up with his own interpretation.

This problem would only get worse; it is a problem inherent in Protestantism that all the appeals to Scripture have never been able to resolve. Not to put too fine a point on it, the problem is that "sola scriptura" makes a mockery of the very concept of truth.

CHAPTER 7

The Austere Scholar: John Calvin

B y Christmas of 1525 and the end of the peasant's revolt, much had happened. Leo X had excommunicated Luther back in 1521; that same year, Charles V had condemned Luther at the imperial Diet of Worms and then returned to Spain. Yet Luther remained a free man, protected by the princes of Germany. Many regions of Germany had gone over to the Lutheran reform entirely, sometimes peaceably, and sometimes by the forcible ejection of Catholic clergy. The revolt of von Sickingen and von Hutten had petered out in 1522; the nobles of Thuringia and Saxony were wrapping up the bloody reprisals against the peasants who had vainly attempted to upend the existing order. Erasmus and Luther were engaged in a bitter public debate over freedom of the will. All over the continent, the question of the reform was on everybody's mind.

We here call it the "reform" because this is how the movement was still viewed by many; the term Protestant would not be coined for another three years. Devout and educated Catholics like Cajetan and Johann Eck had recognized the heresy in Luther's teachings from the outset. Yet it must be noted for many average Christians, it was hard to tell the difference between heresy and a legitimate reforming zeal. In chapter 3, we examined this problem in the context of Erasmus, who condemned abuses in the Church but sometimes strayed into attacking Catholic practice itself. Many good and pious Catholics had condemned abuses in the Church for decades. For many Christians, Luther represented nothing more than the same call for reform—perhaps delivered in a more crude and bombastic fashion, but not essentially different from what had come before.

But by the end of 1525, it was becoming less possible for any educated person not to see that the reform movement was questioning fundamentals of the Catholic faith. Let us take stock of the message that was coming out of Wittenberg by the end of 1525.

Martin Luther had begun the movement known as the Reformation with his teaching that faith alone saves man and had subsequently dispensed with the entire penitential system of the historic Christian faith. When it was pointed out that neither the ecumenical councils nor the Church Fathers supported his premises, Luther responded by casting doubt on the authority of the councils, fathers, and popes, appealing instead to the text of the Bible alone. This handily dispensed with having to deal with the authority of the Church, as well as established Luther as the authoritative interpreter of scriptural text. Without any tradition to give context to biblical passages, Luther—or any man—became the authoritative expositor of Christian revelation.

Of course, the sacraments were obstacles to this extreme individualization of the Christian faith. While Catholic tradition had always viewed the sacraments as means of grace (tangible ways that man can come in contact with God), Luther viewed the Church's sacramental theology as obstructing man's access to God. Transubstantiation had to be rejected as a superstition that kept people enthralled to the quasi-magical power of priests; marriage was no longer sacramental, and Holy Orders, the sacrament that makes other sacraments possible, was denied. Hence, by overhauling the very concept of a sacrament, Luther was able to dispense with the necessity of the hierarchy, replacing it with an ethereal "priesthood of all believers" divorced from any divinely instituted sacerdotal authority.

Of course, the efficacy of relics and indulgences had been denied, which in turn led to a denial of the authority of the pope, the successor of St. Peter, whom Luther called Antichrist. The authority the pope claimed over the Church was viewed by Luther as a usurpation. Yet the Church must be governed and order must be maintained. If the hierarchy and the papal office were denied, to whom would Christians look to set right the affairs of the churches in their realm?

The natural answer, as we have seen from Luther's appeal to the German princes, was that power would devolve to the secular authorities. The conflict between the secular power and the ecclesiastical power was an old one, and a conflict with very sharply defined fault lines in Germany, with its history of conflict with the papacy. Luther expected the state to step in and take a more active role in ecclesial affairs. All subsequent Protestant movements would share a common belief in the secularization of church properties and an expanded role of the state in governing the affairs of the Church. As we saw in the revolt of von Hutten, von Sickingen, and the peasants, and as we shall see time and again, what would become Protestantism was typically established by the arm of secular authority.

Doctrinal deviations led to practical changes in Christian worship. In those parishes under control of the "reform," services were said in the vernacular; Gregorian chant was eliminated in favor of vernacular hymns; Mass was replaced by a kind of communal meal, where a Eucharist (in which Christ's real presence was denied) was offered on structures more reminiscent of tables than altars of sacrifice. This was done to wean the common people away from the traditional belief in the sacrificial nature of the Mass.

These elements of the Lutheran movement were all present by 1525 at the end of the Peasants' War. The breach was growing and had become violent. It was becoming increasingly clear to many that this was no reform, no continuity, but a positive rupture.

When the Peasants' War erupted in Germany, Peter Canisius was only four years old. He was probably just beginning to learn his letters, recite his prayers, and get an understanding of the world beyond Nijmegen. We can imagine his father, Jacob Kanis, standing at the shipping docks along the Waal, talking to his fellow merchants about the events in the world beyond, wondering what implications they might have for the life and business of their city.

The affairs of Germany were of no mere academic interest to the people of the Netherlands. In the sixteenth century, the Netherlands, too, were part of the dominions of Charles V, and the men of Nijmegen followed the affairs of Germany with careful interest. Though Luther had few partisans in the Netherlands, there was always a strain of religious dissent in the Low Countries. Throughout the late Middle Ages, the Low Countries had spawned several pious lay associations that had occasionally crossed the line into heresy. Erasmus, the man many accused of laying the egg of the Reformation, was a Dutchman. In 1525, the Netherlands was still firmly within the Catholic fold, but the situation was watched with apprehension.

Indeed, the reform was spreading. It was no longer a disagreement among monks, as Charles V had once quipped, nor was it any longer a mere German problem. By 1525, it is not right to continue to speak of it simply as the Lutheran movement, for by that time many other men were taking up the attack against the Catholic Church, but under different banners than that of Luther.

In 1523, while Thomas Müntzer was preaching apocalypticism to overflowing crowds in Allstedt, an industrious young clerk from Picardy was traveling to Paris to begin his philosophy studies. The boy, Jean Cauvin, was only fourteen. Cauvin came from a family that had tied their fortunes to the service of the Church. Cauvin's father had been a cathedral notary and registrar to the ecclesiastical court. When Jean was twelve, his father procured his employment as a clerk for the bishop of Noyons, where the young man was tonsured, like all episcopal clerks. When he left for Paris to study philosophy in 1523, it was assumed he would enter the priesthood.

Cauvin, or John Calvin as history remembers him, studied at the Collège de la Marche and the Collège de Montaigu and was formed in the Humanist-reformer mold. There is no indication that Calvin was particularly religious as a student, showing little Catholic devotion and no affinity for Martin Luther. When Calvin completed his studies in 1527, Luther was engaged in a fierce debate with fellow reformer Ulrich Zwingli over the presence of Christ in the Eucharist. The united Lutheran edifice had cracked; reform movements were cropping up outside Germany that strongly clashed with Luther on many fronts. Though Calvin favored reform, he was reluctant to side with the Lutherans or Zwinglians and kept his religious opinions to himself.

Calvin entered the University of Bourges in 1529 to study law, at the behest of his father. Here he studied under the famed Humanist lawyer Andreas Alciati. It was at Bourges under the masterful tutelage of Alciati that Calvin honed the erudition and precision of thought that would make him the preeminent scholar of the Protestant Reformation. A thin-faced young man with a powerful nose and dark, thoughtful eyes, Calvin's studious intellect was naturally suited to the intricacies of law.

He spent some time at the law school in Orleans and returned to Bourges in 1531. By then he was an eminent scholar in the Humanist ideal, knowledgeable in Latin, Greek, Hebrew and well-studied in civic law; he had even won some notoriety for a commentary on Seneca. His scholarship paid off, and by 1532 Calvin was installed as a doctor of law at Orleans.

Of course, it is not as a lawyer but a reformer that Calvin is remembered. There are varying accounts of his conversion. Calvin spoke of his turn to religion sometimes as a sudden conversion, other times as a gradual development. It is certain that throughout the late 1520s, John Calvin increasingly came to ponder eternal truths. Like so many other Christians before him, Calvin began to worry about the state of his soul. He began to lament the irreligiosity of his past life; he had never been a notorious sinner, but still, he brooded over the years spent in secular pursuits. In one of many passages he wrote about his conversion, Calvin, in the preface to his *Commentary on the Book of Psalms*, said, "God by a sudden conversion subdued and brought my mind to a teachable frame, which was more hardened in such matters than might have been expected from one at my early period of life. Having thus received some taste and knowledge of true godliness, I was immediately inflamed with so intense a desire to make progress therein, that although I did not altogether leave off other studies, yet I pursued them with less ardor."

A hundred years earlier, a young man of such skill and devotion would have given himself up to the service of the Church. Perhaps joining the Dominicans or one of the teaching orders, he would have undertaken a life of penance and preaching in the service of Christ and his Church and perhaps died in the odor of sanctity. But the medieval spirit was passing from the world; Luther had rent Christendom, and controversy and confusion reigned everywhere. As a Humanist, Calvin had already sympathized with those calling for reform, but unlike Erasmus, he threw his lot in definitively with the reformers.

As a professor, Calvin's initial gestures toward the reform were to ally publicly with other reform-minded faculty. He returned to Paris in 1533 where he publicly associated with Nicholas Cop, rector of the Collège Royal of Paris. Cop was devoted to reforming the Church in France along Protestant lines. In his inaugural address on November 1, 1533, Cop called for the full reform of the Catholic Church in France. The address infuriated the conservative faculty of the college, who secured a condemnation of Cop for heresy. Cop was compelled to flee France; Calvin, too, as a public associate of Cop, made himself scarce to avoid incrimination. Thus 1533 ended with Calvin's first show of public support for the reform, ending in his hiding.

France at the time was ruled by King Francis I. Protestantism had begun to creep into France throughout the 1520s. Though Catholic, King Francis was not averse to the Lutheran movement. His sister, Marguerite of Angoulême, was sincerely attracted to Luther's theology and may have softened her brother's heart to Lutheranism. Francis supported the movement politically, as any disorder in Germany served his political interest by weakening the authority of his rival, Emperor Charles V. Francis welcomed Lutheran refugees into France and encouraged religious toleration, despite the wishes of the Parlement de Paris, which suspected Lutheran refugees imported into France would eventually turn on their host kingdom. Francis believed these suspicions were unfounded. He would be proven very wrong.

On the morning of October 17, 1534, the people of Paris awoke to find the city littered with anonymous anti-Catholic placards. The posters attacked the Mass, saying it was a horrific, unbearable abuse invented in direct contradiction to the teaching of Jesus. A blatant attack on the Blessed Sacrament was offensive enough to Catholics, but what made the event particularly disturbing was that the placards also appeared on the door of the king's bedchamber. This shook the security of King Francis, who suspected a massive anti-Catholic conspiracy that reached right up to the royal household.

Immediately, the royal policy of tolerance was scrapped. Francis offered rewards for information leading to the apprehension of the culprits, promising they would be burned at the stake for the offense. In the meantime, Eucharistic processions of reparation were organized throughout Paris, with King Francis himself participating. The perpetrators were soon apprehended and executions began that fall. Every Protestant fell under suspicion. The king's former disposition of geniality and tolerance turned and gave way to the most severe rigor.

Calvin, in Paris at the time, thought it best to flee France altogether. He made his way to Basel, Switzerland. Switzerland had become a sort of clearinghouse for Protestant refugees from around Europe, as well as for German Protestants who opposed Luther. It was a land full of contention, where Catholic and Protestant populations contested hotly for supremacy in each town, and where Protestant sects vied with each other in a war of tracts over what was the most authentic interpretation of the Gospel.

The situation in Geneva furnishes us with a decent example of the state of affairs in Switzerland as a whole. Protestant preachers had first arrived in 1519; by 1527, the new faith had sufficiently divided the city that the populace was in open revolt against the House of Savoy, whose duke claimed sovereignty there. By 1530, the power of the Catholic Church in Geneva was broken, and Geneva was effectually independent from the Savoy. The city council held a series of public disputations in 1535 to determine whether to remain Catholic or formally establish some form of Protestantism as the official faith. The Catholic party was defeated, which resulted in the destruction of altars, the smashing of images, and the formal prohibition of the Mass by legislative decree. In the new regime, church and state were fused in the city council, which enforced religious as well as secular law. Priests were arrested and people were fined for not attending Protestant worship. Protestant militias from Berne were sent to Geneva to lend muscle to the council's decrees.

It is strange that Calvin, with his natural timidity and academic mind, should have settled in such a place. It seems his first inclination was to go elsewhere; after leaving Basel, he traveled to Italy and back to France. He visited Geneva in 1536 and intended to only stay a single night before passing on, but the local Protestant preacher, William Farel, implored Calvin to stay and help him organize the reformed church in Geneva. It had been scarcely a year since the Catholic Church had been dismantled there, and the reform was in a state of disorganization. Calvin's austere demeanor and his orderly, legal mind would help stabilize the reform of Geneva. Calvin agreed, and thus began his residence in the city with which he would forever be associated.

Calvin's reputation was growing fast in the Protestant movement, bolstered by the publication of his monumental work *Institutes of the Christian Religion*, published only a few months before his coming to Geneva. The work is voluminous and very different from the writings of Luther. Martin Luther preferred to explain his teaching in scores of short letters for the general public, full of all the emotion and vitriol of a man caught up in the midst of the struggle between God and the devil. Calvin, on the other hand, embodied his theology in a single massive tome, written for scholars and theologians. While full of deep conviction, the mood of the *Institutes* gives no indication of the tumultuous conditions under which they were written. If Luther writes passionately from the midst of the struggle, Calvin writes from above it, looking down calmly upon the whole drama of the cosmos with the unshakable conviction that God has already won.

Books much longer than this one have tried and failed to adequately summarize the content of Calvin's teaching. Here, we shall only attempt to sketch the main outlines of his dogma.

The one teaching that the entire first generation of reformers held in common was a denial of free will. Luther had debated bitterly with Erasmus about free will; Luther's companion Melanchthon called free will an impious dogma. Calvin shared his peers' negative estimation of free will. The Protestant reform ultimately asserted a kind of monism in God's relation to the world. God alone was the only agent in man's salvation; no role could be played by anyone else, even in the minutest sense. Gone were the concepts of participation, mediation, and communitarianism that had characterized Christianity from the very beginning. Men did not participate or contribute to their salvation in any sense.

Hence, the sacraments, the hierarchy, and the very concept of meritorious works could find no place along the Protestant spectrum. Autonomy does not even exist within the will of man; God is the sole power, the sole actor in the universe, even unto the remotest corner of every man's heart.

Traditional Catholic theology affirmed that God's will was supreme, of course, and that God was the ultimate power in the universe. But it also affirmed that in creating man in his image and likeness, God endowed us with a will that was truly free, even as God's will is free. In Catholicism, our free will does not detract from God's will; rather, it only exists as a participation in the will of God, and when properly formed, our wills actually glorify God. The highest thing a man can do with his free will is align it with the divine will; this alignment is, in a very real sense, the definition of sanctity. Free will is necessary for our love of God to be perfected.

Calvin denies that God positively forces our wills, but he views the working of human will as a mechanical effect of God's will. We all do such-and-such because God wills it, just as water inevitably winds up at the bottom of a slope. It is irresistible, for God's grace renders it so. For the Catholic, grace was a gift of God that made it possible for a man to freely do God's will; for Calvin, grace was a name for the mechanism by which God imposes his will on a man.

All Christians agree that God is sovereign. How then do we account for things that go against God's will? Catholicism had distinguished between things God positively decrees and things he merely allows; those things he decrees are part of his positive will, those he merely allows are part of his permissive will, which is necessary so that the freedom of man might be preserved. Between the poles of these two dimensions of God's will, all human acts are accounted for. God could positively will a man to repent of his sins, but if the man persisted in his evil, God would will to allow him that choice permissively, even though it contravened God's positive will. Thus, man truly has a choice and is truly responsible before God.

Calvin denied this distinction, considering it a blasphemy to assert that any man could contravene God's will in any sense. Calvin obliterated the distinction between the positive and the permissive will of God, seeing every event under the sun as positively decreed by God. This presents an obvious dilemma when we consider human evil. If God positively decrees everything, then he must positively decree sin, including the original sin of Adam that brought ruin upon the human race. The traditional Catholic understanding of free will holds that God permits (but doesn't decree) room for sin, but with free will abolished, sin must be directly attributed to God.

Calvin saw where this logic led and did not deny it. Rather, he affirmed it as an immutable teaching of the Gospel. If a man sinned, it was because God had willed him to. Thus he writes in the *Institutes*, "man by the righteous impulsion of God does that which is unlawful," and that "man falls, the Providence of God so ordaining."[15]

It could be asked why God then commands men to be righteous in the Scriptures if he positively wills them to sin? Calvin solves this dilemma by introducing a duality into

---

[15]   John Calvin, *Institutes*, IV, 18, 2; III, 23, 8.

God's will, positing a public or "apparent" will of God that commands men to do good and avoid evil, but behind this is a secret, unsearchable will, unknown to any man, whereby God arbitrarily determines who will in fact succeed at carrying out his will and who will fail.

This obviously ties in with the most well-known Calvinist doctrine, the idea of predestination—or rather we should say Calvin's version of predestination, because all Christians admit that God predetermines things to one degree or another. What makes Calvin's predestination so unique is that it makes the salvation or damnation of man absolutely arbitrary and dependent solely on a predetermining decree of God, which is not tied to anything a man may or may not do and which can admit of no appeal. If a man goes to hell, he does so because from all eternity God decreed that he should wind up there.

This is quite consistent with Calvin's system. God is the cause of sinful deeds in men. The penalty of sin is eternal punishment. Ergo, God positively wills certain souls to damnation and certain souls to salvation. It is pointless to ask by what criteria God makes this judgment; it is buried in the unsearchable mist of his eternal decrees. Thus, a man is damned to hell not by virtue of anything he has done; rather, his decree of damnation is pronounced in eternity past before he is ever born. His sins merely confirm his immutable sentence already pronounced.

Those who go to heaven are the elect. But if one is predestined to heaven, how would one ever know? Here is where Calvin identifies the value of good deeds. God commands us to do good and avoid evil, not because the completion of good works actually contributes to our salvation, but because by good deeds a man demonstrates the fact of his election. A member of the elect possesses the grace of God, which moves him to do good deeds. By this the elect are discerned from the reprobate. Thus, external works become for the Calvinist signs pointing to his election: an austere, frugal lifestyle, diligent work, fidelity to prayer and weekly services, charitable works, and irreproachable morality—these things all signify that a man *is* saved, though they cannot contribute one iota to *whether* or not he is saved.

The effect of this cast-iron logic was paradoxical and terrifying. While preaching this system as the "liberty of the Gospel," its practical effect was that it laid on its adherents a works-based mentality more oppressive than anything of which Luther accused the Catholic Church. Nobody wants to think they have been predestined to hell from all eternity. The only way to have any demonstrable proof to the contrary is to perform good and pious works relentlessly in hopes that this sufficiently establishes one's election in his own conscience. It places a regimen of works on the believer far more burdensome than the Catholic system. If a Catholic passed up an opportunity to do a good deed, it meant he was spiritually lax and at worst that he had sinned by omission. This posed no real problem, because the Catholic could always amend his life, go to confession, and begin again. A Calvinist, however, who failed to do a good deed now had to grapple with the anxiety that his omission might mean he has been predestined to hell from all eternity. After all, if he was in God's grace, why would he willingly pass up an opportunity to do good?

Of course, one cannot pass judgment on the consciences of individual Calvinists, but it is not difficult to see how such a system would wreak havoc in the hearts of the scrupulous or even any Christian whose faith was less than perfect. Whatever Calvin's original intentions, his system has historically been identified with rigor and austerity. The adjective *puritanical* enters the English language with reference to the social effects of Calvinism, as Calvinists strove to outdo one another in godliness to prove they were not all part of the mass of damnation.

Nowhere was this Puritanism more pronounced than in Calvin's Geneva, where the reformer reigned as a theocratic monarch for the remainder of his life. The labors of Calvin in Geneva are impressive by any measure. He pastored the church of St. Pierre, preaching hour-long sermons extemporaneously multiple times per week. He penned commentaries on the Scriptures and produced scores of pamphlets, both doctrinal and devotional. He maintained a constant correspondence with eminent persons all over Europe, orchestrated missionary efforts, and trained disciples to preach his gospel throughout Christendom.

At the time of Calvin's arrival, few persons in Geneva were willing to subscribe to his confession of faith. Thus, when Calvin began implementing his reform, he faced bitter opposition, not so much from theological rivals as from a party loosely known as the "libertines," people who simply wanted to live their lives unhindered by the intrusive theocracy Calvin established. Calvin would struggle with these people for most of his life, and when he had the opportunity, they were strictly punished.

Officially, Geneva was ruled by a city council and a religious "consistory," established at Calvin's behest for the trying of ecclesiastical offenses (later the city council would assume power to punish for even these). Calvin's role was officially pastor of the church of St. Pierre, but in practice, he had broad authority to regulate the affairs of the city. He sometimes came into conflict with the council—once he had to relocate to Strasbourg for several years because of opposition from different factions within Geneva—but from 1541 on, Calvin more or less retained undisputed control of the city. In that year, the city council passed the "Ecclesiastical Ordinances," which defined the roles of the clergy and gave clerics broad political influence.

Historians debate whether Calvin's Geneva was truly a theocracy in the strict sense; it depends upon one's definitions. It is certain that the regime was essentially religious, that political and religious matters were hard to disentangle, and that the secular authority enforced criminal penalties for religious offenses. Francoise Favre, wife of one of Calvin's political opponents, was tried and imprisoned for the offense of dancing in 1547. A man named Ami Perrin, another political rival, was sentenced to have his hand cut off for resisting Calvin's rule but fled before the sentence could be carried out. Jacques Gruet, a drunken atheist who mocked the Scriptures and left a blasphemous note in Calvin's parish, was arrested and beheaded in 1547. Most famous of the victims of Geneva was Michael Servetus, a Spanish physician who denied the Trinity and had ridiculed Calvin's *Institutes*. When Servetus passed through Geneva in 1553, Calvin had him arrested and burned alive.

The point is not to try to paint Calvin as a bloodthirsty villain; Catholic kingdoms had civil penalties for religious offenses as well, and Servetus had previously been sentenced to death by burning by a Catholic tribunal in Vienne before fleeing to Geneva. Rather, these cases exemplify the more or less theocratic nature of Calvin's regime, the union of the religious and secular authority in Geneva, the sorts of offenses Calvin considered worthy of death, and the influence of Calvin personally.

Though after the 1550s Calvin was not challenged politically for the rest of his life, he suffered personal discouragement at the lack of unity among Reformers as he watched the groups coming out of the Reformation continue to divide and subdivide. Calvin spent his final years establishing a school for children in Geneva. He died after a prolonged fever on May 27, 1564 at age fifty-four. He was hastily buried in an unmarked grave, intentionally left anonymous to discourage homage to Calvin becoming a kind of Protestant saint-cult. Calvin would have disapproved of such a thing.

Calvinism would become perhaps the most virile and prolific Protestant sect to come out of the sixteenth century. During Calvin's own life, it made inroads into France, the Holy Roman Empire, and the Low Countries, but it would attain special prominence in England and Scotland, where Calvinist movements would topple monarchs.

It is not difficult to understand the appeal of Calvinism. It provided a system of rigorous social and personal discipline attractive to those who found other forms of Christianity too lax. The denial of free will and the belief in predestination

embellished every good deed with an aura of divine certitude—whether repairing a wagon wheel, sitting through an
hour-long sermon, or flogging the town drunkard for playing cards, the sixteenth-century Calvinist had an iron-clad
certainty that his actions were the infallible outworking of
God's inscrutable providence.

Still, Calvinism has been characterized as a joyless system, and this, too, is understandable. The man who was less
than saintly in his religious observance could be tormented
by the idea that he was predestined to hell. The very idea
of the arbitrary predestination of certain souls to hell is an
admittedly depressing thought, no matter how one spins it.
Furthermore, the Calvinist polity was of necessity always one
of great rigor; recreation was often mistaken for moral laxity, and simple joys for sins. The eighteenth-century satirist
Voltaire, no friend to religion of any sort, wittily noted, "If
[Calvinists] condemned celibacy in the priests, and opened
the gates of the convents, it was only to turn all society into
a convent. Shows and entertainments were expressly forbidden by their religion; and for more than two hundred years
there was not a single musical instrument allowed in the city
of Geneva."

In chapter 10, we will see the fruit Calvinism bore in Scotland, but first we must travel from Geneva to the island of
merry England to see how the Reformation unfolded there.

Chapter 8

Two Witnesses:
Sts. Thomas More and John Fisher

The German Peasants' War ended in the winter of 1525 with the southern kingdoms of the Holy Roman Empire awash in blood. As we have noted, the causes of this conflict were not essentially religious, but the revolutionary diatribe of Martin Luther against ecclesiastical authority, coupled with his bold proclamations on the freedom of Christians, had certainly exacerbated existing tensions. The religious question had become political, and every prince in the empire would have to confront it.

The princes of the Holy Roman Empire convened at Speyer the following summer. The gathering was presided over by Ferdinand, brother of Emperor Charles V and Arch-duke of Austria. The assembly was initially summoned to deal with the Turkish threat on the empire's eastern reaches, but once gathered, the princes clamored for settlement to the religious question. Emperor Charles V's 1521 Edict of Worms condemned Lutheranism, yet throughout the empire, Lutheranism was spreading, often with the open approval of secular princes who saw the Lutheran movement as an occasion to seize ecclesiastical property. Was the Edict of Worms policy, or was it a dead letter?

To Ferdinand and the notables of the realm, it seemed that the Edict was unenforceable. Lutheranism was simply too deeply entrenched. After considerable debate, the princes issued a decree in August 1526 that each prince within the realm could establish whatever religion they wished—Lutheranism and Catholicism being the only two options. This policy of religious liberty was a triumph for the Lutherans. Even if Catholic princes retained the right to keep Lutheranism out of their domains, at least it gave Lutheranism legal standing within those realms where it was already established.

This situation was quickly reversed, however. Charles had not given much attention to the German empire in 1526, for he was occupied with a war with King Francis I of France. The following year saw him in Italy, and it was not until 1529 that his military affairs with France were settled. That spring, he again turned his attention to the affairs of the empire. What he saw alarmed him; despite proscribing Lutheranism in 1521, the succeeding eight years had seen the proliferation and consolidation of Lutheranism throughout southern Germany. Whatever the situation on the ground, Charles was committed to the Catholic faith and rescinded the decree of 1526, insisting on the full implementation of the Edict of Worms.

This turn of events seriously threatened the existence of Lutheran communities throughout the empire. Not only was Catholicism reestablished as the only legally recognized faith, but Lutheran pastors—and princes—who had seized Catholic property over the past eight years faced the prospect of having to return it to the Church. Various reformers of different persuasions—Lutherans, followers of the Swiss Ulrich Zwingli, and radicals in the mold of Thomas Müntzer—all united to protest the emperor's decree. On April 19, 1529, they issued a joint declaration protesting Charles's policy. The protest was signed by six imperial princes and the representatives of fourteen imperial free cities. The signatories of the 1529 document became known as "Protestants" by virtue of their protest against the reintroduction of the Edict of Worms. The term quickly expanded to denote any individual who denied the claims of the Catholic Church and embraced the core principles of the reform. And Germany would endure another twenty-five years of warfare.

Thus, as the first decade of the Reformation era closed, the religious landscape had been divided into two camps, Catholic and Protestant. In 1529, the Catholics were still in the majority, by far, and presented a well-organized, culturally monolithic front against the spread of Protestantism. The bulk and organization of the Church, however, also made it difficult to move swiftly to check the advances of the reform. In 1529, many Catholic dioceses did not yet grasp the threat posed by Protestantism or, if they had, were responding in a purely reactive mode. There had been talk of an ecumenical council to address the crisis, but so far nothing had materialized. By contrast, the Protestant movement was smaller, fragmented, and torn by internal divisions and dissension (both Luther and Calvin were appalled at the disunity among the reform movements). Yet the Protestants often benefited from the allegiance of land hungry members of the lower nobility and merchant middle class, a missionary fervor, and a fluidity of organization that made it easier to react to changing conditions on the ground.

The monarchs of Christendom found themselves compelled to take sides. Some wanted to make a political game out of it, like Francis I of France, who remained Catholic but toyed with Protestantism to score diplomatic points against his rival, Charles V—or Elector Frederick of Saxony, who was a devoted Catholic but went out of his way to shelter Luther. These monarchs often found they were playing with fire: recall that the Protestant refugees welcomed by Francis I turned against him in the affair of the placards, and Frederick's Saxony became the site of Müntzer's failed rebellion. Some monarchs were sincere devotees of the new faith— King Christian III of Denmark had adopted Lutheranism before ascending the throne and implemented it with zeal, officially making Lutheranism the religion of his kingdom in 1528, despite considerable political unrest. Other monarchs piously defended the Catholic Church on principle, adhering to the faith of their fathers; Charles V was a steadfast son of the Church who was determined to uphold its position at any cost.

In this latter group, we could place King Henry VIII of England, who at the outset was a very devoted Catholic and remained more or less opposed to Lutheranism throughout his reign. Henry was of the royal house of Tudor, which had only been in power for thirty-two years at the time of Luther's *95 Theses*—the Tudors were of relatively recent vintage as far as European royal dynasties go. Henry was never destined for the throne; his elder brother Arthur had been groomed for succession from birth by their competent and penny-pinching father, Henry VII. The succession plan had been formalized by the marriage of Prince Arthur to the gentle Catherine of Aragon, the daughter of the famous Ferdinand and Isabella of Spain and the aunt of Emperor Charles V.

Henry, as the younger son, was relegated to the care of the foremost tutors in the realm: John Skelton, Bernard Andre, Giles D'Ewes, Richard Croke, and John Fisher, the respected bishop of Rochester. His education was exceptional, and the young Henry proved to be intellectually astute. He was fluent in Latin, Spanish, and French and had a working knowledge of Italian. He was studied in the Scriptures and articulate in the finer theological points of the Christian faith. Raised in the full blossom of the Humanist age, young Henry was well acquainted with the writings of the classical era (he was particularly knowledgeable in Cicero and Livy) and the philosophies of the Humanists. He also had a deep piety and attended Mass daily.

Henry's destiny changed in 1502 when his brother Arthur died. It became apparent that young Henry—then ten years old and being raised as a scholar—was going to have to be prepared for a life of statesmanship. Though his education changed drastically, Henry maintained a vigorous interest in all things academic. As he grew, he began fruitful corre-spondences with famous Humanists Erasmus and Thomas More, both of whom considered Henry to be exceptionally intelligent and well rounded.

As Henry grew to manhood, he became something of a prodigy. The prince was physically imposing, with a tall, confident gait, broad shoulders and a muscular chest, and a love of all things athletic. He was equally at home hunting or engaging in philosophical sparring with eminent scholars. He was shrewd but generous, and had an encyclopedic memory. Humanists like More, Erasmus, Skelton, and Fisher saw in Henry a kind of rising luminary of the Humanist ideal—an educated and powerful prince who would apply the principles of Humanism to the governance of his realm. Thus, good things were expected of this young prince, who maintained a constant circle of scholarly companions. When his father was finally dead and buried in 1509, young Henry ascended to the throne of England as King Henry VIII.

We have mentioned Thomas More in passing several times in this book. More was Henry's senior by thirteen years. Coming from a respectable upper middle-class background, Thomas More studied under the noted Humanists Thomas Linacre and William Grocyn at Oxford, enthusiastically embracing the "new learning." More's father was the reputable attorney Sir John More, who insisted that Thomas follow up his education at Oxford with a training in law at Lincoln's Inn, London.

More began his practice in 1502, but immediately experienced a kind of spiritual conversion. He seriously contemplated entering religious life and actually relocated to a small home near the Carthusian monastery of London. There, he spent the better part of a year joining in the spiritual life of the monks and imbibing Carthusian spirituality. Though More eventually returned to the world and ran successfully for Parliament in 1504, the spiritual discipline he developed with the Carthusians endured. For most of his life, he wore a hair shirt and practiced rigorous penances.

After More entered law and Parliament, his star only rose higher. He was chosen to formally address Henry's coronation procession in 1509, where he declared that England was now entering a golden age. He was renowned for his erudition and wit and eventually became privy counselor in 1514, the sixteenth-century equivalent of an attorney general for the court. He distinguished himself in various undertakings, serving as secretary for Chancellor Thomas Cardinal Wolsey, carrying out a diplomatic mission to Emperor Charles V (who was deeply impressed with More), working in the office of Exchequer, and eventually becoming the secretary of King Henry VIII himself in 1521. This was an extremely influential position; besides putting More in the personal confidence of the king, he became the liaison between the king and other royal officials, the gatekeeper to foreign diplomats seeking royal audience, and a ghost writer of official documents.

The other great Humanist of the period was Bishop John Fisher. When Henry was a boy, Fisher was a renowned theologian at Cambridge. Fisher had some nominal contact with King Henry when the boy was young and seems to have tutored him in some degree, but Fisher's real connection with the court was through King Henry's grandmother, the Lady Margaret Beaufort. Lady Margaret was an extremely pious soul who had taken Fisher as her personal confessor. Old King Henry VII sought to reform the Church in his realm by appointing good and virtuous men to the episcopacy, and in a letter to Lady Margaret in 1504, he explains that John Fisher was a model candidate:

> I am well minded to promote Master Fisher, your confessor, to a bishopric; and I assure you, Madam, for none other cause, but for the great and singular virtue that I know and see in him, as well in cunning [knowledge] and natural wisdom, and specially for his good and virtuous living and conversation. And by the promotion of such a man I know well it should encourage many others to live virtuously and to take such ways as he doth, which should be a good example to many others hereafter.[16]

Fisher became bishop of Rochester in 1504. Rochester was the poorest diocese in England, but that did not stop him from quickly becoming a beacon of the English church. Fisher's renown was in both his theological insight and his powerful preaching, gifts that were rare in an age when most bishops were canonists or statesmen.

The English church was perhaps one of the best organized in Christendom; the moderate influence of northern Humanism had brought a quiet reform of piety and ecclesiastical governance. Education was better among the English clergy than on the continent, and the first two Tudor kings were sincere proponents of genuine ecclesiastical reform. Nevertheless, many of the problems of late medieval Catholicism persisted, notably a dearth of skilled preachers and over involvement of bishops in political affairs. Erudite and a

---

16   Henry VII to Lady Margaret Beaufort, 1504. *St. John Fisher*, E. E. Reynolds (Mediatrix Press: Post Falls, ID.), 2015, pg. 39.

powerful orator, Fisher countered that trend and became not only the best-known English preacher but a model bishop. He regularly preached to the people in their churches or in open fields, and he visited the sick of his diocese even if they were in a smoky hovel that others would dare not to enter. Judging from the number of editions in both English and Latin, his "Sermons on the Penitential Psalms" were extremely popular.

Fisher's fame was such that he was called upon to preach at the funerals of King Henry VII and Lady Margaret (both in 1509). His reputation also extended to the continent, and he was able to persuade the famed Erasmus to visit Cambridge University upon the latter's visit to England. Erasmus was impressed with Fisher's piety and scholarship, and the two became friends. In 1516, when Erasmus was again in England and staying with Fisher, Thomas More came to pay his old friend a visit. One can imagine Fisher, More, and Erasmus all sitting in Fisher's library together, laughing merrily and discoursing on matters of religion, polity, and morals.

The new king, Henry VIII, also held Fisher in high regard. Henry VIII, like his father, had a vision for the reform of the English church. With the king's good graces, Fisher regularly preached against corruption and urged his fellow clerics to adopt disciplinary reforms. Fisher, however, harbored no Protestant sympathies. He was a loyal son of the Church, his calls for reform proceeding from a sincere desire for the glory of Christ's body and the salvation of souls, not from any nationalist or anti-Roman prejudice—still less from any sympathy for those who would try to separate kingdoms from unity with the successor of St. Peter or steal Church property under the guise of reform.

When word reached England of Luther's break with Rome, St. John Fisher entered the controversy by composing a work refuting Luther's re-assertion of the articles that had been condemned by Pope Leo X. King Henry was also indignant at the actions of the Saxon monk. Though an amateur theologian, he was astute enough to understand Luther's basic attack on the sacramental system of the Catholic Church. In 1521, the year Luther was excommunicated, the king himself published a treatise entitled *Assertio septem sacramentorum* ("Defense of the Seven Sacraments"), a point-by-point rebuttal of Luther's sacramental theology. St. Thomas More, as Henry's secretary, edited the work.

As an interesting aside on Henry's book, we should note that Thomas More suggested to Henry that he leave out the defense of the papacy in the dedicatory epistle to Pope Leo X. Henry, however, insisted on keeping it in the book. The reason for this, odd as it seems from our modern vantage point given Henry's later actions and More's martyrdom, is that the king believed that the papacy was of divine origin, while More did not. In ten years' time, their positions would be entirely reversed. Henry would abandon the papacy in order to have his way in regard to marriage and control of the Church, but More, reading John Fisher's writings against Luther, would come to be convinced from the weight of Fisher's argumentation that the papacy was indeed a divine institution.

At any rate, Henry won the praise of Pope Leo X, who conferred upon him the title "Defender of the Faith." In

1526, Cardinal Wolsey presided over a massive burning of Lutheran books, in which John Fisher gave a rousing sermon against the pernicious doctrines of Luther. Henry had made it perfectly clear that the "reform" had no place in his kingdom.

In the 1520s, both More and Fisher enjoyed the respect and confidence of the throne. More, at the recommendation of Chancellor Cardinal Wolsey, was made speaker of the House of Commons in 1523; in 1525, he became chancellor of the duchy of Lancaster, which gave him broad authority over much of northern England. More's ultimate promotion came in 1529 when he became lord chancellor upon Wolsey's fall from power. As chancellor, More became, in effect, the chief legal representative of the crown and its interests. Fisher's star was also in the ascendant as he became the most notable ecclesiastic in the realm. Though he could have been promoted—and though some pegged him as successor to archbishop of Canterbury William Warham—the good bishop dutifully stayed on in the poor diocese of Rochester and continued his affiliation with the University of Cambridge.

The spread of Protestantism continued to occupy the energies of both men. In 1526, Fisher, at the insistence of Henry VIII, preached a series of famous sermons at St. Paul's against the errors of Luther. The Peasants' War had just ended and all Germany was in chaos. Rightly or wrongly, these disorders were popularly attributed to Luther, and Henry VIII wanted no penetration of Lutheranism into his domains. As we saw, throughout the 1520s, Fisher would devote considerable energy to vigilantly defending the Catholic faith against

Protestantism, which was slowly seeping into England from the continent. Preaching and writing occupied most of his time, but Fisher also was not averse to handing notable heretics over to the secular arm, though when he handled them in his own diocese, he generally succeeded in returning them to the Catholic faith. His motto was "Either I shall make them a Catholic, or they shall make me a Lutheran." With his deep knowledge of the Scriptures and the Fathers, the latter was scarcely possible. In 1529, nevertheless, Fisher and Archbishop Warham of Canterbury presided over the trial of one Thomas Hitton, a renegade English priest who had been caught smuggling Protestant tracts in from the Netherlands. Warham secured Hitton's condemnation for heresy, and Thomas More ensured Hitton was punished by the secular arm. Hitton was subsequently burned at the stake.

Henry's zealous opposition to Protestantism and the systematic efforts of More, Fisher, and others to oppose the spread of heresy drove Protestant agitators from the kingdom. Many English Protestant exiles wound up just over the Channel in the Netherlands. Yet even while political pressure kept Protestantism at bay, it crept into the very heart of the kingdom through other avenues.

Catherine of Aragon, the Spanish wife of Henry VIII, had borne Henry one daughter, Mary, the future Mary Tudor. Five other pregnancies resulted in stillbirths or children who died shortly after birth. By 1520, Catherine was past childbearing age and had no subsequent pregnancies. This was of considerable concern to Henry. His dynasty was still relatively young, having taken power only in 1485 at the end of a bitter civil war. Without a male successor, the realm could fall back into chaos, especially given the destabilizing threat posed by Protestantism. True, he had a potential successor in his daughter Mary, but England had never been ruled by a queen since Matilda in the twelfth century, a reign renowned only for its anarchy. Henry's lack of a male heir could potentially mean civil war and the dissolution of his house.

In 1525, Henry became enamored with Anne Boleyn, one of Queen Catherine's ladies-in-waiting. At eleven years Henry's junior, Anne was beautiful, educated, and receptive to the king's attention. Anne had been educated on the continent and had adopted some of the tenets of Protestantism. While Henry had vigorously opposed the spread of Protestantism in his realm, the tender graces and gentle, persuasive conversation of Anne somewhat softened Henry's heart to some of the ideas of the reform.

Traditionally, a relationship of this sort usually came to nothing. Monarchs typically married for political purposes, not love; most, save for the saintly, kept mistresses for companionship and to attend to their physical desires. Henry VIII had certainly kept mistresses. Anne Boleyn's own sister, Mary, had formerly been the mistress of the king. Anne, however, refused the king's amorous advances. A devout Protestant, Anne refused to become Henry's mistress, though in all other respects she reciprocated his attention. This refusal drove Henry's ambition even further, for he was the sort of man who wanted nothing so badly as that which he was told he could not have.

This led Henry to reflect on his marriage with Catherine. Why had he failed to produce a male heir? Perhaps, he surmised, the marriage had been cursed by God. Henry had latched onto two passages from the Old Testament Book of Leviticus: "You shall not uncover the nakedness of your brother's wife; she is your brother's nakedness" (Lv 18:16), "If a man takes his brother's wife, it is impurity; he has uncovered his brother's nakedness, they shall be childless" (Lv 20:21). The second passage in particular had special relevance to Henry; in marrying Catherine, had he not taken his brother Arthur's wife? And had Henry not suffered for it by Catherine's inability to produce an heir?

Throughout 1525–1527, Henry began cobbling together an argument that his marriage to Catherine was contrary to divine law, based on the text of Leviticus. Typically, a previous marriage to a sibling was considered an impediment to marriage. Pope Julius II had dispensed Henry from this impediment back in 1503, allowing the marriage of Henry and Catherine to proceed. Henry had to find a way to get the present pontiff, Clement VII, to invalidate the papal dispensation, clearing the way for Henry to have the marriage to Catherine annulled. He sent out for opinions from learned theologians and universities in England as well as on the Continent. He also sent Cardinal Wolsey to see St. John Fisher to elicit his opinion. Fisher replied that the original dispensation would have to be examined but was entirely skeptical as to the merits of the argument. In fact, he said that the Church Fathers traditionally put the passages from Leviticus and Deuteronomy together—that a man *must* marry his brother's wife to raise up children to his name so that if the brother died childless, the marriage was legitimate. Wolsey was troubled by this, as it was a serious challenge to the arguments that he and Henry had been developing over the last few months.

It is important to understand that Henry was not seeking a divorce but an annulment. Practically speaking, the effects of the two were the same; Henry wished to terminate his marital relationship with Catherine of Aragon in order to be free to wed Anne Boleyn. Yet the two are logically distinct; a divorce is the termination of an existing marriage, while an annulment is a declaration that no valid marriage ever existed to begin with. Since the Catholic Church has never recognized divorce as something permissible under divine law, Henry had to find a way to get the pope to declare that his marriage to Catherine had never been valid to begin with. The first step was for Wolsey to set up a private ecclesiastical trial to adjudicate the matter in England in the hopes that a favorable decision from himself would convince the pope to concur without any further issue. But Wolsey stalled, he found the matter too hard, or else discovered conscience late in his career and realized he could not manage a canonical process of this nature to his liking.

Thus, in 1527, Wolsey referred the matter to Rome for Pope Clement's judgment, hoping to use his contacts in the Curia to sway Clement to his side. Unbeknownst to Wolsey, however, in 1527—the very year Henry made it plain to Catherine that he intended to annul the marriage—Charles V's army in Italy saw its pay fall into arrears, mutinied, and sacked the city of Rome. The reasons for this are complex (we will examine them more closely in chapter 10). The sack of the city was devastatingly destructive. So calamitous was the sack of Rome that many historians date the sack of 1527 as the moment the Renaissance ended. Pope Clement was severely shaken by the incident and was terrified of arousing the anger of Emperor Charles V.

Seeking to put further pressure on the pope, Henry marshaled some of the greatest theological minds in Europe to address the case. Theological masters from the University of Paris debated the king's "great matter," some arguing for, some against invalidity. For Catherine's part, Henry had hoped she would consent to go away quietly to a monastery, but when faced with this proposal, she reacted with indignation and resolved to fight the king's efforts. Catherine brought to her defense none other than the best theologian in the kingdom, Bishop John Fisher. Fisher would appear in courts on the queen's behalf and argue against Henry's case with appalling bluntness; he compared Henry to King Herod Antipas and stated that, like John the Baptist, he was ready to die in defense of the indissolubility of marriage. This enraged Henry, who felt betrayed by the bishop he and his father had so favored. He composed a long Latin diatribe against Fisher, whom he would never forgive for publicly opposing him.

More was in a much different position. As chancellor, More had the job of publicly arguing in favor of the royal policy, much like an attorney general who must argue the government's case. Personally, however, More had misgivings about the king's argument. He was initially willing to argue in favor of the king's annulment, but when the debate shifted from marital impediments to papal authority, More would be caught in a crisis of conscience.

It is beyond the scope of this chapter to comprehensively expound King Henry's argument. It went through various stages of refinement, had multiple angles, and incorporated arguments historical, canonical, and biblical. Henry believed Leviticus plainly forbade marriage to a brother's widow (ignoring that Deuteronomy seemed to have an exception for when a brother died without heirs, which was exactly Henry's case). The Church, however, had frequently issued dispensations for cases where the brother had died before the marriage had been consummated. Henry argued that the marriage of Catherine to Arthur had been consummated; Catherine, that it had not. Thus, for a time, Queen Catherine suffered the embarrassment of all Europe debating whether or not she had sex once in 1501.

The real question, though, was whether the marriage to a brother's widow was an impediment of divine law. If it was, the pope could have no authority to dispense from it. If it was not, popes could make such dispensations. Thus, the ground of the question began to shift to papal authority, with Henry obviously arguing that the pope had no power to dispense from impediments of divine law. Ecclesiastical courts in England had been unable to come to a decision on Henry's case. And so, in 1528, the papal legate Campeggio arrived in England with authority from Pope Clement VII to render judgment.

Little known to Henry, however, was the fact that Clement intended to delay the case indefinitely. Considered of itself, Henry's request was not completely unprecedented; in fact, annulments had been granted before for monarchs in precisely Henry's situation. Clement, however, saw a broader picture, for he could never forget that Catherine was the aunt of Charles V, the Holy Roman emperor, and during the sack of Rome, the pope had witnessed, helplessly, the destruction of the city by Charles's troops. Thus, when messages began arriving from England insisting that the pope help Henry put away the emperor's aunt, Clement was loath to grant the request for fear of offending Charles. The legate Campeggio made some efforts to persuade Queen Catherine to withdraw her opposition voluntarily but declined to take any further action when she refused.

Between 1527 and 1529, as the drama with the annulment played out and Henry sparred with Campeggio, Henry's mood took a decided turn against the pope. Among the king's supporters, anti-clericalism was rife. As the parliamentary elections of 1529 drew near, all around the kingdom men either sympathetic to Protestantism or at least willing to risk a breach with Rome began standing for Parliament. Wolsey wrote to the pope to warn him that Henry would break with Rome to get his own way. This veiled threat failed to move Clement, however. By this time, Henry was tiring of Wolsey's failures and stripped him of the chancellorship in 1529. Wolsey took ill, and was only saved from being executed as a traitor by dying of illness instead, crying out, "If only I served my God as well as I served my king!"

Still, though Henry's mind was darkening on Rome, and though he listened respectfully to Anne Boleyn's Protestant sympathies, being a Protestant in Henry VIII's England was still extremely dangerous. Even while Henry was preparing an all-out assault on papal authority and pushing anti-clerical legislation through Parliament, he was still burning Protestant heretics. The very year the Catholic clergy would be suppressed, Henry burned a man for denying transubstantiation. It is one of the great ironies of the English Protestant Reformation that it was rammed through by a king who fancied himself an enemy of Protestantism even while he was in the act of establishing it.

When it became clear that the papal legate Campeggio would not render a decision, Henry got the case transferred to Rome in 1529. Pope Clement was under significant political pressure from Henry; the pope, however, continued his characteristic indecision and refused to rule on the case. Meanwhile, Henry's new Parliament, the so-called "Reformation Parliament," began establishing the legal machinery that would allow Henry broad control of ecclesiastical affairs. Canonical courts were abolished, and it was made a criminal offense to appeal to any authority outside the realm of England. This latter piece of legislation was drafted with the intention of prohibiting appeals to Rome. The Parliament passed a bill threatening to cut off all payments to Rome if Henry's annulment was not granted within a year. English clergy were prohibited from attending any religious gatherings abroad.

For those, like John Fisher, who supported the queen's position, the situation was growing precarious. Fisher had appealed to the Holy See against the king's legislation in 1530 and was immediately imprisoned. He was soon released, but his troubles were not over. In 1531, when the clergy came together for convocation, Henry angrily renewed the old *Præmunire* statutes dating from the reign of Edward I (1272–1307), which forbade appeals across the sea to Rome. He accused the clergy of breaking these statutes and demanded payment of a fine of one hundred thousand pounds. More than just money was demanded, however; under the influence of his new councilor Thomas Cromwell, Henry insisted that the clergy recognize the king as the supreme head of the Church of England with an oath.

The 1531 "Law of Supremacy" essentially forced the English church to choose between their king and their pope. Henry was trying to establish a position that would allow an English court to annul his marriage without regards to the pope; Henry surmised that if the king was recognized as the head of the Church by the English clergy themselves, the annulment could be legitimized. For faithful Catholics like Fisher, the oath Henry imposed upon the clergy was a denial of the primacy of Peter. It was to St. Peter that Christ had entrusted his Church, not to the kings of the nations.

Fisher and his fellow clergymen met in consistory in 1531 to debate King Henry's proposal. Through Fisher's efforts, Henry mitigated the oath, adding the phrase "insofar as the law of God allows," which was more palatable to the clergy. The phrase gave room for the clergy to affirm what was essentially a tautology, saying, "The king has authority over the Church, except where he doesn't."

The peace of the compromise did not last long. In 1531, Fisher survived what appeared to be two attempts on his life, one by poisoning and the other from a cannon shot from the home of Thomas Boleyn. Fisher continued to preach publicly against the divorce, supporting Queen Catherine's position as he always had. Henry, meanwhile, continued to push the royal supremacy by every avenue he could.

Thomas More, in the meantime, resigned the chancellorship in 1532, alleging poor health. Though he swore the oath with the clause "insofar as the law of God allows," More was becoming increasingly isolated politically and could no longer support the policies the king was formulating. Thus, by 1532, both More and Fisher had put themselves definitively outside the king's favor, More by attempting to withdraw from public life, Fisher by challenging Henry's actions boldly from the pulpit.

The same year More resigned, William Warham, the elderly archbishop of Canterbury, passed away. Henry secured the nomination of one Thomas Cranmer to the post. Cranmer was a priest of Cambridge, who was the chaplain to Anne Boleyn's family as well as a noted supporter of the annulment with strong Lutheran sympathies. Like Luther, he had renounced his vow of celibacy and taken a wife. Cranmer approved of Henry's direction thus far and made himself a creature of the crown in order to advance his religious agenda. Cranmer's appointment to the highest ecclesiastical office in the land would open the way for Henry to do whatever he wished with the full approval of the English church. Fisher was temporarily arrested a week after Cranmer's appointment. Presumably, Henry knew that Cranmer's appointment would elicit more public opposition from Fisher; arresting him was a convenient way to forestall more open criticism.

With Cranmer in place and Fisher out of the way for the time being, Henry moved quickly. In January, 1533, Henry was secretly wed to Anne Boleyn by Cranmer. In April, an ecclesiastical court presided over by Cranmer formally annulled Henry's marriage to Catherine. That year, Parliament passed the Act of Succession, which declared Henry's daughter Mary by Catherine a bastard and designated the royal succession through Anne Boleyn. Once this was accomplished, Fisher was released. Fisher would again be arrested, fined, and released in 1534 in what amounted to a campaign of harassment by Henry.

More had disappeared from public life in 1532, but Henry continued to pester him about his allegiance to the new regime. Thomas Cromwell, in particular, sought various means to implicate More, first charging him with taking bribes, later attempting to condemn him for his association with a certain nun who had vocally opposed Henry's marriage to Anne. More successfully evaded both of these traps.

In the end, however, it was the Act of Succession that proved the undoing of both More and Fisher. More had conspicuously failed to show up at Anne Boleyn's coronation. This was not treason, but Henry took it as a personal insult to Anne. In April of 1535, both More and Fisher were summoned to Lambeth Palace to take the oath of succession, acknowledging Anne as queen and the offspring of Henry and Anne as legitimate heirs to the throne, on pain of treason. Both Fisher and More were willing to swear part of the oath, namely that the right of succession would go to Henry and Anne's children, since kings and parliaments might choose the succession as they like. They would not, however, swear to the preamble that declared Anne as queen and the marriage to Catherine invalid. As a result, both were sent to the Tower of London to think it over.

Pope Clement had finally roused himself from inactivity and pronounced Henry's marriage to Catherine valid in 1534, but by then the situation was out of control. Henry had effectively broken all institutional ties with Rome and used his new-found domination of the English clergy to legitimize his marriage to Anne. Pope Clement died shortly after excommunicating Henry and Cranmer. The new pope, Paul III, tried to get Henry to soften his treatment of Fisher by making Fisher a cardinal, but this only made Henry more determined to destroy him.

Cromwell's men interrogated both Fisher and More for the better part of the year, but they were never able to obtain any evidence of treason, even by the new "thought crime" definition of the Act of Succession. More and Fisher passed notes in the tower and both agreed not to take the oath even if they would be told the other had, as well as to be silent so as not to be condemned. Time was running out for Henry, as both men were popular in England, while Anne was hated; sympathy for More and Fisher grew daily.

At last, on the seventh of May, 1535, a royal informer was sent to John Fisher to ask him what his real opinion was on the Act of Royal Supremacy—could Henry be the head of the English church, even if only in theory? He added an oath that the king merely wanted to know what Fisher thought and that this would not be used against him. Fisher, after hearing the oath, revealed that he did not believe Henry could be head of the English church. The unknown early biographer of Fisher suggests this informer was Richard Rich, who tried the same trick with Thomas More. More was more street-wise, however, and revealed nothing. Fisher was tried for treason on June 17, where the same man appeared to confess that Fisher maliciously and traitorously denied the Royal Supremacy. Fisher admitted it was so but asserted the man had made an oath that it would not be used against him. It was to no avail; the verdict was of course a foregone conclusion. Fisher was condemned to be hanged, drawn, and quartered, but the sentence was subsequently commuted to beheading. Fisher went to his death with a peaceful, dignified certitude in the righteousness of his cause. He was beheaded on June 22, 1535. His naked body was left on the scaffold until evening and his head stuck upon a pole on London Bridge. Fisher never performed any miracles in his life, but in his death, he performed a singular one; his head on London Bridge emitted the fragrant smell of roses that permeated the entire area of the heavily trafficked bridge. This proved yet another embarrassment to Henry's regime, and he ordered Fisher's head to be removed so that it could be replaced with that of Thomas More!

Thomas More lasted only a fortnight longer. He was tried for the same charge and had astutely refused to swear or deny the acts of Succession and Royal Supremacy, using the legal principle *Qui tacet, consentit* ("He who is silent, seems to consent") as a way to avoid denying what the Church taught and at the same time avoiding a death sentence for treason.

In the end, since there was no proof and Cromwell was desperate to get More's condemnation, he brought forth the solicitor general, Richard Rich, who testified that he heard More deny the king's headship over the Church while he visited him in the tower. Despite the dubious nature of the testimony (which most historians regard as false), the jury quickly arrived at a guilty verdict. More was sentenced to be hanged, drawn, and quartered, but like Fisher, had his sentence commuted to beheading. Still, once he saw he was condemned, More at last spoke his mind. He declared that the king could not be head of the Church, because Englishmen had long ago recognized that title as unique to the pope, before England was even England, and as such the parliament has no right to bestow this title on the king.

Thomas More was beheaded on July 6, 1535. His last words were, "I am the king's good servant, but God's first." His head, too, was left to rot on a pike suspended from the Tower of London.

The Church's two witnesses, St. Thomas More and St. John Fisher, would both eventually be raised to the altars as saints and martyrs for the true Faith. The year they died, Thomas Cromwell took over practical management of the ecclesiastical affairs of England. Henry and his councilors were busy preparing to seize the wealth of the kingdom's monasteries. Cranmer was in the early phases of Protestantizing the English church. Queen Anne was pregnant with a child who would one day give the Church many more martyrs. The story of the English Reformation was only beginning.

CHAPTER 9

Thomas Cromwell and Mary Tudor

W e cannot consider the establishment of Protestantism in England apart from the fascinating character of Thomas Cromwell. Cromwell had risen from humble mercantile origins to become a lawyer attached to the retinue of Cardinal Wolsey. When the latter fell from power and subsequently died in 1529, Cromwell managed to secure a seat in Parliament and became a royal favorite, entering King Henry's Privy Council in 1530. He held a dizzying array of posts in the service of the crown: twenty-five major offices, not counting additional minor ones. Cromwell was possessed of an exceptional intelligence and wit that made him a valuable counselor, but he was also unyieldingly faithful to Henry, his king. These two traits were rare in a counselor; the stereotypical royal advisor is either a witless stooge who is little more than a yes-man, or else a clever deceiver always scheming to undermine royal power. In Cromwell, Henry found a servant as conniving as a serpent but as loyal as a lapdog.

Cromwell was behind all the extensions of royal authority throughout the 1530s. As noted in chapter 8, it was

Cromwell who secured the executions of More and Fisher and who became lord privy seal and chamberlain after their deaths. Cromwell was the architect behind much of the legislation that granted Henry the supreme control of the English church. Catherine of Aragon, who had been imprisoned since 1532, died in January, 1536—at the news of which Henry rejoiced, a gesture considered vulgar by many. With More, Fisher, and Catherine all gone, and with sycophants like Cranmer and Cromwell behind the apparatuses of church and state, Henry was about to embark on one of the most ambitious power grabs in Western history.

The Act of Supremacy had established Henry VIII as the supreme head of the Church in England. This gave him ultimate say over the disposal of all ecclesiastical appointments and more importantly, ecclesiastical property. Of particular interest to King Henry were the kingdom's monasteries. England had always benefited from a very lively monastic presence throughout the Middle Ages. By 1536, the year Queen Catherine died, there were nearly nine hundred religious houses in England, comprised of twelve thousand souls. To put it in perspective, about one adult Englishman in every fifty was in a religious order.[17] This represented a phenomenal amount of wealth, both in land and hard assets. In 1534–35, Henry had Cromwell undertake a massive inventory of the wealth of all the monasteries. This was a monumental task that necessitated Cromwell making personal visitations

---

[17]   This statistic and others about the state of religious life on the eve of the dissolution of the monasteries can be found in the article "The Dissolution of the Monasteries" by G. W. Bernard, *History* (2011) 96, #324.

to most of the monasteries. Of paramount importance was assessing the wealth of each monastery, but Cromwell was also to instruct the monasteries on their duty to obey the king and reject papal authority, as well as to reform religious practices by looking for evidence of moral laxity and "superstitious" practices, such as the veneration of relics.

The state of the monasteries was a subject of great debate. Erasmus had considered most monasteries of the day to be places of moral laxity and spiritual sloth, where the idle contributed nothing to society but sat on the means of production, consuming but not producing. This view was prevalent among contemporaries sympathetic to Protestantism. While there were certainly abuses—and while many English monastic houses were small and barely able to sustain themselves—historians have also noted that monastic life was generally much sounder in England, where strong reforming impulses had already taken root prior to the introduction of Protestantism. In England, the critiques of Erasmus and others were often mere caricatures.

Cromwell brought back scandalous reports of monastic excesses, lax morals, and corrupt clergy. While there is no doubt some truth to these reports, it should be noted they were far from impartial. The purpose of the visitation was to inventory the monastic wealth for presumed seizure by the crown, a seizure that was to be carried out by Protestants who were predisposed against monasticism. In addition to this, given Cromwell's attempts to fabricate evidence against both More and Fisher, we should presume exaggeration in his reports. He was actively seeking to condemn the monasteries to justify the seizure of their wealth.

Regardless of the truth or falsity of Cromwell's visitation reports, they served their purpose. Henry came to the conclusion that England was glutted with too many religious houses whose members were not living their vocations. He also saw them as hotbeds of resistance to the royal supremacy, particularly the Carthusians, Observant Franciscans, and Bridgettine monks and nuns, all of whom were notable critics of the royal policy. Ultimately, Henry was planning a grand military adventure in Europe against Francis I, and the wealth of the monasteries would go a long way toward funding his continental campaign.

The First Suppression Act of 1536 dissolved what were termed the "lesser houses," those whose value in land, rents, and other assets did not amount to more than two hundred pounds. The assets of such houses were confiscated by the crown, and their monks and nuns sent to live at larger monasteries. Somewhere around 350 monasteries were dissolved under this act. Meanwhile, Cranmer sermonized on the benefits of the suppression, calling the monasteries dens of iniquity and promising the people that with the wealth of the monasteries, the king would never need to raise taxes again.

The centerpiece of the monastic dissolution came with the Second Suppression Act of 1539, which called for the dissolution of the remaining 552 monasteries, regardless of their assets or the quality of their religious observance. The wealth of the monasteries was transferred to a Court of Augmentations, which organized the revenue and paid out pensions to monks and nuns deprived of their living.

Suppression of monasteries was not necessarily a novel thing. Throughout the Middle Ages, kings had often dissolved monasteries that had fallen into disrepair or whose endowments could no longer support their vocations. There was a long precedent in England of kings consolidating smaller monasteries into larger monastic houses. Furthermore, even considered objectively, England had a very large number of monasteries and convents relative to its size. Thus, when Henry began closing the smaller monasteries in 1536, few Englishmen suspected the king was planning the total eradication of monasticism in the kingdom. This was only gradually realized—and by then it was too late.

The real nature of the suppressions became clear by the behavior of the royal officers sent to oversee the suppression. No sooner had the monks been turned out than royal agents began dismantling the monasteries and carting off their physical assets for sale. Workmen stripped copper from the roofs. Chalices and vestments were carried off. The once quiet chapels and crypts were profaned by the sound of hammers and chisels prying precious jewels from reliquaries. Triptychs and other pieces of art were seized and sold to the rich to adorn their private chapels. When all else that could be removed had been, even the timbers themselves were torn out to be resold, leaving many monasteries to collapse. Such measures made it clear that the dissolution was little more than organized state-sponsored looting. By 1540, the last monastery was closed.

This was not all done without resistance. Many religious suffered martyrdom for refusing the king's will in some manner. Occasionally a zealous abbot would resist the royal commissioners; such resistance was met with fierce reprisals. In the fall of 1539, Abbot Richard Whiting of Glastonbury resisted Cromwell's agents who had showed up without warning to dissolve the monastery. Whiting had formerly signed the Act of Supremacy, recognizing Henry as head of the Church in England. This did not save him; for his resistance, he was hanged, drawn, and quartered. Abbot John Beche of Colchester had similarly refused to hand the lands entrusted to him over to the crown. He was arrested, tried for treason, and hanged in December of 1539. Abbot Hugh Cook Farringdon of Reading was also initially supportive of King Henry's annulment but was subsequently condemned as a traitor and hanged, drawn, and quartered in his own abbey in November 1539. He would be beatified as a martyr in 1895.

It was not only monks who resisted. While King Henry enjoyed strong support in London and the southeast (where Protestant sympathies were strong among the London merchant class), the west and north of England were staunchly Catholic. The people in those regions grumbled with disapproval at the news from London that Henry was seeking to put away Queen Catherine. They watched with dismay as England's relationship with the papacy deteriorated. They stood, mouths agape and hearts downcast, while they watched royal workmen dismantle the ancient monasteries throughout the late 1530s. Changes to the traditional Catholic liturgy unnerved them; royal officials appeared in isolated villages and hamlets, ensuring that the local priests were conforming to new theological ideology emanating from London. All over England, frustration with Henry's policies was rising.

In late 1536, a spontaneous uprising of tens of thousands of Catholics burst out of northern England after the closure of a Cistercian abbey in Lincolnshire. Their grievances were both economic and religious; their demands included remission of certain taxes and reform of property laws, but they also demanded an end to the monastic dissolutions, the ejection of Protestant heretics from government, and a repudiation of the Protestantizing theology of Thomas Cranmer.

The rising, called the Pilgrimage of Grace, was largely peaceful. As the crowds moved south through Yorkshire, ejected monks and nuns were returned to their abbeys and Catholic observances were restored in parish churches. Unfortunately, a gathering of royalist nobles persuaded the pilgrimage to disband by promising redress of grievances. The leaders of the rising came to London to meet with Henry VIII but were subsequently arrested and hanged when disorders continued in the countryside. An armed insurrection that rose in the west shortly afterwards was similarly crushed. Throughout 1537 and 1538, plots, smaller uprisings, and executions continued as Henry brought the full machinery of the state to bear against all opposition to his program.

It is interesting that it was not the divorce proceedings and remarriage that brought the countryside to rebellion but the dissolution of the monasteries and the religious reform. While Cromwell was Henry's agent of political change, it was Thomas Cranmer, the archbishop of Canterbury, who pushed through Henry's religious reform. Henry's original vision for the English Church appears to have been something very close to Catholicism but without the pope, which makes sense given that Henry's original grievance with Rome was about authority, not doctrine. Thus, we see that in the convocation of 1536, the "Ten Articles" of faith promulgated under Cranmer retained many traditionally Catholic elements. The cult of the saints and prayers for their intercession are encouraged, as are prayers for the souls in Purgatory; transubstantiation and infant baptism are affirmed; and the traditional Creeds of the Church are retained. However, ecumenical councils are omitted as sources of faith; papal pardons are ridiculed; and sacred images, though retained, are not to be venerated. The "Six Articles" of 1539 also affirmed transubstantiation, auricular—that is, private—confession, and clerical celibacy. Essentially, Henry wanted to retain the faith of his fathers but remove any aspect of it that could rival his authority, such as the papacy and Church councils.

This tack made it possible for the common folk to continue enjoying their faith as they always had—for a time at least. Altars, candles, communion, readings, statues, stained glass, hymns all remained the same in the beginning. To the uneducated layman, what really was the tangible change? The prayers for the pope might be omitted, but much else seemed the same. Mass was still being said in Latin through most of the realm. How much difference did the layman really notice?

While this was helpful for ameliorating the concern of the public, the Protestants of England saw it as a compromise with Rome. Since Henry broke with the papacy, English Protestantism had been growing steadily. By 1540, many English bishops were essentially Protestant, some more sympathetic to Luther, some to Calvin. Henry had never quite felt at ease with the presence of these men within his realm, and their influence remained muted for most of his reign. They would soon have their moment, however.

Henry's marriage with Anne had not brought him the happiness, nor the heir, he anticipated. It was on account of Anne that Henry had broken with Rome, executed More and Fisher, incurred excommunication, and turned the whole kingdom Protestant. Henry had gambled that this would all be worth the procurement of a son. On September 7, 1533, Anne gave birth to a girl. The little princess was christened Elizabeth a few days later in a ceremony Henry did not attend. The king's disappointment was palpable; Anne had promised a son, and the king's astrologers had told him the child would be a boy. Elizabeth was perhaps the most unwanted royal child in European history.

Anne would soldier on bravely, giving Henry three more pregnancies—three miscarriages. We can imagine the chilling of relations between Henry and Anne as it became clear that the misfortune of Queen Catherine had followed Henry into his second marriage. By 1536, Henry had lost interest in Anne and was courting Jane Seymour, a maid of honor who had served both Anne Boleyn and Catherine. Restless to try again with his new lover, Henry had Anne arrested and charged with treason, incest, and adultery with seven different men. The charges were absolutely ridiculous but sufficient to secure a condemnation for Anne. She was beheaded the day before Henry wed Jane Seymour.

Jane would give Henry his long-desired son, who would become Edward VI, but she died from complications of childbirth in 1537. But Henry at last had his male heir, and

Elizabeth was bastardized along with her half-sister Mary, the daughter of Catherine of Aragon. Henry would go through three more wives before his death in January 1547. Henry VIII's reign, which had begun with such promise, had become an endless and gruesome spectacle of executions of friends, relatives, wives, churchmen, and others. Even the faithful Thomas Cromwell eventually lost Henry's favor—and his own head. It is estimated that as many as seventy-two thousand people may have been executed during Henry's reign, though there is no way to know for sure.

Despite his constant tinkering with his new royal church, religion in England was in chaos by the time of his death as Catholics, Anglicans, and a growing "Puritan" branch vied for influence. His reforms had caused political upheaval and an upending of traditional European alliances. Henry had not even been able to enjoy the wealth pilfered from the monasteries. The revenue of what was perhaps the biggest land grab in European history quickly dissipated as properties were sold off to royal favorites in order to raise funds for Henry's continental wars. His military adventures floundered, and the government was heavily in debt by the time of his death. Thus, all Henry's scheming, confiscations, and bloodletting ultimately brought him nothing and cost England dearly.

Edward VI was the son of Henry VIII and his third wife, Jane Seymour. The boy was ten when he came to the throne in 1547 and would only reign for six years. As he never enjoyed ruling in his majority, Edward was dominated by a regency council, led first by his uncle Edward Seymour and later by John Dudley, Earl of Warwick and Duke of

Northumberland. Both Seymour and Dudley had favored a more aggressive Protestantism, influenced by Calvinism. Cranmer, too, freed from the sentimentality that had bound King Henry to Catholic trappings, became more progressive. Edward was amenable to these influences, and in his brief reign, the English church shifted from the pope-less Catholicism of Henry to something recognizably Protestant.

The year 1549 saw an important move in this direction with the Act of Uniformity. This act mandated the use of Cranmer's *Book of Common Prayer* throughout the realm. The *Book of Common Prayer*'s greatest novelty was the introduction of the vernacular liturgy (which sparked an armed rebellion in Cornwall), but it was much more than a liturgical book. It was a kind of missal, with daily prayers for private use and Scripture readings for the year. Fit to be used by clergy and laity alike, the *Book of Common Prayer* created a kind of social uniformity around a Protestantized worship service.

Following the introduction of Cranmer's *Book of Common Prayer*, King Edward began to utilize his role as supreme head of the church to reform the doctrines of Anglicanism along Protestant lines. In 1550, the rite of ordination was revised to omit all reference to the sacrifice of the Mass. Justification by faith alone would become Anglican doctrine. The laity were encouraged to receive both the Host and the chalice, and the elevation of the Host at communion was eliminated. References to prayers for the dead were omitted in the new rite of worship, as were any references to the Mass as a sacrifice. For some Protestants, however, these changes did not go far enough. Some of the more radical among them decried the retention of an episcopacy and other vestiges of "popery"; in some places, there were incidents of iconoclasm as angry Puritans smashed images or broke stained glass. Even if Protestants debated about the degree of the reform, the reign of Edward VI had thrown the English church definitively into the Protestant camp.

But Edward was not long for this world. Always frail and of a weak constitution, he fell seriously ill in January of 1553. The illness became grave and Edward was suddenly faced with a succession crisis, as he had no offspring. Though Henry had bastardized both Mary and Elizabeth in 1536, the 1544 Act of Succession (passed after the birth of Edward) restored them to the royal succession, with Mary designated to succeed Edward if he died childless and Elizabeth to succeed Mary in similar circumstances.

Of course, nobody had expected Edward to die childless. When Edward took the throne in 1547, it was assumed he was the beginning of a Protestant dynasty. With his sudden death in 1553, England was immediately faced with the prospect of a Catholic restoration in the person of Mary Tudor, daughter of Catherine of Aragon. Mary spent much of her adolescence in seclusion after her initial exclusion from the succession. She was denied contact with her mother and was frequently ill. It was only after Anne Boleyn's execution that she was returned to court, though relations with her father were always tense. Through all her sufferings, Mary had clung steadfastly to the Catholic faith of her mother. At Christmas 1550, King Edward publicly humiliated Mary at court by demanding she renounce Catholicism, which she boldly refused, though the episode brought her to tears.

Thus, as Edward lay dying, England faced the prospect of a Catholic restoration. Edward wished to disinherit Mary, but his advisers told him that the law did not permit him to disinherit only one sister; he had to disinherit both of his sisters or neither of them. After some anguished indecision in the throes of death, Edward disinherited both of his sisters and conferred succession on Lady Jane Grey, a Protestant grand-niece of Henry.

Mary was summoned to London to bid farewell to Edward, but being warned of a plot to capture her, she fled to the Catholic strongholds of East Anglia. In the meantime, Edward died on July 6, 1553. Once settled in hiding, Mary wrote to the Privy Council demanding they recognize her as Edward's successor. Whatever one might want to say about the Protestant leanings of the Privy Council, at least Mary was a known entity. She had spent her life on and off at court, had an impeccable royal pedigree, as well as the sympathy of many of the common folk, who had the common sense to realize that Princess Mary had been treated rather shabbily by her father. Support for Lady Jane dwindled and Mary was crowned in October 1553. An unsuccessful coup was launched to put Mary's half-sister Elizabeth on the throne, but this was put down swiftly, and after a round of executions (including that of Lady Jane), Mary was secure on the throne.

Mary faced an immediate problem, as almost the entire royal administration at this point was Protestant; most of the Privy Council had initially supported the claim of Lady Jane. Mary was a sensible woman and knew that a policy of clemency was necessary to maintain unity in the government.

And the Parliament seemed open to conciliation. Negotiations were opened up with the Holy See to restore relations with Rome; Reginald Cardinal Pole, an eminent English ecclesiastic who had been living in exile in France, was made papal legate and archbishop of Canterbury. The restoration began in earnest. The ancient Mass was restored, though without any penalties for non-conformity. New bishops were consecrated. Clerical celibacy was restored. The title "Supreme Head" was repudiated. Everywhere, the ancient Catholic faith was being restored.

It might be wondered why the Parliament and nobility who had for so long been eager abettors of Henry VIII's designs would so suddenly turn and support Mary with such vigor. The answer was in the question of Church lands. If England were reconciled to Rome, would it therefore follow that all the monastic lands confiscated under the dissolution would need to be restored? Would the rising class of young moneyed nobles who had gotten fat off of monastic properties be compelled to give back their plunder? Mary and Cardinal Pole seemed to understand that the path to reconciliation would be nigh impossible if they tried to enforce compulsory return of monastic lands, which by this time had been in the hands of their new owners for almost twenty years. Thus, Cardinal Pole was able to secure a papal dispensation for the new owners of confiscated monastic lands to retain them. It seems that as long as the nouveau riche were allowed to keep their property, they were willing to tolerate Mary's restoration of Catholicism. Parliament declared the marriage of Henry and Catherine valid and rescinded all of Edward VI's religious laws. On November 30, 1554,

Cardinal Pole pronounced absolution over the kingdom of England and her Parliament.

Mary's restoration, however, was fated to be short-lived. One of the factors that worked against her was her unpopular marriage. As Edward VI had schemed to keep the throne from passing to Mary, Mary now attempted to secure the throne from passing to her Protestant half-sister Elizabeth. When she took the throne, Mary was already thirty-seven years old and most likely past child-bearing age. Furthermore, she was habitually in bad health and probably sensed her reign would not be of long duration. Marriage was her first priority, and she quickly contracted a marriage with Prince Philip II of Spain, the son of the Holy Roman emperor, Charles V.

The English peerage reacted with extreme hostility toward the marriage. They were zealous that none of England's sovereignty should devolve to Spain, and to this end, a flurry of legislation was passed ensuring Philip's titles and powers as king of England could only be exercised jointly with Mary and would expire entirely upon her death. But beyond that, there was a kind of visceral hatred for Spain that had taken hold of the English psyche. Throughout the long reign of Henry VIII, much animus had been directed by the state against the Catholic Church, which refused to grant Henry his annulment from his Spanish queen. The Spaniards, angered by Henry's treatment of Catherine and reflexively Catholic to the core, became a kind of sinister Catholic foil against which to contrast the godly, or at least English, reform of Cranmer, Cromwell, and the rest. This had been going on for almost three decades by the time Mary was wed to Philip. English sentiment toward Spain in the 1550s was one of deep, guttural aversion. Though Mary must have known this, she may have miscalculated the depth of English disapproval, as she loved Philip deeply.

For Philip's part, the marriage was one of political expedience. The Spanish prince spent several months in England in 1554, dutifully making love to the sickly queen in an attempt to conceive an heir. A false pregnancy in 1554 seems to have convinced Philip that the queen was beyond childbearing, and he soon after departed England to go attend to Spain's wars abroad. She would only see him one more time during her life.

The English lords, however, were fearful of the throne falling into the hands of a permanent Anglo-Spanish Catholic line. Violent insurrections broke out in Kent, and several prominent nobles were found orchestrating it. The rebellion was crushed before it even got off the ground, with the customary executions that followed. The revolt, however, had fazed Mary. Among the rebel lords were Protestants she had initially exercised leniency toward and been willing to work with for the good of the realm. Her sense of safety was greatly shaken, causing her to reconsider her previous policies of toleration.

The rebellion brought with it a wave of religious repression of Protestants. The former archbishop Cranmer, who had been deposed and kept in various degrees of confinement, was burned at the stake in 1556, calling the pope an antichrist and enemy of God as he was led away to death. Mary's "Heresy Acts," which were little more than restatements of traditional English law that predated the Tudors, took a hard line against Protestantism. Somewhere around 283 Protestants suffered death during Mary's reign; many more fled to the continent, where they took up their pens and wrote scathing denunciations of "Bloody Mary" and her policies. The ambassador from the Holy Roman Empire warned Mary that the executions were very unpopular and could lead to a revolt, but Mary seemed convinced that the rigidity of the Heresy Acts was the only way to extirpate Protestantism in the kingdom and end the political and social instability that had characterized the previous thirty years.

Mary's Protestant half-sister Elizabeth was an enigma. Should she be considered friend or foe? Mary and Elizabeth had both suffered under the reign of Edward VI, when both had been removed from the succession. Both had endured the indignity of having their mothers repudiated (in Elizabeth's case, beheaded) by Henry. Both had been publicly declared bastards. There was a kind of solidarity in hardship that existed between the half-sisters, though religion divided them. When Mary had taken the throne, she rode into London with Elizabeth at her side.

This quickly changed, however, as Protestant nobles made Elizabeth the center of their conspiracies against Mary. Elizabeth spent much of Mary's reign either confined to the Tower or under house arrest, while Mary debated what to do with her. Some advisors urged her execution, as the mere existence of the Protestant princess would make her a perpetual rallying point for political dissent. Others argued that whatever Elizabeth might have symbolized to the Protestants, she herself had never been implicated in any wrongdoing and it would be unjust to put her to death, as well as needlessly provoke Mary's Protestant subjects.

The debate was cut short, however, when it became clear that Mary was dying. By 1556, Elizabeth's succession seemed assured. She was returned to court, and Europe's monarchs—such as Mary's husband Philip II, now king of Spain—began cultivating relationships with Elizabeth. In the fall of 1558, Mary was in her last extremity and the kingdom was preparing for the return of Protestant rule in the person of Elizabeth. On November 7, Mary recognized Elizabeth as her successor and then died days later. Cardinal Pole died only twelve hours after Mary. He would be the last Catholic archbishop of Canterbury.

When Mary died on November 17, 1558, an era came to an end. With the ascension of the Protestant Elizabeth, it would become clear that the religious shift toward Protestantism that occurred under Henry VIII and Edward VI was not going to be some aberration, but represented a permanent shift in English society. It was Mary's attempted restoration, rather, that proved to be the aberration. England, which had once been so devoted to the Church that she was known as "Our Lady's Dowry," had been launched into a new trajectory by Henry VIII. By 1558, Protestantism was so firmly entrenched, at least among the ruling class of England, that it could no longer be undone.

Similar realignments were happening over the border in the kingdom of Scotland, England's northern neighbor.

CHAPTER 10

Kirk and State: John Knox and Mary, Queen of Scots

Whereas the establishment of Protestantism in England was pushed through by the crown, in Scotland it was established despite the opposition of the crown. In both cases, the role of the nobility and the seizure of ecclesiastical properties would be central. But while the driving character of the English turn to Protestantism was King Henry VIII, in Scotland it was the fiery preacher John Knox.

The origins of Knox are uncertain; scholars even debate the decade of his birth. He was born sometime in the first two decades of the sixteenth century, of middling yeoman stock in the coastal country east of Edinburgh. He had a decent education and a working knowledge of Latin and French. Based on fleeting references in his own works, it appears Knox was originally a Catholic priest, though he seems to have repudiated the Catholic faith by 1540, the same year St. Peter Canisius was graduating college in Cologne and in which the Jesuits received papal approval. After leaving the priesthood, Knox hired himself out as a tutor in the homes of the Scottish nobility.

In the 1540s, Scotland was still officially a Catholic kingdom, though there was a strong Protestant movement brewing. Scotland's king was James V, a nephew of Henry VIII. After England's break with Rome, Henry sought to forge a political alliance with Scotland by pressuring James to repudiate the Catholic faith, something the devoted king would not consider. James enjoyed the full support of the Church, represented in Scotland by David Cardinal Beaton of St. Andrews. Together, James V and Beaton attempted to steer the Church and state through the ever-stormy seas of Scottish politics.

In 1542, Henry VIII invaded Scotland in an attempt to force his northern policies on the Scots. James V rode off to battle against England, never to return, for he was killed at the Battle of Solway Moss. The death of a king is always devastating, but James's was even more so as his solitary heir was his infant daughter Mary, his only child by his French wife, Mary of Guise. As the kingdom wept for the tragic death of their king on the bloody field of Solway Moss, the small but influential Protestant faction amongst the nobles began plotting to take advantage of the political destabilization. Meanwhile, James's widow, Mary of Guise, assumed control of the kingdom. Politically vulnerable, the French queen began trying to find the most advantageous marriage arrangement for her daughter, something that would keep her safe while strengthening Scotland.

In those troubled days, John Knox was a kind of theological rabble-rouser—half-preacher, half-thug—a man who preached reformed doctrines at Protestant gatherings but also swaggered about wearing a long sword, a kind of Protestant hired muscle. Knox fell in with Beaton's most determined opponent, the Protestant itinerant George Wishart. Wishart had traveled all over England and the Continent spreading Protestantism of the Calvinist brand. Wishart had a special affection for the zealous young Knox and made him his bodyguard.

The year 1546 saw Wishart, Knox, and companions in St. Andrews, the seat of Cardinal Beaton. The cardinal had lost some political influence at James's death, but he was unwilling to tolerate the presence of the troublemaker Wishart in his diocese. Wishart was subsequently arrested; Knox, his bodyguard, pleaded to stay and suffer with the preacher, but Wishart told him to flee and return to tutoring. Wishart was condemned and burned on March 28, 1546.

Beaton did not long survive Wishart, however. Wishart's disciples were thirsty for revenge, and two months after his execution, an armed band of Protestant nobles burst into the cardinal's castle at St. Andrews. They stormed into his private chambers and murdered Beaton, afterward mutilating his body and hanging it from the window of his castle for the entire city to view. Knox, who had returned to tutoring, was ecstatic at the grisly murder. He wrote exultantly about the killing of the cardinal, whom Knox derisively called a son of the devil. Obviously, Knox was still grieving for the death of his master, Wishart. Even so, his exultation at such a brutal murder seems unbecoming for any sort of Christian preacher. But Knox held a strange interpretation of the fifth commandment, asserting that notorious sinners and criminals could be put to death by private individuals, especially if these men had usurped authority or were being protected by oppressive rulers. For Knox, the murder and mutilation of Cardinal Beaton by private individuals was not only a justified exercise of legitimate law but something to be rejoiced in and even laughed at.

Knox's entire theological system was marked by a kind of crudity. He held to the ubiquitous Protestant doctrines of justification by faith alone and the secularization of ecclesiastical lands, but his system completely lacked the refinement of Calvin or even the consistency of Luther. His theology was ensconced in the austere spirit of the Old Testament, evidencing little of the gentleness or mercy of the teachings of Christ. He was a talented preacher and could draw large crowds to his lengthy sermons, but his words were often laced with calls to violence that exceeded anything ever spoken by Luther and shocked even his supporters. His hatred of Catholicism was almost phobic.

Knox's life was as tumultuous as his doctrine. Always at the center of political and religious intrigues, he spent two years as a galley slave in a French ship before setting himself up as pastor of an Anglican parish in northern England, where he came into conflict with Anglican authorities over his condemnation of kneeling during communion as idolatry. Knox eventually had to flee England with the accession of Mary Tudor. He made his way to Geneva, where he met and worked under the now-elderly John Calvin. The restoration of Catholicism under Mary Tudor was extremely disconcerting for Knox, who saw her Catholic policies as the triumph of idolatry over "the Gospel." Knox pressured

Calvin to endorse the violent overthrow of Mary. Calvin's response was lukewarm and cautious, but that did not stop Knox from publishing *A Faithful Admonition to the Professors of God's Truth in England*. The *Faithful Admonition* is both an exhortation to the Protestant preachers of England and a scathing condemnation of Mary Tudor in tones evocative of the direst judgments of the Old Testament:

> [N]ever let that obstinate woman come to authority. She is an errant Papist. She will subvert the true religion, and will bring in strangers, to the destruction of this commonwealth . . . assuredly as our God lives, and as we feel these present troubles, our God himself shall rise to our defense; he shall confound the counsels of our enemies, and trouble the wits of such as most wrongfully trouble us. He shall send Jehu to execute his just judgments against idolaters, and against such as obstinately defend them. Jezebel herself shall not escape the vengeance and plagues that are prepared for their portion. The flatterers and maintainers of her abominations shall drink the cup of God's wrath with her.[18]

Knox returned to Scotland briefly in 1555 and was greatly impressed with the gains the Reformation had made there since his departure. Though absent from his homeland since 1547, he had garnered an international reputation as one of the greatest of all reformed preachers and a light of Scottish

---

[18]   http://www.swrb.com/newslett/actualNLs/faithadm.htm. As extracted from: *Selected Writings of John Knox: Public Epistles, Treatises, and Expositions to the Year 1559*. Reed, Kevin, (Dallas, Presbyterian Heritage Publications, 1995).

Protestantism. His support among the largely Protestant nobility of southern Scotland was considerable, and Knox was something of a celebrity. He decided the time was ripe to address the queen regent, Mary of Guise. His famous letter of 1556 pleaded with the French dowager to accept Protestantism. Mary of Guise treated this letter with a mixture of contempt and ridicule. Knox resented this and left Scotland to take up a post as pastor in Geneva. Shortly after his departure, he was condemned in Scotland and burned in effigy.

Women in power were always a thorn in Knox's side. Both Mary Tudor and Mary of Guise had opposed his preaching. The heir to the Scottish throne was the Catholic princess Mary, now living in France and betrothed to Prince Francis II. Fulminating at the women who opposed him, in 1558 Knox composed *The first blast of the trumpet against the monstruous regiment of women*. The treatise attacked the very idea of women in authority as contrary to natural law and abominable in the eyes of God. Though Knox's intended targets were Mary Tudor and Mary of Guise, both Catholics, the work had the unintended effect of alienating the Protestant Elizabeth Tudor, who took the throne later that year. Elizabeth was deeply offended by Knox's tract and forever disliked him on account of it.

The female who would most vex Knox, however, was Mary Stuart. Mary was the daughter of the late King James V of Scotland and Mary of Guise. After James's death at Solway Moss, the infant had immediately become a pawn in the national-religious conflict of the day, with Scottish barons and Henry VIII both hoping to use the child to their advantage. Instead, Mary of Guise betrothed Mary to Prince

Francis II of France and shipped the child off to the French court, where she could be insulated from the political and religious instability of Scotland and England—for a time, at least.

Mary grew into a splendid young woman. Tall, graceful, and crowned with a full head of luxurious red hair, Mary Stuart was considered extremely beautiful. Yet she was not merely a pretty face, for she was also fluent in six languages and competent both in literature and domestic arts such as needlework and horsemanship. Though vivacious and worldly in the Renaissance sense, she was a devoted Catholic and would be unwavering in her dedication to the Faith throughout her troubled life.

Though her mother-in-law, Catherine de' Medici, treated her coldly (we shall learn more about Catherine in chapter 16), she was beloved by the French court. The wedding of Mary and Francis was solemnized with great fanfare in April 1558, when she was sixteen years old. Within one year, Mary's husband, Prince Francis, ascended the throne as king of France upon the unexpected death of his father. Young Mary found herself queen of the oldest and most powerful monarchy in Christendom.

Mary was not destined to remain long in France, however. After scarcely a year on the throne, her young husband fell ill and died. Catherine de' Medici was declared queen regent of France as different factions positioned themselves for the inevitable struggle to fill the power vacuum left by Francis's death. Divisions followed mainly along religious lines, with Catholics and French Calvinists (called Huguenots) siding against each other.

With the political situation in France deteriorating, Mary was sent back to her native Scotland. Her mother, Mary of Guise, having recently passed away and young Mary now in her majority, it was time for her to take her place as queen of the Scots, the name by which she would forever be remembered. Mary landed at the port city of Leith north of Edinburgh on August 19, 1561. She was given an icy reception by the local Protestant nobility, whose resentment of her began the moment she stepped foot on Scottish soil.

Though she was born in Scotland, Mary had left her home for France when she was but five years old; culturally, she was French. Her long absence meant she was unacquainted with the complex and dangerous nature of Scottish politics. Since her departure from Scotland in 1548, it had become a much more hazardous place. Subsequent to the murder of Cardinal Beaton, Protestantism was in the ascendancy throughout the kingdom. The queen regent, Mary of Guise, had maintained official unity with Rome, but a powerful cadre of Protestant Scottish nobles had coalesced against the hated French queen. John Knox had returned to Scotland the summer prior and immediately caused a rebellion in the town of Perth. His fiery denunciation of Catholic religious orders whipped the crowds into frenzied agitation. Mobs looted the city's parish before destroying the Dominican and Franciscan friaries, attacking the local Carthusian house, and carrying off everything of value.

The Protestants soon evacuated Perth, but Knox moved on to St. Andrews, preaching a similar sermon followed by more looting. As word of the events in Perth and St. Andrews spread, riots broke out in other cities across central Scotland.

Monasteries were pillaged and destroyed. Ancient cathedrals dating from the time of Scotland's great King David and his holy mother Queen St. Margaret were torn down. A wave of angry iconoclasm surged over the realm, while Protestant nobles either looked on or else aided the mobs, knowing that property wrested from the Church would inevitably end up in their own hands.

The surge of violent anti-Catholicism had been too great for the queen regent to withstand. With scores of her supporters daily abandoning her, Mary of Guise had to retreat to the fortress of Dunbar. Meanwhile, the Protestant nobility had taken charge of the rebellion and were calling themselves the "Faithful Congregation of Christ Jesus in Scotland," or the Lords of the Congregation for short. The Lords of the Congregation occupied Edinburgh and, though unable to take the imposing fortress there, pillaged the city's ancient church. They agreed to withdraw from the royal capital only after Mary of Guise agreed to allow them freedom of conscience in all religious matters. Mary of Guise reluctantly agreed to the terms in the summer of 1559. Before long, however, violence broke out again, this time with Knox soliciting military aid from England. The forces of Mary of Guise were defeated, and Mary was declared deposed by the Lords of the Congregation. She retreated to Edinburgh Castle, where she died suddenly in June 1560. Following the death of Mary of Guise, the Lords of the Congregation declared Scotland a Protestant kingdom. A gathering of the Scottish Parliament declared Calvinism the official faith of Scotland and formally repudiated the jurisdiction of the Catholic Church in the kingdom. Scotland was now a

Protestant kingdom, politically dominated by the close-knit circle of the Lords of the Congregation and under the fiery spiritual vision of John Knox.

All of this happened in the twelve months prior to the arrival of Mary Stuart from France. Mary thus found herself a Catholic queen in a kingdom that had violently rejected the Catholic faith. Like Mary Tudor, she initially believed that some sort of reconciliation with the Lords of the Congregation was necessary to govern effectively. Noble as this idea was, she fundamentally failed to understand the strident opposition of Knox and the Lords to being ruled by a papist, no matter how accommodating she was. The situation was complicated by the fact that the chief of the Lords of the Congregation was her half-brother, James, Earl of Moray, bastard son of James V. Thus the already tense religious situation was further muddled by familial rivalry.

It is beyond the scope of this chapter to detail every misstep Mary made during her six years on the throne. We shall note only some of the most significant. As a gesture of goodwill, she retained a majority of Protestant advisors on her Privy Council, which had the effect of alienating the remaining Catholic nobles. She would take as her secretary the Italian Catholic musician David Rizzio, whose presence as a foreigner so close to the queen could not but excite jealous fury among the Scottish lords. Militarily, she was entirely dependent on the cooperation of the Lords of the Congregation. Then there was the English question. As a cousin of Elizabeth and potential heir to the throne of England, should Elizabeth die childless, Mary was the heir presumptive. Much of her attention seems to have been focused on settling the English succession rather than strengthening her own position in Scotland, which consequently weakened her.

The local Protestants also went out of their way to make it extremely difficult for Mary. When she appeared in public to attend a private Mass in Edinburgh, her chaplain and other members of her entourage were furiously attacked by the Protestants of Edinburgh. The Lords of the Congregation sternly warned her that the people of Edinburgh had repudiated Catholicism, root and branch, and would tolerate no public displays of popery.

One of the burdens of ruling Scotland was having to deal with John Knox, whom the Lords of the Congregation regarded with the reverence of a prophet. Knox was summoned to five audiences with Mary between 1561 and 1563, each time precipitated by some public disturbance or incendiary sermon that reached the ears of the queen. We know of these interviews only from the recollections of Knox, so they are a bit one-sided. Even so, cutting through potential bias, we can clearly discern what sorts of audiences these were. The picture that emerges is of the imposing presence of Knox dominating the young Mary. Knox preaches boldly to the queen as if she were one of his congregation. He calls the Catholic Church a harlot, the Mass an offense to God, and told her she was completely lacking in knowledge. In one audience, Knox's severity reduced Mary to tears.

Haughty speech in the presence of a queen! It is perhaps questionable why Mary continued to torment herself by permitting these sessions, which were little more than occasions for Knox to bully the queen on religious matters. She certainly felt helpless against the influence of the gloomy prophet, whose mission was backed by the swords of the nobility. In their final session, Knox is flatly accused of treason for encouraging Scotch Protestants to violently resist Mary's attempts to prosecute two Protestants for disrupting a Mass. The record of the meeting shows Knox shouting her down, and Mary casting about for anyone who would support her; even her own Privy Council gave her but a lukewarm defense. Finding little support among her councilors, Knox was dismissed without penalty.

The encounters with Knox are indicative of Mary Stuart's relationship with the new Scottish Calvinist order: indignation on the part of the queen at the insults and open disobedience of her subjects but impotence to do anything because she was hopelessly outmaneuvered by the Protestants who dominated the government apparatus.

Mary continued to have her private Masses and maintain a gay Renaissance lifestyle in the privacy of her quarters at Edinburgh, but meanwhile, Scotland was transformed into a Calvinist kingdom. Episcopacy was preached against in favor of the Presbyterian model of church government, new "books of order" were promulgated reforming worship along Calvinist lines, and a brutal iconoclasm destroyed the remnants of the kingdom's medieval Catholic heritage. The energy behind the transformation was swift and violent, but it was not as popular as its effects might suggest. As in England, the main proponents of the reform were the nobility who resided in southern and central Scotland, near the royal capital of Edinburgh. In the highlands and the western isles, the ancient Faith clung tenaciously to life.

Mary's isolation was exacerbated by her lack of a husband. She had been contemplating a match since her arrival in Scotland and in 1565 settled on her cousin, Henry Stuart, Lord Darnley. Darnley was tall and handsome and had a jolly disposition that suited Mary well. He had strong dynastic connections to both the Stuarts and the Tudors—and as a Catholic, he could be a bulwark against the Protestant party. Mary and Darnley were wed in a private ceremony according to Catholic rites in July 1565.

Things went bad almost immediately, as Darnley unexpectedly refused to attend the nuptial Mass following the ceremony. Mary was soon with child, but it became apparent that Darnley was a vain, senseless fellow who gave little care to anything but drinking and debauchery. His religious practice was indifferent; Darnley was formally a Catholic but sympathized with the Lords of the Congregation, though this was probably political—his only real religious devotion seemed to be to his belly. Mary was appalled by Darnley's loose manners and refused to grant him the Crown Matrimonial, which would have made him successor to the throne if she died childless. This infuriated him, and within a few months, the two were estranged and no longer living together.

The sad queen turned for comfort to her secretary, David Rizzio, the Italian musician she had taken into her confidence. Though he served only as Mary's translator, the Lords of the Congregation had never approved of Rizzio. The presence of a foreign Catholic so close to the queen's ear had always been unsettling. The lords disliked him, but Darnley was mad with jealousy; he even suspected Rizzio might be the father of Mary's child. Given Darnley's unstable mind and poor character, history has little reason to assume this. But to Darnley it was an all-consuming paranoia. The estranged Darnley thus found common ground with the Lords of the Congregation in their mutual hatred of Rizzio.

This hatred boiled over on March 9, 1566. Mary, then seven months pregnant, was dining in the evening with Rizzio in her private quarters at Holyroodhouse. Suddenly, Darnley and a band of armed nobles burst into her chamber. Led by Lord Ruthven, one of Mary's own Privy Councilors, they demanded she hand over Rizzio. Mary stood up and boldly refused. Rizzio hid behind the queen, but the men shoved Mary aside and stabbed Rizzio to death in her presence. Rizzio was stabbed fifty-six times while Mary looked on and screamed. Then Darnley and the lords dragged the bloodied corpse out and flung it down the main staircase, stripping Rizzio of his jewels and fine clothing before departing.

A whole coterie of Protestant nobles were implicated in the plot, but investigations ultimately came to nothing. In fact, the murder of Rizzio simply threw into relief how helpless Mary truly was. If the sovereign queen of a kingdom did not have enough weight to keep her own secretary from being murdered in her private quarters, what security could she expect? How she must have puzzled over the question in quiet moments before the Blessed Sacrament in her private chapel. How does one govern such a people?

Mary's child was born a few months later and baptized James. With the succession secure, Darnley and Mary seemed close to reconciliation. They often visited one another's quarters and things seemed on the mend. How Mary found the heart to reconcile with a man who had murdered her secretary before her eyes, we shall never know, but she tried nevertheless. Darnley's erratic behavior continued to erode his support amongst the nobles, however. Furthermore, he continually badgered Mary to grant him the Crown Matrimonial, which she steadfastly refused. To make matters worse, a bout of smallpox in early 1567 left Darnley pockmarked and deformed.

In February of 1567, Mary left Darnley to recover from his infirmity in a country house at Kirk O'Field outside Edinburgh while she attended a wedding. On February 9, two explosions rocked the house where Darnley was staying, leveling it to the ground. It was subsequently discovered that the blast was caused by two barrels of gunpowder hidden beneath the floor. Darnley, however, was not in the house. His body and that of a servant were found laid out in the field outside the house. They showed no signs of being injured by the blast and were found to have died from strangulation.

The murder of Darnley has long been a matter of speculation. The political opponents of Mary naturally suspected her involvement. But suspicions were also swirling around another character—James Hepburn, Earl of Bothwell.

Bothwell had known Mary casually since her days as queen of France but had become closer to her in the months leading up to Darnley's death; some suggest the two may have been lovers. Whatever the case, Bothwell and Mary clearly had a special relationship that made him naturally suspect. Bothwell was tried for the murder and acquitted, though one of his soldiers who was unfortunate enough to happen upon the crime scene first was hanged, drawn, and quartered as a scapegoat.

Though Bothwell was a Protestant, he was not a religious zealot. His character was adventurous and individualistic, perhaps embodying what most people associate with the quintessential Scottish spirit. The stifling moralism of Knox and the Congregation held no appeal to him. Ever an outsider, Mary, who had never been able to find her place, found a kindred spirit in Bothwell. They drew even closer in the months after Darnley's death, and as the Scottish lords had expressed their will that Mary should marry a native Scotsman next, it was widely rumored that Bothwell would be the one.

Events were about to take a very unexpected turn. On April 24, 1567, Mary was progressing toward Edinburgh when her entourage was ambushed by Bothwell and eight hundred of his men. Bothwell declared that he had uncovered a conspiracy against Mary and forcibly conveyed her to Dunbar Castle. There Bothwell allegedly raped her, perhaps in an attempt to secure her marriage to him. Shortly thereafter, she created him a duke and married him on May 15 in Protestant rites.

The events of April through May 1567 are bizarre and have been debated by historians for ages. Even as these events were unfolding, many suspected a ruse. Sir William Drury, an observer of the English court in Scotland, wrote back to London that the kidnapping was prearranged and Mary was complicit in the entire affair. What woman would want to marry a man who had raped her, let alone create him a duke? That something had been prearranged was a common opinion among those who saw the whole saga as a scheme of Mary's to foist an unwanted king upon the throne without the consent of the Lords of the Congregation.

And unwanted he certainly was! While certain notables had expressed support for the union of Bothwell and Mary, the events of the spring had jarred even those sympathetic to the pair. Catholics considered the marriage invalid. Despite Bothwell's acquittal, it was widely believed that Bothwell was involved in Darnley's murder somehow, and Scots from Edinburgh to the western isles scratched their heads and wondered why Mary would wed the man accused of murdering her husband. The Lords of the Congregation mistrusted Bothwell as an outsider and resented the influence he would have on the queen. By June, the Lords of the Congregation were in open revolt.

Mary, Bothwell, and an army of supporters met the rebels at Carberry Hill on June 15. Bothwell proved reluctant to engage and allowed the initiative to be lost in lengthy negotiations; meanwhile, Mary's soldiers began to melt away as it became clear that the rebels had the advantage. By afternoon, it was clear that Mary could not prevail. Her forces were largely dissipated. Bothwell embraced his bride one last time—this woman he had only been wedded to for thirty days—and fled, never to see her again. On promise of her freedom, Mary surrendered to the rebels.

The queen was conducted to Edinburgh, where the whole populace of the city turned out to jeer her as an adulteress and a murderer. Mary bore these insults patiently, expecting vindication. She had surrendered in anticipation of her freedom. The Lords, however, had her in their power and were not about to let a crisis go to waste. Rather than releasing her, they imprisoned her in the island fortress of Loch Leven. On July 23, she miscarried Bothwell's twins. The very next day, still sick and bleeding from the miscarriage, she was visited by the rebel lords who forced her abdication in favor of her son James, then scarcely a year old. When she refused to sign the abdication document, one of the lords roughly grabbed her hand and forcibly affixed her signature to the paper.

With Mary out of the way, the Scottish Parliament leaped into action. Knox had been out of the kingdom visiting England and so was absent for the saga of Darnley's death, the marriage to Bothwell, and subsequent rebellion. But by June, he was conveniently back in Edinburgh to preach on the occasion of Mary's abdication and guide the Lords in their management of the realm. Mary's son, James, was to be educated by Protestant tutors. Until his majority, the kingdom was to be governed under the regency of James, Earl of Moray, the bastard half-brother of the imprisoned queen of Scots. Oblivious to the momentous events occurring around him, the thirteen-month-old James was crowned King James VI of Scotland on July 29, 1567, with much fanfare. John Knox, now at the pinnacle of his career, preached the coronation sermon. The monstrous regiment of women was over in Scotland. The crown was on the brow of a Protestant heir who, guided by the stern discipline of the Congregation, would usher in a reign of godliness. The era of the "Kirk," the Scottish Presbyterian church of Knox, had dawned.

Bothwell, meanwhile, fled Scotland and was pursued by ship until a storm forced a landing in Norway, then under the control of Denmark. The king of Denmark locked him up, for he recognized in the exiled lord a powerful political bargaining chip. When it became clear, however, that Mary would never regain power, he cast Bothwell into the notorious Dragsholm Castle prison and forgot about him. The miserable conditions in the prison quickly drove Bothwell to insanity; he spent the last decade of his life chained to a pillar, where he raved and paced the floor so incessantly that a circular groove in the floor around the pillar can still be seen today.

Mary, meanwhile, lingered in captivity for the better part of a year. But by May of 1568, she had managed to sufficiently win over the younger brother of the owner of Loch Leven castle. With the aid of this young man, she was able to escape. Her flight came at a fortuitous time for her cause. Mary's forced abdication had been unpopular with many Scots, even Protestants. Support for the Lords of the Congregation was greatest around Edinburgh, but in the kingdom at large, Mary had many supporters who, whatever their religious opinions, knew she was the rightful monarch. The regency of Moray had also been plagued with ineptitude and division in the months since Mary's abdication. Thus, as news spread of the queen's escape, men flocked to her standard. Within a week, she had raised a considerable force of six thousand men, led by some of the most eminent nobles of the realm, many of them Protestant.

The regent Moray raised a force and met Mary at a narrow pass called Langside on May 13, 1568. Unfortunately, though Mary's army was larger than Moray's, her forces suffered from lack of organization. The battle that followed was a confusing mess of pistol fire and interlocked pikes.

Eventually, Mary's flanks collapsed and her army fractured. The Battle of Langside ended in a victory for Moray. Forces loyal to Mary would continue to do what they could on her behalf for another five years, but ultimately the queen's men would go down in defeat.

With her cause defeated in Scotland, Mary fled to her cousin Elizabeth in England, surrendering to English officials on May 18, 1568. Whatever differences Mary might have had with Elizabeth relating to religion, policy, or succession, Mary had confidence that the bonds of blood and their common royal title would engender both empathy and sympathy from her cousin. She initially hoped Elizabeth would lend support to restore her to the throne. Elizabeth, however, received Mary cautiously. Mary bided her time at Carlisle Castle, near the Scottish border. She was certain that her cousin would help her vindicate her cause. What she did not know was that she was not a guest but a prisoner and that she would never taste freedom again.

CHAPTER 11

The Visionary Pope: Paul III and the Council of Trent

Thus far, we have considered the events of the sixteenth century as driven by the Protestants. We should not imagine, however, the Catholic Church was merely passive or reactive throughout these historic events. Because Protestantism ultimately triumphed in places like England, Scotland, and northern Germany, it is easy to read a kind of historical determinism back into the past, as if the march of Protestantism was irresistible and the Catholic Church was helpless against the inexorable rupture of Christendom.

It is natural to read history through the lens of what ultimately happened—to understand historical causes in light of their ultimate effects. While this might aid us in understanding how events fit together in the great narrative of the past, it is not always helpful in grasping what the characters of history were actually thinking and what motivated them, as facts that do not fit easily into the narrative tend to become discarded. For example, because of the wide acceptance of the narrative of the bold reformers speaking out against a corrupt, powerful Catholic hierarchy, it is often forgotten that there were numerous reform movements within the Catholic Church herself, both before and during the Reformation.

In Spain, there was a general reform of learning and discipline under the Franciscan cardinal Francisco Jiménez de Cisneros (1436–1517). Under his guidance, the Franciscan order in Spain was entirely reformed. Priests were ordered to hear confessions regularly, care for the education of the young, and preach the Gospel faithfully. Monks were compelled to remain in the monasteries where they were professed, and offenses against clerical celibacy were strictly punished. To foster learning, the cardinal founded the Spanish University of Alcala entirely out of his private funds. Cisneros was also a Humanist who published a new edition of the Bible in multiple languages so readers could verify the translations. Under Cisneros's long tenure, the entire Spanish Church was reformed and laxity weeded out with a determination that sometimes bordered on inflexibility. The great cardinal died in 1517, only eight days after Martin Luther posted his *95 Theses*.

In Italy, there were vibrant movements founded by lay persons that sought to live out the Christian vocation to love in an active manner. These organizations, called Oratories, promoted pious works and a spirituality suited to lay persons. The Oratory of St. Jerome was founded in Vicenza in 1494. Its members practiced communal and private prayer, frequent confession and communion, and charitable works among the sick and poor. The Oratory of Divine Love, founded in Rome in 1517, emphasized work in the city's hospitals and counted among its members many important persons of both the lay and ecclesiastical rank.

In England, an educational renaissance was ushered in by John Colet, a friend of Erasmus and dean of St. Paul's Cathedral, and an individual who was briefly mentioned in an earlier chapter. In Colet's 1512 sermon for the convocation of the cathedral chapter, he condemns worldliness of the clergy and calls for a general reform of education and discipline. Colet, who died in 1519, became the exemplar of a Catholic prelate dedicated to reform while remaining unwaveringly loyal to the Catholic faith.

The Netherlands were home to a vibrant movement of lay piety known as the *devotio moderna*. Originally associated with an organization called the Brethren of the Common Life, the *devotio moderna* was an approach to spirituality that stressed simplicity of living, humility, and obedience. Its popularity spread throughout the Low Countries and Germany in the fifteenth century; its principles were adopted by Thomas à Kempis, a Dutch canon who incorporated them into his famous book *Imitation of Christ*. Kempis's *Imitation* was one of the most widely read spiritual books in the decades leading up to the Reformation; St. Thomas More read it daily and said every Christian should own it.

Many new religious orders were formed as well. Cardinal Cajetan (whom we met in chapter 5 as an antagonist of Luther) founded the Theatines right around the time Luther was leading Germany into chaos. The Theatines established rigorous new standards for the Italian priesthood and episcopate, devoted themselves to pastoral ministry, and promoted regular communion and veneration of the Blessed Sacrament. Other reform orders such as the Regular Clerics of St. Paul, the Barnabites, and the Brothers Hospitallers of St. John of God would soon follow. Many traditional orders, such as the Camaldolese, Dominicans, and Franciscans also undertook reforms in the early 1500s. The Franciscan reform led to the establishment of the Capuchins, who were first conceived by Matteo Bassi in 1520, before Martin Luther had even been excommunicated.

Reform was also on the minds of the highest leaders of the Church. The Fifth Lateran Council, which sat from 1512–1517, took up the mantle of reform. Convened under Julius II, the so-called "Warrior Pope," Lateran V required all pastors to have a minimum level of demonstrable competence in preaching, condemned certain episcopal abuses, and called for the establishment of financial institutions that could make low-interest loans available to the lower classes, an idea that was quite ahead of its time. Unfortunately, the reforms of the council had little time to take effect, as Luther's *95 Theses* came only seven months after it closed.

The point is that reform was not merely a Protestant battle cry. God has never left the Church without men and women, of whatever estate, who have taken up the call to reform when it was needed. The various lay and ecclesiastical movements of the 1400s and early 1500s demonstrate that authentic piety and commitment to disciplined Christian living were alive and well in pre-Reformation Europe. The Church never "needed" the Protestant Reformation in order to get its house in order.

Even so, the most penetrating minds of the age had recognized that an ecumenical council was probably necessary if authentic reform were to be implemented universally. Calls for a council had come immediately after the close of Lateran V, which was poorly implemented and left some of the most grievous abuses untouched. It was the outbreak of the Lutheran crisis that added greater urgency to these calls. Luther himself had appealed to an ecumenical council in 1518 because he was convinced he would be condemned if he went to Rome. This appeal was met with derision; Pope Pius II had in 1469 condemned those who "presume to appeal from the pope to a future council, in spite of the fact that the pope is the vicar of Jesus Christ."[19] This dictate, however, was generally ignored in Germany. As Lutheranism sprawled into a nationalist movement, many German ecclesiastics and secular rulers sympathetic to Luther called for a German national council to set the affairs of the German church in order.

Both Pope Clement VII and Emperor Charles V opposed such a plan, for the attitude of many Germans toward the pope was so toxic that a national council could only result in the ossification of anti-Roman prejudice. Charles, however, did think an ecumenical council would be advisable and even offered the imperial city of Trent as a location. Plans were stunted, however, by the political rupture between Charles V and Clement VII that culminated in the 1527 sack of Rome, which we mentioned in chapter 8. Furthermore, the peace established in Germany at the end of the Peasants' War was broken in 1529 when Charles V revoked the

---

[19]   Pope Pius II, *Execrabilis*, 1469.

decision of the Diet of Speyer and insisted on strict enforcement of the Edict of Worms. This decision led to a massive
rebellion by an alliance of Lutheran princes and Protestant
free cities throughout northern and central Germany. Formalized in 1531, this alliance called itself the Schmalkaldic
League. The League was a kind of religious defense alliance.
Lutheran states pledged mutual self-defense should their territories be invaded by Charles V. Since the members of the
League were generally contiguous with each other, it quickly
became a kind of territorial secession movement. This could
not have come at a worse time for Charles, as he was already
engaged in a protracted military struggle with France and
was also distracted by renewed aggression by the Ottoman
Turks on the empire's eastern borders. Thus, the Lutheran
states pursued their political and religious secession without
much opposition.

This chaos made it difficult for the pope and emperor to
lay the necessary groundwork for a council; until the 1530s,
Protestantism was almost exclusively a problem within the
Holy Roman Empire, so the emperor's collaboration was
essential. Furthermore, King Francis I of France brought all
the political pressure he could muster to bear against the
summoning of a council. Though a Catholic himself, Francis tended to support the Schmalkaldic League in Germany.
The reason was simple: Charles V was Francis's enemy. The
purpose of an ecumenical council was to hash out the grievances of the Protestants and hopefully reconcile them back
to full unity with Rome and Charles V. And full unity of
Charles V's subjects was the last thing Francis wanted. Thus,
the Protestant Schmalkaldic League was supported by the

Catholic king of France, who continually obstructed all attempts at reconciliation.

A strong opponent of a general council was the papal legate Lorenzo Campeggio, the same legate who had gone to England to arbitrate Henry VIII's divorce case. Campeggio doubted the sincerity of Protestants who claimed they wished for a council. Tensions mounted when Pope Clement VII told Charles V that a precondition of convening a council would be the repudiation of Protestant doctrines by the lead reformers. This was of course abhorrent to Protestants, who far from seeing the council as a means to reconcile them to Rome, hoped Rome would embrace the reform. Clement VII was again discussing a council in 1532 and even got as far as drafting briefs to the kings of France, Germany, and England. Francis, however, reacted with indignation; Henry VIII, by that time embroiled in the divorce proceedings, refused to respond.

When Pope Clement VII died in 1534, the council was still only a dream. It was the vision and determination of the next pope, Paul III, that brought the council to fruition. Paul III was born Alessandro Farnese. At the time of his election in 1534, he had already been a cardinal for forty-one years. He had weathered the pontificates of the Medici and Borgia popes and emerged with a sterling reputation for piety and zeal. It is a testament to the character of Alessandro Farnese that the various factions of the Roman curia elected him nearly unanimously.

Farnese took the name Paul III. Despite his age, he undertook the work of reform with considerable zeal. His frail figure concealed a leader of exceptional fortitude and vision.

His portrait, painted by the Renaissance artist Titian, shows a bent little man with a broad nose, small, penetrating eyes, and a hoary beard resting on his breast. Looks can be deceiving. This unassuming little pontiff would be the one to undertake the enormous task of shepherding the Catholic Church from the Renaissance into the Counter-Reformation.

A veteran diplomat with decades of experience in the Vatican, Paul filled the Sacred College with men of the most eminent learning and piety. A brief sketch of some of these men will help us to appreciate this pope's vision of reform. One of his appointments was Reginald Pole, the brilliant Englishman who would help Mary Tudor reestablish Catholicism in England. Another important appointment was Jacopo Sadoleto, an eminent theologian and model bishop who, unlike many bishops of his day, would not absent himself from his diocese save on express orders of the pope. Paul valued Sadoleto's insights on episcopal governance and hoped to use his advice in a general reform of the episcopacy. Also worthy of mention is Cardinal Carafa, the future Pope Paul IV. Carafa was an ascetic who had helped found the Theatines. He was a rigorous opponent of the Protestant heresy and unyielding in his defense of orthodoxy.

But perhaps the most important appointment was the Venetian Gasparo Contarini. Contarini was elevated to the cardinalate shortly after Paul's election. Contarini was also a zealous reformer who suppressed abuses in the Roman Church and aided Paul in implementing his vision. To him, Pope Paul entrusted the task of finding suitable, reform-minded candidates for the Sacred College. Thus, throughout Paul's fifteen-year pontificate, the Curia was consistently stocked with men sympathetic to reforming discipline and morals. Paul knew that it was not enough to simply issue decrees and publish documents. He was old enough to have participated in the proceedings of the Fifth Lateran Council and witnessed how many of that council's disciplinary decrees became dead letters for lack of reform-minded bishops and cardinals to implement them. He knew that personnel is policy, and the meaningful reform of the Catholic Church could not happen without the right men in the right places.

In 1536, Paul appointed Contarini to head a commission charged with providing the pope with recommendations for reform. Sadoleto, Carafa, and other eminent ecclesiastics joined Contarini's commission. Their task was to create a catalog of abuses within the Vatican and the Church at large and make recommendations to Pope Paul for reform. The result was the 1537 document *Consilium de emendanda ecclesia*, an ambitious program of reform that called for a total overhaul of discipline from the diocesan level right up to the Roman Curia. The sheer scope of the recommendations was daunting, even to a pope with the mettle of Paul III. We can imagine the old, wizened brows of the aged pontiff furling at the size of the task before him. Contarini, however, encouraged him to be faithful to the great jurisdiction placed in his hands and himself led by example by zealously reforming his own diocese of Cividale di Belluno.

The path laid out for Pope Paul was clear. Contarini was thanked for his services and sent to Germany at the request of Charles V to help reconcile Protestants to the Faith. Paul had already been laying the groundwork for an ecumenical council to be assembled at Mantua. Protests from various bishops and kings, however, postponed the council until 1539, by which time its location had been moved to Trent. Charles V again asked the pope to delay, as at the time there were religious conferences being held throughout Germany which Charles hoped would reconcile the Protestants. The cautious emperor thought an ecumenical council might needlessly antagonize the Protestants and jeopardize the talks.

However, by 1541 it was clear that reconciliation was as far away as ever. Pope Paul finally issued a convocation of the council in May 1542, but again opposition from Charles V and King Francis stalled matters, such that on the day appointed for the opening of the council, only a handful of bishops had trickled into the northern Italian city of Trent. It was not until 1545 that Paul was finally able to settle all the political and logistical obstacles and the Council of Trent was officially opened on the feast of the Annunciation in 1545.

The beginning of the council was inauspicious by modern standards; its first session was sparsely attended by four cardinals, four archbishops, twenty-one bishops, and a cluster of theologians and papal legates. The early sessions were bogged down by dull but necessary discussions of procedure. Council fathers disputed what the council should be named; other arguments broke out over whether bishops who could not attend the council because of religious disorders in their dioceses should be able to vote by proxy.

Still, despite its beginning, Trent would go on to become one of the most important ecumenical councils of all time, with decrees touching every aspect of Catholic life and doctrine. Its sweeping decrees reformed the discipline of the

Church and stamped its image on Catholic culture for the next four centuries.

It is ironic that Pope Paul III, the determined old pontiff who had seen the council through to fruition, did not attend. As a matter of fact, the council would sit intermittently for eighteen years with no pope ever attending. Still, even if Paul was unable to attend, the zealous pontiff was able to die content, knowing that the Council of Trent had taken up the important work of reforming the Church.

The first sessions of Trent took up matters of doctrinal disagreement with Protestants. Protestants had been invited to the council and granted safe conduct, although the nature of their demands quickly made it clear that reconciliation was impossible. Outlandish suggestions, such as a decree releasing all bishops from their obedience to the pope, were bound to go nowhere. This perhaps shows the different mentalities of the Catholic and Protestant participants. Most Catholic bishops assumed that if certain disciplinary reforms were undertaken and disputed matters of theology cleared up, reconciliation with the Protestants would be possible. The Protestants were not particularly interested in reconciliation. They viewed the council as a means to persuade the Church universal essentially to Protestantize itself. When it became clear that the Protestants were unwilling to reconcile and the Catholics unwilling to repudiate the papacy, Protestant participation in the council ceased.

Even so, the first period of the council rolled on and saw some of its most important doctrinal pronouncements. Luther had initially challenged the authority of Catholic tradition in his early conflicts with Johann von Eck and

Cardinal Cajetan; Charles V had appealed to Catholic tradition in his condemnation of Luther, whereas Luther had exalted the Scriptures alone as the sole rule of faith. Trent reaffirmed that Sacred Tradition as well as Sacred Scripture constitute the rule of faith and that Scripture should never be interpreted outside of the consensus of Tradition and the Fathers.

Of particular importance was the council's decree on original sin, which addressed some of Luther's most fundamental errors. Luther's essential mistake was in equating the inclination to sin with sin itself, which led him to despair and ultimately to abandon the Church's teaching on sin and grace in favor of his doctrine of justification by faith alone. Trent reaffirmed the traditional understanding that through the original sin of Adam, all mankind is by the mere propagation of the species born deprived of sanctifying grace. This grace, however, is restored by Baptism, in which a man is translated from the state of being a son of Adam to a son of God in Christ. Despite this, however, concupiscence— the inclination to sin—remains, even among those who are redeemed. Yet this inclination to sin is not to be confused with sin itself. It is to be manfully resisted in the grace of Christ and in fact becomes the occasion of crowning merit to those who resist it. Those who are in grace are truly pleasing to God. This view contrasts sharply with that of Luther, who taught that even in a state of redemption a man was not substantially pleasing to God.

Against Calvin, the council taught that while man may have moral certainty of the remission of his sins, no one could boast with absolute certainty of remission of their sins, least of all merely because they believe it. This is not to say we do not have confidence in God's mercy when we emerge from the confessional, but such confidence is distinct from the absolute knowledge of predestination favored by Calvin. The council condemned the idea that a person can know whether or not he is predestined for heaven as a rash presumption.

Some of the most important reforms of the early sessions concerned the problems of multiple benefices and absentee bishops. A benefice is a name for an ecclesiastical property destined for the support of ministers or the care of souls— traditionally, a diocese, abbey church, cathedral building, or any such revenue-producing property. One of the greatest sources of medieval ecclesiastical dereliction was the amassing of several of these properties by individual bishops, who lived in none of them, collected revenue from all of them, and farmed out their management to others. This system allowed bishops to be practically absent from their dioceses (which were mismanaged), allowing them the freedom to pander for influence at the courts of kings or popes. One can easily see how detrimental this was to the good of souls, to say nothing of the extent to which it scandalized the faithful. The Council of Lyons in 1274 had already prohibited anyone from holding more than one office with the care of souls; further decrees by subsequent medieval pontiffs attacked the practice but to little effect. It took the reforming zeal of Trent to end the practice definitively. The sixth session required bishops to live in their diocese and not absent it without grave reason, while the seventh session commanded all holders of multiple benefices to resign all of their holdings except for one. Henceforth, a diocese would actually be managed by its resident bishop who, more dispensed from political concerns, would give primary attention to the care of souls.

One of the great theologians of the Council of Trent was none other than St. Peter Canisius, the Jesuit theologian from Holland we met in chapter 1. St. Peter's life was roughly contiguous with the great events of the Reformation. The great saint was ordained to the priesthood in 1546 and attended the council as the personal theologian of Cardinal Otto Truchsess von Waldburg, bishop of Augsburg. He spent 1547 with the council fathers and spoke several times before the congregation of theologians before moving on to Rome to spend time under the personal direction of St. Ignatius. St. Peter would return to Trent in its final sessions to speak on matters relating to the celebration of the Eucharist and report on popular opinion about the council.

Pope Paul III would not live to see the conclusion of Trent. The first period of the council closed in September 1549 in the wake of deteriorating relations between the pope and Emperor Charles V, largely surrounding Paul's attempt to move the council to Bologna to avoid a pestilence that had broken out in Trent. Paul did not long survive the closing of the first sessions; he died suddenly in November 1549. It would be two years before the new pope, Julius III, reconvened the council in 1551.

If Paul III was the father of the council, St. Peter Canisius embodied its vision. You may remember that Peter was born the year Luther was excommunicated. Raised on the stories of the religious troubles of Germany and England, he came of age in the years when devoted Catholics had committed themselves to answering the challenge of Protestantism with their own reforming zeal. We saw in chapter 1 how the piety of Peter led him to the Jesuits. The Jesuits, whom we will examine more closely in the next chapter, were the shock troops of what would become known as the Counter-Reformation, the great renaissance of discipline and theology that accompanied the Church's response to Protestantism.

St. Peter's life embodies the dynamism and piety of the Counter-Reformation. His evangelical labors are so varied it is dizzying to recount them all. If we were to follow this great Jesuit master about in the 1550s and 60s, we would see him now assisting secular princes in settling the religious affairs of their kingdoms, now serving as a preacher or adminis-trator to some bishop. From Rome, Vienna, Ingolstadt, Strasbourg, Munich, and everywhere in between, founding colleges, preaching in cathedrals, and attending imperial diets. His surviving sermons could have been drawn from the canons of Trent. The Catholic understanding of tradi-tion, the veneration of Mary and the saints, the efficacy of indulgences, and the Catholic doctrine of salvation are all recurring themes of his homilies. He served as administrator of the ancient diocese of Vienna, where he implemented the reform program of Trent with fortitude. Everywhere he went he established educational foundations, preached tirelessly, and made the disciplinary vision of Trent his own.

This was no small feat, as the vision of Trent was broad. The second period of the council under Julius III sat from 1551–1552 and issued decrees on the sacraments and reform of clerical life. Unexpected reverses in Charles V's war against the Protestant princes endangered the city of Trent, however, and forced the council to disband for a time. It would continue in hibernation under the unpopular papacy of Paul IV, to be summoned for the third and final time in 1559 upon the ascension of Pope Pius IV.

Pius IV announced the opening of the council shortly after taking the Chair of Peter. The reconvening of Trent was a very delicate affair. Many of the reforming decrees issued by Trent were meant to secure the independence of Catholic prelates from undue political influence, something against which many monarchs pushed back. Pope Pius needed a strong, dependable bishop to model the reforms of the Council in his own diocese. Pius would find his man in his nephew Charles Borromeo, of whom we shall say more in the next chapter.

The last sessions of the council were particularly important for the faith and morals of the Church. Doctrinally, the nature of the Sacrifice of the Mass was considered. The sacrificial nature of the Mass had been denied by Luther, Cranmer, and Calvin, each of whom saw it as fundamentally opposed to salvation by faith alone. This criticism was answered in the twenty-second session, in which the Catholic doctrine of the Mass was masterfully laid out. Indeed, Trent's session on the Sacrifice of the Mass is one of the most concise and beautiful explanations of Catholic teaching in the Church's tradition. The council grounds the sacrificial nature of the Mass in its institution by Christ himself, who willed the Mass to be the means through which the merits of his sacrifice were perpetuated throughout time in an unbloody manner under the forms of bread and wine. Because the Sacrifice of the Mass is nothing other than the sacrifice of Christ himself, it can be offered for the living as well as the dead, for the channel of its merits is as wide as is the grace of God. Masses offered in commemoration of the saints are not offered to those saints but in honor of them, for the purpose of supplicating them for their intercession and recalling their holy lives. The ceremonies and externals of the Mass were not detractions from the glory of God but were rather incentives to piety.

Session twenty-three of 1563, the last year of the council, sought to address the problem of ignorant and immoral clerics by ordaining the establishment of ecclesiastical seminaries in every diocese. Candidates to the priesthood were to be trained in the practice of virtue and educated in Scripture and sacred theology. The seminary was not intended to merely impart knowledge, but form character. Austerity, patience, wisdom, erudition were all to be inculcated in priestly candidates in the seminary, which would operate under the watchful eye of the attentive bishop. Thus was the method of priestly formation that has given the Church thousands of priests over the past five centuries born.

The council was closed on December 4, 1563, after some final decrees reaffirming the veneration of relics and the cult of the saints. The import of Trent is best summarized by the 1913 *Catholic Encyclopedia*:

> The Ecumenical Council of Trent has proved to be of the greatest importance for the development of the inner life of the Church. No council has ever had to accomplish its task under more serious difficulties, none has had so many questions of the greatest

importance to decide. The assembly proved to the world that notwithstanding repeated apostasy in church life there still existed in it an abundance of religious force and of loyal championship of the unchanging principles of Christianity. Although unfortunately the council, through no fault of the fathers assembled, was not able to heal the religious differences of western Europe, yet the infallible Divine truth was clearly proclaimed in opposition to the false doctrines of the day, and in this way a firm foundation was laid for the overthrow of heresy and the carrying out of genuine internal reform in the Church.[20]

As Trent ended, so passed the first generation of the Reformation. Martin Luther died the year after it was convened; Calvin died the year after it closed. St. Ignatius Loyola died in the midst of the council. Gone were Henry VIII, Thomas More, Cranmer, Erasmus, and all the men who lived through the first tumultuous years of the rending of Christendom. The zeitgeist of the Renaissance in Rome had evolved under the reforming spirit of Paul III and Pius IV into the modest piety of the Baroque era. Charles V, who had fought the Protestants of Germany indecisively for thirty years, finally gave up and agreed to the 1555 Peace of Augsburg, a meeting attended by eminent Catholic and Protestant figures throughout the empire, including St. Peter Canisius. The settlement agreed to adopt the principle "Cuius region, eius

---

[20]   J. P. Kirsch (1912). Council of Trent. In *The Catholic Encyclopedia*. New York: Robert Appleton Company. Retrieved February 15, 2017 from New Advent: http://www.newadvent.org/cathen/15030c.htm.

religio," loosely translated, "Whose realm, his religion." In other words, each prince within the empire would be allowed to choose either Catholicism or Lutheranism for his realm. Having finally achieved peace and worn out from decades of war, Emperor Charles abdicated the throne in 1556 and retired to a monastery to prepare to meet God. According to legend, he spent his final years trying to make a room full of clocks keep perfect time. Some believe this is an allegory signifying Charles's troubled reign and his inability to bring all the affairs of the empire into order.

Yes, the first generation of the Reformation was passing. But the drama of the age was far from over.

CHAPTER 12

Soldiers of the Counter-Reformation: Ignatius & Borromeo

The Catholic Church's response to the Protestant Reformation is generally called the Counter-Reformation. From a Catholic viewpoint, this is a misnomer. The Protestant Reformation should be called the Protestant Rebellion, and the Counter-Reformation should simply be called the Reformation. Alas, history is written by the victors, and at least in the English language the narrative we have inherited comes through a Protestant lens. Thus, we will use the conventional language of Reformation and Counter-Reformation, even though we know the reality was quite different.

The Council of Trent set the agenda for the Counter-Reformation. As we saw in the last chapter, in many respects the key aspects of this reform had been fleshed out before the council was even summoned. Yet it was Trent that took this reforming zeal and solidified it as the Church's official policy. It was a lofty vision, a vision in which educated, disciplined clergy taught, governed, and sanctified a devout flock nurtured on beautiful Catholic art and music and edified by the celebration of reverent Masses. Of course, this had *always* been the Catholic ideal; the vision of Trent was nothing other than that the Church should return to her roots and become what Christ willed her to be. This principle is at the heart of every authentic reform of the Church.

The Counter-Reformation progressed along two main tracks. The first was oriented outward, toward the immediate mission fields of Protestant Europe as well as the more remote mission fields of the New World. On this outer track, the Catholic faith progressed by means of evangelism and public disputation, whether in face-to-face debates or a flurry of polemical writings. The other track of the Counter-Reformation was more internal, focused on reforming the life of the clergy and the administration of diocesan government. On this inner track, the reform progressed by means of holy, disciplined bishops willing to implement the vision of Trent in the management of their dioceses. The missionary impulse is best exemplified by the Spaniard St. Ignatius of Loyola; the administrative reform, by St. Charles Borromeo of Milan.

St. Ignatius Loyola (1491–1556) was a Castilian born at the dawn of the Spanish golden age. The Spaniards, Castilians in particular, possessed a deep martial spirit forged in centuries of battles with the Muslim Moors. Spain had been overrun by Muslim conquerors from Africa back in the eighth century. The *Reconquista* was an eight-hundred-year conflict in which the beleaguered Christian kingdoms of Spain attempted to push the Islamic invaders back out of the peninsula. The last Moorish outpost in Spain was conquered in the year 1492, the year after Ignatius was born.

The long struggle against the Moors imprinted the Spanish people with a strong sense of national identity, as well as a love for all things military. In many ways, the young Ignatius was a typical Spanish boy of the age: an adventurous, swaggering braggadocio raised on stories of knights and the military heroes of Christendom. He also had a kind of bullish zeal for the Catholic religion; a Moor who once made the mistake of denying the divinity of Christ in front of Ignatius found himself challenged to a duel. The greater glory of Spain, the wooing of young maidens, the excitement of battle—these were the ideals that motivated young Ignatius. In 1509, he took up arms under the service of a local duke and participated in many military campaigns. As far as we can tell, he conducted himself honorably and was a valued member of the duke's army. Ignatius seemed to have a promising military career ahead of him.

His dreams were soon dashed, however, when he was grievously wounded at the Battle of Pamplona in 1521. His left leg was shattered by a cannonball while defending a Spanish castle against an invading French-Navarrese force. The wounded soldier was carried to his father's estate in Loyola to recover. We can only imagine the horror of Ignatius's treatment. In an age before anesthesia, when the existence of bacteria was unknown, he underwent several surgeries to repair his leg, including having the bone set and then having it subsequently re-broken and reset when the first procedure was done incorrectly. We can only imagine the agony of the young man as he drew on all his soldierly fortitude to try to remain calm as the doctors mangled his broken limbs; at one point, a protruding piece of bone had to be sawed off. In the end, Ignatius was left with a severe limp due to one leg being shorter than the other. With such a deformity, it was clear his military career was over.

As he lay recovering in his ancestral castle of Loyola, Ignatius asked for some reading material to pass the time. He hoped to nourish his mind on the tales of knighthood and chivalry such as he was accustomed, but none were available. Instead, he was brought devotional books on the lives of Christ and the saints. These books had a profound influence on Ignatius. He began to notice in the saints the same competitive spirit that had attracted him to chivalry. Instead of excelling in horsemanship or the joust, the saints aimed to excel at charity and penance. He began to consider what his life would be like if he applied his natural discipline and competitiveness to works of piety rather than feats of arms. He frequently returned to these ruminations during his long convalescence. Grace slowly moved his heart until he wept for his past sins and was inflamed with zeal to pursue holiness. By the end of 1521, Ignatius appears to have resolved to pursue some form of religious life. The same year Martin Luther incurred excommunication and was raising hell all over Germany, the man who would be one of the Church's greatest saints was undergoing spiritual conversion.

After his recovery, Ignatius divested himself of his fine clothes and donned a rough sackcloth. He went on a pilgrimage to Monserrat and afterward took up residence in a small cave outside Barcelona. He spent several months in this cave, wrestling with scruples about his past sins and laboring to devote his life wholly to God. Hours of prayer coupled with rigorous fasts and the advice of a kindly confessor eventually brought him the peace he sought. During this time, Ignatius took notes about the spiritual experiences he was going through. These became the framework for his later masterpiece, *The Spiritual Exercises*.

Ignatius possessed a strong sense of mission, but he was uncertain how to best direct that pious impulse. He made a pilgrimage to Jerusalem and briefly entertained thoughts of laboring for the conversion of Muslims in the Holy Land, but by March of 1524, he was back in Barcelona. He endeavored to spend his time furthering his education and spent the next decade in various universities, eventually winding up in Paris. He obtained a licentiate in theology, but poor health prevented him from ever going on to his doctorate. Ignatius was never known as a great scholar; the value of his university years was not in any depth of erudition, but rather in the practical wisdom of dealing with people and understanding human motivations. His youthful boldness, softened and formed under the power of grace, had matured and turned Ignatius into a natural leader. He learned to find the best in different types of people, leading them based on their strengths. His discernment of the movements of the soul and the varied motivations of human action was extraordinarily keen.

It was only natural that such a man should have attracted the society of wholesome friends wherever he went. Whether in the Spanish universities of Alcala and Salamanca or at

Paris, he never wanted for companions. These companions would join with Ignatius in his discipline and viewed him as a spiritual father. Thus were forged the initial friendships that would blossom into the Society of Jesus.

No truly pious endeavor can flourish without opposition; wherever he went, Ignatius faced accusations from people hostile to his manner of living. He was dragged before the Inquisition on occasion and once publicly flogged for a misunderstanding, for which he received a public apology. Despite all opposition, Ignatius and his companions persevered. In 1534, the same year Henry VIII was tossing Sts. Thomas More and John Fisher into prison, Ignatius and his companions took vows of poverty and chastity. They were ordained to the priesthood soon after. Even so, it was not until 1540 that the order received the formal approbation of the pope. The approval of the order was made by Paul III, the great father of Trent we met in the last chapter. Paul knew Ignatius personally and had witnessed the holiness of the companions up close. The Society of Jesus was officially constituted by the bull *Regimini militanis Ecclesiae* of September 27, 1540.

Pope Paul III originally envisioned the Society of Jesus (Jesuits) as a missionary order. Before the society had even been approved, Pope Paul already had designs to send Ignatius's order out as missionaries. The Jesuits, of course, would become extremely prolific in the foreign missions. They were the first to penetrate China and Japan with the message of Christ. They have merited undying glory for their labors among the native tribes of North America throughout the seventeenth century, efforts which were crowned with many notable martyrdoms. But it was not only in the foreign mission fields that they made an impact. In 1540, Europe was rife with religious conflict. The monasteries were being dissolved in England. Charles V was waging war against the Protestant Schmalkaldic League, which was backed by Catholic France. John Calvin was establishing himself as dictator of Geneva. Pope Paul III was struggling to bring the Council of Trent into existence. Missionary work was needed as desperately in the old world as it was in the new.

The Jesuit charism exemplified the spirit of the Counter-Reformation superbly. Their constitutions prohibited them from accepting certain ecclesiastical offices that could interfere with their manner of life. Concerned with the problem of uneducated or poorly formed clerics, the constitutions also proscribed a lengthier novitiate than was common at the time. In keeping with the zealous spirit of the Counter-Reformation, the Jesuit constitutions officially bound them to the active life, including not only foreign missions at the behest of the pope but also education of the young and care of the sick and imprisoned.

It was the Jesuits who brought the vision of Counter-Reform to the cities and villages of Europe. Everywhere some Protestant preacher or theologian was making inroads, he would find himself countered by a Jesuit priest. Such was the case with St. Peter Canisius, who spent the better part of his life with the Jesuits countering the spread of Protestantism in writing and public disputation. As the Society spread throughout the 1540s and 50s, they became a bulwark of Catholic orthodoxy and manfully combated Protestantism through a variety of mediums. They ran printing presses,

taught in seminaries, ran grammar schools, sent out traveling preachers, organized parish missions, engaged in theological disputations in person or writing, advised bishops,
and much more. Christendom was a battlefield, and the
Jesuits were the shock troops of the Counter-Reformation.

The interior world of the soul was also a battlefield eagerly
engaged by the Jesuits. Beginning with his time as an ascetic
in the cave outside Barcelona, Ignatius had been compil-
ing written records of his spiritual experiences. Over the
years, these crystallized into a series of observations about
the movements of the spirit in general, coupled with practical guidelines for the spiritually sensitive on how to discern
God's will. These, of course, became the *Spiritual Exercises*.
In its final form (published originally in 1548 as a handbook for priests), the *Spiritual Exercises* were divided into
four weeks of meditations following the life of Christ. The
Exercises contained a trove of spiritual wisdom: how to pray,
how to avoid scrupulosity, how to choose one's vocation in
life without being swayed by improper concerns—in short,
how to discern the will of God and follow it faithfully.

The meticulous, discerning precision of the *Spiritual Exercises* suited the mood of the Counter-Reform perfectly, for
Ignatius's *Exercises* sorted through and reformed the habits of
the soul just as surely as Trent sorted through and reformed
the habits of the Church. The *Exercises* were to the spiritual
life what the canons of Trent were to the administration of
the Church. As the Jesuits spread the Counter-Reform, they
brought the *Spiritual Exercises* with them, thus becoming a
true source of evangelical renewal and devotion throughout
Christendom.

Ignatius himself would spend his last years in Rome. His life there was consumed with two great labors: the founding of the Roman and German colleges, and the thankless task of sorting out a power struggle within the Society that threatened the stability of the Portuguese province. Ignatius took ill on July 30, 1556. His doctors did not presume the illness would be fatal, but Ignatius sensed otherwise and asked for the last sacraments. He received a papal blessing from Pope Paul IV and then retired to bed for the evening. When he was found the next morning, he was laying with such peaceful composure it was not immediately apparent he was in the throes of death. He expired shortly thereafter, while attendants were running to fetch the holy oils for his last anointing. St. Ignatius would be canonized in 1622. At the time of his death, the Society of Jesus numbered close to a thousand members with one hundred religious houses scattered throughout ten provinces.

We mentioned above that the Counter-Reformation progressed along two tracks, one being a kind of externally oriented activism, the other being an internal reordering of the administration of the Church. If St. Ignatius Loyola symbolizes the first, the second is exemplified by St. Charles Borromeo (1538–1584). At first glance, there is not much in Charles Borromeo to suggest he would become one of the luminaries of the Counter-Reformation. He was born to wealth and privilege in the Castle of Arona near Lake Maggiore in northern Italy in 1538. His family connections and early career reeked of nepotism. His father was a powerful count and his mother one of the notorious Medici family. Through his mother's side, he was a nephew of Pope Pius IV

(r. 1559–1565), and through the influence of his father's family, he was made the abbot of a monastery at age twelve.

Yes, young Charles Borromeo could have easily become one of those ubiquitous members of the Italian nobility who treated the Church like a cash cow to be used for political gain. Yet such was not the disposition of young Charles. Almost as soon as he was placed in charge of his monastery, he made it known that he would take only a fraction of its revenues for himself and designated the rest for the succor of the poor.

He pursued studies in nearby Milan and later at the University of Pavia. From his youth, Charles was skilled with money and managed to get by on the very small pittance allowed him by his father. Though the scarcity of cash sometimes left him in desperate circumstances, it helped him develop a talent for thrift and administration that would prove his greatest natural strength. When his father died in 1558, Charles's entire family asked him to assume responsibility for managing the family's property and business interests, even though Charles was not the eldest son. With constancy and diplomatic skill rare in a twenty-year-old, Charles successfully negotiated competing claims upon his family's estates while simultaneously completing his thesis for a doctorate in civil and canon law in 1559.

In 1559, the Church was in the midst of the Council of Trent, the sessions of which had started to fizzle out. Pope Paul III had died a decade earlier, and Pope Julius III had suspended the Council in 1553 because of political troubles. Thus, the Church was caught up in the midst of the Tridentine reforms but had not yet seen them implemented by the

Church universal. A man of Charles's energy and organizational skill could serve the Church admirably. Soon enough he would get his opportunity.

The year he received his doctorate, Pope Paul IV died. Pope Paul had been an original member of Paul III's reform commission, and though he was unpopular as a pope, he had imposed a rigid discipline on the Roman Curia that destroyed, root and branch, the abuses associated with the Renaissance papacy. Charles was still at the University of Pavia when he got word that his uncle, Giovanni de' Medici, had been elected pope on Christmas Day of 1559 and taken the name Pope Pius IV. His uncle requested that Charles make his way to Rome with all haste to aid him in the government of the Church. Thus, with great excitement, the twenty-one year-old future saint set out for Rome.

Charles's uncle knew of his nephew's talents and placed him in a role of considerable influence as administrator of the Papal States. Once again, Charles would utilize his skills as an administrator, this time for the temporal holdings of the Church under the immediate auspices of the pope. In this office, he excelled, and promotion followed promotion with a rapidity that must have left him with little time to breathe. He was made a cardinal-deacon, as well as supervisor of the Franciscans, Carmelites, and Knights of Malta. He founded and took charge of a literary academy at the Vatican, and was given charge of reorganizing the stalled Council of Trent. His most notable appointment, however, was to the vacant archbishopric of Milan in 1564. In the interim since his uncle's election, Charles's eldest brother had died, and the family had begged him to leave the clerical estate to return and manage the affairs of the Borromeo clan. But Charles had devoted himself to the well-being of the Church, and on December 7, 1563, he received episcopal consecration in the Sistine Chapel, thus forever taking the Bride of Christ as his spouse. He entered into the episcopal government of Milan the following spring. Charles could not have known it at the time, but Milan would become the crucible where the vision of the fathers of Trent was forged into a workable program of diocesan administration that would be adopted by the universal Church.

That Charles had a talent for governance was obvious, but the ecclesiastical honors heaped upon him caused him to take a deeper look at the state of his own soul. He desired not only to administer the Church's affairs well but also to administer his own soul with excellence. When he came to Rome, he made the acquaintance of men who were already living lives of holy discipline who became role models. St. Ignatius had been dead for three years when Charles came to Rome, but he had left behind the Roman College, the labor of his later years. Charles had ample opportunity to converse with the Jesuits of Rome and was deeply moved by their discipline and blameless lives. He also made the acquaintance of the Theatines, the order of St. Cajetan. Another profound influence on Charles was the Dominican Bartholomew of Braga, a Portuguese bishop he met in Rome during the reconvening of Trent. Bartholomew was well-respected by the Roman Curia for his learning and holiness. Bartholomew had devoted himself to the founding of hospices for the sick while also publishing Portuguese catechisms to teach Catholic doctrine. Bishop Bartholomew's erudition, just government, and labors for the sick all impressed Charles and instilled in his own soul a desire to imitate these godly examples. Thus, Charles not only distinguished himself for his capable administration but he also began to exhibit the character of a true saint.

Pope Pius charged Charles with overseeing the organization of the reconvening of the final sessions of Trent. This was a monumental task: problems with the Holy Roman emperor, disputes with the French delegation, logistical difficulties, and many other troubles demanded his constant attention. We can get an idea of the sheer magnitude of this work by the immense volume of correspondence that survives between Charles and the cardinal legates of the council. Various times, it looked as if the council itself would break up. Yet Charles persevered and helped bring the Council of Trent to a successful close.

Charles's interior life had deepened significantly during the council. He had considered retiring to a monastery to work out his salvation removed from the troubles of the world, but his friend Bishop Bartholomew convinced him that a man of his talent should remain engaged in the world for the building up of the Church. Around this time Pius IV visited his nephew and gave him his most important charge yet: to begin adopting the reforms of Trent as an example. In other words, Charles should devote himself to the zealous implementation of the Council of Trent and become, in his own diocese, a model bishop along the lines envisioned by Trent. Other cardinals had been entrusted with this task as well, but the bonds of blood between Pius and Charles, as well as Charles's history of successful administration, gave his work a special value in the eyes of Pius.

Affairs in Rome prevented Charles from immediately returning to Milan, and thus the work of reform was carried out by his representative, Msgr. Nicolo Ormaneto. Ormaneto had worked in the household of Cardinal Pole in England while the latter worked restoring the ancient Faith during the reign of Mary Tudor. In England, Ormanento dealt with restoring Catholicism in a kingdom of Protestants; in Milan, he would face another challenge: restoring Catholicism in a city of lax Catholics, a task no less daunting. Charles always had a keen eye for detail, and Ormanento was given very precise instructions as to how to begin the reform of Milan.

A diocesan synod was called in summer of 1564, announcing the implementation of the reforms of Trent to Milan's twelve hundred priests. It was with the clergy that Charles began the reforms, reasoning that the Christian faithful would only rise to the level of piety modeled by their clergy. Like pastor, like people. Ormanento began a visitation of the parishes and convents of the diocese, armed with the letters of Archbishop Charles and the authority to shake up whatever he deemed in need of shaking. One of the immediate objects of Ormanento's attention was the reform of church music, where a creeping secularism had begun to degrade the quality and reverence of liturgical music. Following Trent, Charles commanded the avoidance of any instrument or musical text that was not in keeping with the sacred dignity of the liturgy. Too much focus on the virtuosity of the musician was to be discouraged. Musicians and cantors must display a liturgical sensibility. Secular tunes were to be avoided. Matters of clerical expenses, priestly discipline, and the education of the young were all also addressed in turn.

The reform of the convents brought Ormanento much grief. It had become common for nuns to entertain guests in the parlors of their convents. These visitations, especially by wealthy socialites, turned such parlor visitations into occasions for gossip and chit chat about worldly matters. Charles ordered grilles to be installed in every convent parlor, such that face-to-face meetings with visitors would no longer be possible. Many convents protested that they had no funds for such renovations; in these cases, Charles paid for them out of his own income. Others fought back more openly. The complaints from one convent made it all the way up to Pope Pius IV himself, who had to intervene personally and command the sisters to set a good example by heeding Charles's directives.

Despite his success, Ormanento was discouraged by dogged resistance to Charles's directives and begged to be relieved of his duty. His affairs in Rome being settled, in 1565 Charles himself came to Milan to take charge of the reform. He was met with great fanfare, as he was the first archbishop to reside in the city for eighty years. It may seem strange to us from the vantage of almost five centuries that bishops should so long reside away from their see. But we must recall that until Trent, it was very common for important bishops to reside at the courts of king or pope and hand the administration of their dioceses off to subordinates. Charles Borromeo was known for many important administrative reforms, but merely living in his diocese may ironically be one of the most important.

Of equal importance was the foundation of the seminary of Milan. The seminary was perhaps the greatest administrative reform of Trent. To grasp the importance of the seminary, one must understand what preceded it. Prior to the Council of Trent, there was no systematic education for candidates to the priesthood. Certainly, there were the grammar schools and the universities, but these did not prepare men for the duties of the priesthood in particular. In the late Middle Ages, a newly ordained priest was expected to attach himself to the service of a more experienced pastor to learn how to say Mass, baptize, and preach through a kind of apprenticeship. Because of the mismanagement of so many dioceses, parish income was often siphoned off by diocesan administrators, leaving parish priests in a state of abject poverty. Many pastors were unwilling to take on an apprentice priest, which would only further subdivide their already meager living. Thus, new priests were often pushed to the margins, parishless itinerants, wandering about from town to town hearing confessions for stipends or fumbling through the Mass prayers in some ramshackle country chapel in exchange for food. More often than not, they ended up taking on additional occupations, sometimes as barbers or surgeons. The lack of steady employment drove many to idleness. The vagrant priest is a common foil in late medieval literature where he is found at the local tavern, drinking and whoring with the best of them.

To remedy this problem, Trent had called for the establishment of seminaries for the purpose of providing systematic education for candidates to the priesthood, not just in theology, but in the practical details of pastoring a flock. Charles had begun establishing the seminary of Milan through Ormanento but brought the project to completion himself. Clerical discipline and an orderly life were stressed at Borromeo's seminary. High standards of literacy were expected of his priests. Gone were the days of a semi-literate priest mumbling broken Latin to a gaggle of ignorant rustics. The priests formed in Charles's seminary were models of virtue and education. Other prelates who came to visit Milan were astonished at the good order of Charles's clergy and took his ideas back to their own dioceses.

Neither was the education of children overlooked. Charles established the Confraternity of Christian Doctrine for the systematic education of children in the faith. The Confraternity was the beginning of what is now known as "Sunday School," an institution that has spread far beyond the confines of the Catholic Church and been embraced by almost every Christian body on the planet.

Charles had only begun the great work of reform in Milan when his uncle and patron, Pius IV, died suddenly in 1566. The new conclave elected the Dominican bishop of Mondovi, Michael Ghislieri, pope. Ghislieri was a warm friend of Charles Borromeo and a fellow reformer. Upon being elevated to the papal throne, Ghislieri asked Charles what regnal name he should take. Charles suggested Pius V, symbolizing the continuation of Pius IV's implementation of Trent. Ghislieri took his advice and ascended to the throne of St. Peter as Pius V on January 7, 1566. Pius V's role in the reform of the Church would be just as enduring as Charles Borromeo's, but we must wait until the next chapter to tell his story.

Charles's reforms were not always met with enthusiasm; sometimes they provoked open hostility. Once, when attempting an episcopal visitation, he was physically prohibited from entering the local church. Another time, when solemnly pronouncing an excommunication against a secular duke who opposed his reforms, supporters of the duke opened fire on the archbishop. Charles was unharmed, but his episcopal crozier was damaged.

Another attempt on his life was made in 1569. Charles had for some time been trying unsuccessfully to induce the penitential Order of the Humiliati to undergo necessary reforms. On October 26, 1569, a member of the order crept into the chapel while Charles was at prayer, raised a pistol scarcely a dozen feet from the archbishop, and shot him in the back. The force knocked him to the ground immediately. Charles, hearing the gunshot and feeling the blow, presumed himself to be gravely wounded and began commending his soul to God. His attendants, however, soon found that the ball had been unable to penetrate his thick clerical vestments.

Milan was one of Italy's most ancient and illustrious episcopal sees. Even in Charles's day, it was remembered as the see of the great St. Ambrose. By virtue of its antiquity, it possessed its own distinctive liturgical rite as well. At Milan, Charles Borromeo presided over a diocese with the size and wealth of a small kingdom. A lesser prelate would have used his position to enrich himself at the expense of his flock. But Charles cared only for the good of the Church, and at no time was his saintliness more evident than during the famine of 1571. That year the harvests failed, and the entire region around Milan was struck by a terrible famine. The standard of living was improving throughout the era, but sixteenth-century Europe was still very wedded to local subsistence agriculture. Most people were only one bad harvest away from starvation. When the crops failed in 1571, starvation crept in, striking the lower classes first and hardest. Charles dove into his personal fortune to relieve the starving, feeding as many as three thousand people daily throughout the summer of 1571. He worked around the clock, ministering to the sick and dying. By the cessation of the famine at the end of summer, he had spent the better part of his wealth relieving the poor and had himself become seriously ill from the severity of his toil.

But this was only a precursor for the trial that was to come, for in 1574 the plague made one of its periodic reappearances, striking northern Italy with particular force. Milan became a place of mourning as thousands took ill and died. The clergy were terrified and could only with great difficulty be persuaded to minister to the sick. Charles himself had to lead by example, making personal visits to houses of the ill. His clergy were eventually won over by his example and joined him in his pastoral visits. But his personal labors were not enough for the saintly archbishop; he wished to do penance for the sake of his flock. Going barefoot with a rope around his neck, he led a solemn procession through Milan bearing a relic of the Holy Nail. Thousands joined him in their penitent supplications to God for an end to the plague. There is perhaps no better image than this to sum up the life and work of Charles Borromeo—always at the front, leading by example in carrying the burdens of office for the good of the Church and salvation of souls.

The plague abated in 1577. Charles was only thirty-nine that year, though he had done more in his short life than most men would with thrice that time. He would live and work for seven more years, although ultimately his labors took their toll. By 1584, he was frequently sick with various ailments and died quietly in Milan on November 4, 1584, at age forty-six. The people of Milan began venerating him immediately after his death; he was canonized in 1610.

St. Charles Borromeo was an extraordinary figure in Catholic history. Without his energetic example in implementing the vision of Trent, it is possible that the reforms of the Council could have lost momentum as the force of apathy and long custom pushed back against any change. Such had happened before with previous councils: solemn gatherings of bishops and popes who had vigorously thundered out reform after reform only to return to their dioceses and have nothing happen. Had St. Charles not taken such a vigorous lead in implementing Trent, things may have been different. Fortunately, his example had won over many bishops. By the time of his death, the seminary system of Milan had been replicated in hundreds of dioceses. The Confraternity of Christian Doctrine, the reforms of music and religious life, the discipline of the clergy, the administration of diocesan revenues, episcopal visitations—all of these authentic reforms were being duplicated all over Europe, in accordance with the dictates of Trent and the example of St. Charles.

Ignatius Loyola and Charles Borromeo each exemplified the spirit of the Counter-Reformation: Ignatius its external, evangelical impulse, Charles its internal administrative one.

Both of them stamped a character on the Church that would influence its development for the next four centuries. Both were true soldiers of the Counter-Reformation.

Yet the efforts of holy men such as Ignatius and Charles could not have succeeded without the support of sympathetic popes. In our next chapter, we shall examine the life and work of the penultimate Counter-Reformation pope, St. Pius V.

Chapter 13

Pope St. Pius V

"And I tell you, you are Peter, and on this rock I will build my church, and the powers of death shall not prevail against it. I will give you the keys of the kingdom of heaven, and whatever you bind on earth shall be bound in heaven, and whatever you loose on earth shall be loosed in heaven" (Mt 16:18–19). Our Lord Jesus Christ knew that his Church would undergo tribulation on this earth. Sometimes its challenges would come from enemies without, sometimes from those within. But in order that the faithful might always have access to the true teaching of Christ—and that the unity of the Church with Christ might be gloriously manifest—Christ instituted the office of the papacy, which he established in the person of blessed Peter the Apostle.

The Catholic student of history will inevitably notice that God, in his providence, has always raised up holy men to the See of Peter in moments of crisis. Certainly, there have been scoundrel popes, just as there have been scoundrel presidents and worthless kings. By and large, however, the vast majority of popes have been average men, no better or worse than most leaders. Yet we still cannot fail to be struck by the marvelous way that heroic, saintly popes have arisen in the most pivotal moments to guide the Church through storms to calmer waters. We could note Pope St. Gregory the Great, who reorganized the Church in the wake of the Roman Empire's collapse; Pope St. Gregory VII, that determined opponent of lay investiture who brought an emperor to his knees and secured the independence of the papacy from the Holy Roman emperors; Pope Innocent III, the ultimate medieval pope who reformed the thirteenth-century Church and gave us the Franciscan order. In later days, we could mention Blessed Pius IX, St. Pius X, Pius XII, and St. John Paul II as similarly historic popes—popes who defined an era.

In the sixteenth century, that era-defining pontiff was Pope St. Pius V. We met Pius briefly in the last chapter as a friend of St. Charles Borromeo. Before he was Pope Pius V, he was Michael Ghislieri, a Dominican from the duchy of Milan. He was born in 1504 to a family of middling means. Rather than pursue business or trade, he entered the Dominicans at the young age of fourteen and was ordained at twenty-four. He spent sixteen years teaching theology and philosophy and training novices, eventually becoming prior of several different houses.

Ghislieri's long years with the Dominicans cultivated all the monastic virtues. His penances and fasting were regular but moderate, his prayer life deep and contemplative, and his manner of living austere. He kept silence, save when his duties made it necessary to speak or when he could offer some edifying word to his brethren. His sanctity brought him to the attention of Pope Paul IV, who made him bishop of Sutri in 1556. There, he distinguished himself by his vigorous opposition to heresy and was subsequently promoted to cardinal and placed in charge of the Sacred Congregation of the Roman and Universal Inquisition, which had only recently been established by the reforming pope Paul III in 1542. Ghislieri was soon after appointed bishop of Mondovi by Pius IV (the uncle of Charles Borromeo).

His devotion to discipline knew no respect of person or rank. Once, when Pope Pius IV wanted to appoint a thirteen-year-old member of the Medici clan to the College of Cardinals, Ghislieri protested so ardently that he and Pius IV had a falling out that resulted in Ghislieri's estrangement from the pontiff.

It was, however, this very commitment to discipline and honesty that made Ghislieri so beloved among the cardinals. When Pius IV died in December 1565, the cardinals elected Ghislieri to ascend to the papal throne. The humble Dominican accepted, but only reluctantly and with many tears. During his years as bishop, Ghislieri had earned the friendship of Milan's Charles Borromeo. Borromeo's support had helped Ghislieri's election, in recognition of which, as we already saw, Ghislieri asked Borromeo what regnal name he should assume. Borromeo suggested Pius V, and by that name has Ghislieri ever been remembered.

Borromeo's influence would not end with the papal name. Pope Pius IV had asked Charles Borromeo to implement Trent in Milan. He had done so with great success. Now the new pontiff, Pius V, asked Charles for his help in reforming the clergy in the universal Church. Ever a pastor, these reforms began with his own conduct. Though weighed down by the anxieties of office, Pius V still managed to make two visits to the Blessed Sacrament every single day. He distributed alms among the poor liberally, banished prostitutes from the city, and forbade ostentatious displays of luxury at his court. Pius retained the austere Dominican manner of living at the papal court, which greatly reduced expenses. His personal devotion to the sick was unceasing, and the holy pontiff could always be seen going about the city's hospitals and ministering to the sick. An English Protestant once converted at the mere sight of the saintly man bending down to kiss the ulcerous feet of a leper.

But while the personal blamelessness of clerics was one aspect of Trent's vision, Pius could not lead by example alone. A pope can provide every noble example, but in the end, he must back up his examples with policy. With the recommendations and support of his friend Charles Borromeo, Pius V set about enforcing the decrees of Trent. Bishops who persisted in living away from their dioceses were rebuked and ordered to return to their sees at once. Certain religious orders, such as the Cistercians, were reformed, and secular authorities were put on notice that the Church would henceforth no longer tolerate lay interference in Church affairs for political ends.

One of his most lasting acts was his promulgation of the new Roman Missal in 1570, although "new" is a misnomer. The Council of Trent had called for a revision and reissuance of the Missal, the Breviary, and other important liturgical documents. At the time of the Reformation, the liturgy of the Mass was at its core the same that had been celebrated in the West since the time of Pope St. Gregory the Great. The essential decentralization of medieval society, however, meant that the actual celebration of the Missal was frequently subject to local innovations. In issuing a new edition of the Roman Missal, Pius sought to bring uniformity to the celebration of the Mass in the Roman Rite, as well as bring the Missal into conformity with the revised edition of the Breviary. In *Quo Primum*, the papal bull promulgating the new edition of the Missal, Pius explains his rationale in issuing the new book and discusses the methodology Roman scholars employed in identifying the authentic Roman rite:

> [I]n order that the Missal and Breviary might be in perfect harmony, as is right and proper (considering that it is altogether fitting that there should be in the Church only one appropriate manner of Psalmody and one sole rite of celebrating Mass), [we] deemed it necessary to give Our immediate attention to what still remained to be done, namely the re-editing of the Missal with the least possible delay.
>
> We resolved accordingly to delegate this task to a select committee of scholars; and they, having at every stage of their work and with the utmost care collated the ancient codices in Our Vatican Library and reliable (original or amended) codices from elsewhere, and having also consulted the writing of ancient and approved authors who have bequeathed to us records relating to the said sacred rites, thus restored the Missal itself to the pristine form and rite of the holy Fathers. When this production had been subjected to

close scrutiny and further amended We, after mature consideration, ordered that the final result be forthwith printed and published in Rome, so that all may enjoy the fruit of this labor; that priests may know what prayers to use, and what rites and ceremonies they are to observe henceforward in the celebration of Masses.

Now therefore, in order that all everywhere may adopt and observe what has been delivered to them by the Holy Roman Church, Mother and Mistress of the other churches, it shall be unlawful henceforth and forever throughout the Christian world to sing or to read Masses according to any formula other than that of this Missal published by us.

The bull abrogated the usage of all other forms of the Mass that could not prove a pedigree going back two hundred years, which in 1570 meant prior to 1370. All rites and usages that had been in use prior to 1370 were allowed to continue.

It might seem that Pius was imposing a great novelty on the Church by imposing a single, uniform Mass on Christendom where there had once been multiplicity, but this would be an incorrect understanding of the situation. The multiplicity that existed before 1570 was not so much in different Masses, but in small variations of the Roman rite. The Roman rite had been used almost exclusively in the West since the Carolingian era in the eighth and ninth centuries. In promulgating the Missal of 1570, Pius V established no "new Mass" nor abrogated any other legitimate rites. He merely called for uniformity in liturgical worship by insisting on the celebration of the West's traditional Mass shorn of local innovations that had crept in through the late medieval period. Those forms that were legitimately old enough or distinct enough to be considered a separate rite or usage (such as the Mozarbic rite in Spain or the Ambrosian rite of Milan) were allowed to remain untouched. And ultimately, the Missal of 1570 codified and mandated the faithful celebration of the Mass that most of the West had been using already for a thousand years. It was hardly an innovation.

Pius was well respected throughout the Church and tried to leverage this esteem by supporting Catholics wherever they were beleaguered by Protestants. By the time of his pontificate, France had begun to slip into the chaos of religious violence; Pius offered encouragement to the Catholic League and even contributed money to their cause. The Netherlands, too, had become mired in a war against the Catholic Hapsburg sovereigns, and there, too, Pius lent his aid to the Catholic party.

His biggest conflict was with Queen Elizabeth I of England. When Pius ascended the papal chair in 1566, Elizabeth had been on the throne of England for seven years. It was clear that Elizabeth was no friend to the Catholic Church, for as soon as she took power, she began dismantling the Catholic restoration of Mary Tudor and reestablished the Anglican edifice created under her father and brother. Pius was under no illusions about where Elizabeth's mind was. But toward the end of the decade, two things happened that would bring Pius and Elizabeth into sharp conflict.

The first was the flight of Mary, Queen of Scots, into England in 1568. In chapter 10, we saw how the Puritans of Scotland drove Mary from her throne. She fled to England, hoping her cousin Elizabeth would help her regain her throne. Mary presumed the bonds of blood and royalty would elicit the sympathy of her cousin. But Elizabeth viewed the exiled Scots queen as a bargaining chip and kept her imprisoned until she could determine the most advantageous way to use her. By 1570, the year Pius issued the revised Missal, it was clear that Elizabeth intended simply to keep Mary imprisoned perpetually. This policy was a double-edged sword. On the one hand, the presence of a Catholic monarch on England's northern border was a threat to Elizabeth, especially since Mary had a strong claim to the throne of England—indeed, stronger than Elizabeth herself. Keeping her confined kept a potential rival away from mischief. On the other hand, the unjustly imprisoned queen of Scots could not but arouse the sympathy of those who saw Elizabeth as a tyrant. As long as she remained imprisoned, she became a kind of focal point for resistance to Elizabeth's reign. Pius himself was among those moved by Mary's plight and considered her imprisonment a manifest injustice.

But of more immediate importance was the 1569 northern rebellion. That year, Catholic nobles from across England took up arms against Elizabeth in an attempt to depose her and put Mary on the throne. The rebellion excited the hopes of Catholics across Europe; Pius V himself was a vocal supporter of the rebels. In the midst of the revolt, he offered his aid to the Catholic cause by formally excommunicating Elizabeth in the bull *Regnans in Excelsis*, issued on February

25, 1570. The bull declared Elizabeth the "pretended Queen of England and servant of crime," a reference to her unjust imprisonment of Mary, Queen of Scots. It absolved all Catholics from allegiance to her and actually forbade the faithful from obeying her edicts.

Perhaps Pius was misinformed about the outcome of the rebellion, or perhaps it looked more formidable on paper than it was on the ground. Whatever the case, by the time he issued the excommunication, the northern rebellion had fizzled out. Its leaders were scattered—some were caught and beheaded, others fled England and died impoverished. Pius's excommunication had no meaningful effect upon the rebellion, except to enrage Elizabeth further against Catholics. Indeed, *Regnans in Excelsis* put English Catholics in a terrible dilemma: face excommunication and potential damnation for obeying the heretic queen or face execution for treason for refusing obedience. Anti-Catholic legislation became more oppressive, with many more crimes carrying the penalty of death. We shall look at the status of Catholics in England under Elizabeth in more detail in our next chapter.

Though the revision of the Missal and the excommunication of Elizabeth were noteworthy acts, the name of Pius V will always be associated with the glorious victory of the Christian armies at the Battle of Lepanto in 1571. Thus far in this book, we have given considerable focus to the dynamic between Protestants and Catholics in sixteenth-century Europe, but these two groups were not the only forces at work. Throughout the late Middle Ages, the Ottoman Turks had spread out of central Asia and overrun much of the Middle East. The Turks displaced the older Arabic king-doms of the region but adopted the Islamic religion of the conquered Arabs. This new, aggressive Islamic threat pushed west in the fourteenth and fifteenth centuries, swallowing up the Byzantine Empire with its capital at Constantinople in 1453. Throughout the decades of the Reformation, the Turks had relentlessly pushed west by land and sea, threat-ening the eastern marches of the Holy Roman Empire and raiding the coasts of Italy with impunity. Their ships stalked the Mediterranean, attacking Christian vessels and selling their hapless crews into slavery.

The religious rifts within Europe made the Turkish threat that much more grave. It emboldened the Turks to make sharp advances into the Holy Roman Empire, knowing that Charles V was too preoccupied with the wars against the Schmalkaldic League to devote his attention fully to the east. It also saw Christian rulers seeking Turkish swords against other Christian rulers, as when Francis I of France made an alliance with the Turks in 1536 against their common enemy Charles V. The kings of Christendom played poli-tics with the Turks for decades, using the looming threat of the Turks as a bargaining point in their political squab-bles. But meanwhile, the Turks were conquering huge pieces of Europe and putting them under the dominion of Islam. Under the long reign of Sultan Suleiman the Magnificent (r. 1520–1566), Ottoman armies had marched into places as far flung as Baghdad, Tripoli, and Budapest, bringing mil-lions under the Sultan's rule and pushing the boundaries of the empire from Yemen to Hungary. While the princes of Christendom squabbled, the rapacious Turkish monster was swelling on their eastern borders, poised to devour the entire edifice of Christendom and put an end to the disputes of Christians by burying Protestant and Catholic alike beneath the unstoppable might of the Islamic armies.

Pope Pius V had never been under any illusion about the Turkish threat. As a Mediterranean state, Italy suffered directly at the hands of Turkish raiders. Back when Pius was still teaching with the Dominican order, the Turks had actually invaded the southern Italian city of Otranto with a sizable army and carried off ten thousand Christians as slaves. Their corsairs continued to prowl the waters about Italy and raid Italian towns down to Pius's pontificate. No Italian could ever view the Turkish threat in the abstract. Beyond Pius's cultural memory as an Italian, the successors of St. Peter had always shown a great solicitude about the Muslim threat. Throughout the late Middle Ages and Renaissance, pope after pope pleaded for Christians to unite in crusade against the Islamic foe, while the princes of Christendom yawned and went about their business.

Pius V ascended the papal throne the same year Suleiman died. The new Sultan was Selim II, son of the great Suleiman. Like any prince following in the footsteps of an illustrious father, Selim was anxious to prove his mettle by adding more land to his father's conquests. His early campaigns were lackluster: he managed to win some concessions in east Europe, but these came by treaty; his military efforts in Russia were thwarted by the prowess of Ivan the Terrible. Selim was eager for a resounding military victory that would establish him as a conqueror on par with his legendary father.

Selim settled on the island of Cyprus, which was then under the control of the Republic of Venice. The island of Cyrpus, nestled in the eastern Mediterranean midway between Lebanon and Asia Minor, was deep within Ottoman territory. A Latin Christian outpost so far east was a holdover from the crusades. The crusading era was long gone, however, and though Venice maintained a powerful fleet, the island was relatively isolated. Selim launched a swift invasion in 1570. The capture of the island's two biggest cities, Nicosia and Famagusta, were followed by frightful massacres. In Nicosia, twenty thousand Christians were put to death. Captured women and boys were sold into slavery. After the fall of Famagusta in August 1571, the Christians of the city were massacred after being promised safe conduct. The Venetian governor Bragadin was tortured and then skinned alive; his skin was later stuffed with straw and turned into a war trophy.

Word had come west about the Turkish invasion of Cyprus some months earlier. Pope Pius V had begun promoting the idea of a Christian coalition to counter the Turkish threat and go to the relief of Cyprus. The Spaniards, zealous Catholics that they were, heeded the pope's call. Besides Spain, however, none of the major European powers took part. France was enmeshed in its own civil war; Elizabeth of England, recently excommunicated, certainly would not take part, nor did Emperor Maximilian II. It was rather the smaller states and duchies of Europe who took up the defense of Christendom. Pius committed the Papal States, and the Venetians were, of course, eager to defend their island outpost. They were joined by the Genoese, the duchies of Tuscany, Savoy, Urbino, and Parma, and the military orders of Malta and the Knights Hospitaller. All told, the force, dubbed the Holy League, consisted of a little over two hundred warships and 28,500 infantry manning over 1,800 guns—and this not counting the tens of thousands of oarsmen. Leadership of the enterprise was placed in the capable hands of Don John of Austria, the illegitimate son of Emperor Charles V.

But assembling a navy is always a slow, tedious affair, and was even more so in the sixteenth century. By the time the Holy League was ready to sail, Cyprus had already fallen. News of Governor Bragadin's horrific death—whom the Venetians regarded as a martyr—strengthened the resolve of the League. Cyprus had fallen, but none of the League's members were willing to tolerate the presence of a massive Ottoman fleet in the Mediterranean, especially one in the hands of a warmongering prince hawkish for military glory.

Pope Pius took a deep personal interest in the mission of the League. His personal coat of arms appeared on the League's banner, along with the insignia of Venice, Charles V, and Don John all beneath an image of Christ crucified. The banner was blessed personally by Pius and entrusted to the fleet on August 14. The rendezvous point was at Messina, in Sicily. By the end of the month, all the participants had mustered their forces and Don John had arrived to take command with Pius's blessing.

The fleet of the Holy League departed Messina on September 16, 1571. The Christian fleet crept cautiously along the Greek coast, winding their way east in search of the Ottoman fleet. We can imagine the anxiety of the Christian forces—a disparate hodge-podge of ships from a handful of principalities under command of a bastard prince going up against a larger fleet representing the power of an aggressive empire that straddled three continents. National rivalries threatened to tear the fragile League apart. Bad weather plagued the expedition. From a purely empirical standpoint, the expedition of the Holy League did not seem to be going well.

Of course, the empirical is never the whole of the story. Grace flows imperceptibly, and providence moves through the free will decisions of men and the working of nature to bring about God's ends. Pope Pius had ordered public prayers throughout Christendom for the success of the fleet and himself spent many hours before the Blessed Sacrament beseeching God to bless the Holy League with success. From Rome to Spain to the duchies of northern Italy, the pious invocations of thousands of Christians went up on behalf of the fleet daily. Rosaries were prayed devotedly for the success of Don John and the Christian warriors of Europe.

The Holy League spotted the Turkish fleet in the Gulf of Patras near the town of Lepanto early on October 7, 1571. The Turkish fleet was larger than the Christian, though not by a great deal. Don John formed his ships up in four divisions making a great line running north to south; reserves were deployed behind and others in the fore to stop smaller Turkish ships from harassing the Christian vessels. The Turkish commander, Ali Pasha, formed his ships up in a large crescent to the east of the Holy League. As a great deal of the rowers in the Turkish fleet were Christian slaves, Pasha was worried that they might be tempted to betray their Turkish masters. He allegedly told them, "If I win the battle, I promise you your liberty. If the day is yours, then God has given it to you."

Neither side had a strategic interest in the Gulf of Patras, but both sides were determined to give battle. Don John readied his men—galley prisoners were unchained so they could fight and the Blessed Sacrament was administered to the crews. The banner of the Holy League was raised on the flagship. Don John encouraged all his men to pray to God and the Blessed Virgin for victory. As Don John scrambled to arrange his ships, the Turkish fleet began a cautious advance.

The initial phase of the battle did not bode well for the Christians. The winds were strong against the Christian fleet, which made it extremely difficult for Don John's ships to maintain order. With the wind favoring the Ottomans, the momentum would be all with the Turks. The Christian ships would be caught pushing helplessly against the wind while the Ottoman ships glided through their ranks wreaking havoc.

As the Christian soldiers offered up their prayers and Rosaries, however, the wind slowly began to shift. A breeze began to blow from the west, which gradually gained strength until powerful gusts of wind were beating back against the advancing Turkish fleet. Rejoicing swept through the Christian ranks as the ships of Don John, now aided by the winds that had hitherto hindered them, formed up with ease. The Ottoman ships, meanwhile, lost their momentum and struggled against the wind to maintain cohesion.

An advance force of four galleys from the Holy League fired an opening salvo into the Turkish fleet from close range, further disrupting the Turkish advance. The Turkish right squadron tried to outflank the Christian left, but the Venetians under their admiral Barbarigo stifled this attempt. The fighting was close range, hand to hand and ship to ship. In the end, Barbarigo was killed, but the Turkish outflanking maneuver was stalled. Thousands of Christian galley slaves were rescued from captured Turkish ships. Ecstatic with liberty, these freed Christian slaves were immediately armed and turned with fury upon their former captors.

The center of the Christian line smashed into the Turkish ships. Again, fighting was grueling. Saber rattled against saber upon the decks of a hundred ships as Christian struggled with Turk in the afternoon air choked by cannon fire. The battle was desperate, but the momentum of the battle was with the Holy League. Ali Pasha could not keep his ships together and the Ottoman fleet was in disarray. The Turkish flagship was taken and boarded, its entire crew killed. Ali Pasha himself was slain; his head was shorn off and paraded about on a pike.

The battle went on for two more hours, though the day was already decided. Some Turks fought until their strength was utterly spent and were reduced to hurling lemons and oranges at their opponents, to the uproarious laughter of the Christian forces. At the end of the day, the Holy League had captured some 117 ships and destroyed another 50. Thousands of Christian slaves were rescued and as many Turks taken prisoner. The Holy League suffered 7,500 casualties, the Turks 30,000. The Christian army immediately attributed the victory to the unexplainable shift in winds immediately prior to the battle, which occurred as the men of the League were reciting the Rosary.

But even more stunning was Pius V's miraculous knowledge of the victory occurring hundreds of miles away. On the afternoon of October 7, Pius was engaged in administrative work with some of his cardinals. Shortly after noon, he abruptly paused, opened a nearby window, and looking into the sky said, "A truce to business; our great task at present is to thank God for the victory which He has just given the Christian army." He ordered bells to be rung and victory to be celebrated. When he later received confirmation of the Christian victory, he broke down and wept.

The Turkish defeat at Lepanto did not immediately destroy the Turkish threat; the Ottoman fleet would quickly be rebuilt, and within a year, the Holy League was again engaging the Turks in the eastern Mediterranean. Lepanto's importance was more long term in that it sapped the drive of the Turkish conquests. Selim would recover his fleet, but not his momentum. A treaty formalized in 1573 ended the war and left the Mediterranean permanently divided between a Christian west and a Turkish east. Within the boundaries defined by the treaty, the Ottoman Empire would go into a period of slow decline. They would have a few more strikes in them (the Ottoman invasion of Austria in 1683 pushed far enough west to threaten the city of Vienna itself), but the centuries after Lepanto would see a gradual erosion of Ottoman power. Pius V declared the first Sunday in October a feast in honor of the Rosary and added the supplication "Help of Christians" to the Litany of Loreto.

Pope Pius had helped organize the Holy League that had saved Christendom from the Turks. He did not long outlive this victory. For some time, he had been wracked with illness (believed now to be cancer) and grew progressively worse through spring of 1572. On May 1, he finally succumbed to his illness and died. Pius was buried in a temporary tomb in St. Peter's before being translated to his final resting place—a magnificent crypt in the Basilica di Santa Maria Maggiore—in 1583.

His legacy was immense. The papacy had come a long way since the days of Leo X and Martin Luther. St. Pius V was the first pope to be canonized in almost three hundred years and the last pope to be canonized for over another three hundred. In his personal sanctity, he set a new standard for future popes. The uniformity of worship he made possible by his Missal gave the clergy a renewed sense of unity. Whether a Mass was being celebrated in an Italian basilica or an Irish hovel or in a birch bark hut among the natives of North America, it was according to Pius V's Missal. To this day, whenever the Extraordinary Form of the Mass is said, it is essentially the Mass of St. Pius V. His energetic implementation of Trent charted a course for the Church to which it remained steadfastly faithful for four centuries. He has won undying glory for his role in organizing the Holy League that dealt the Turks their crushing defeat at Lepanto.

The great failure of Pius V's pontificate was his unsuccessful attempt to win England back to the Catholic fold. To England, now, we must again return to see how the Church there fared under the reign of Elizabeth.

CHAPTER 14

The Celebrated Outlaw: St. Edmund Campion

St. Pius V's excommunication of Elizabeth in 1570 exposed Catholics in England to repressive measures by the government while doing no real harm to the queen herself. With the passing of Mary Tudor in 1558, Catholics were again second-class subjects as the new administration of Elizabeth rebuilt the machinery of the Anglican establishment. After 1570, however, things would become much worse for English Catholics. If we stand in Elizabeth's shoes, her anti-Catholic measures are somewhat understandable. She had only recently suppressed a violent rebellion by Catholic nobles in the north. Across the English Channel in Douai, a college had been founded for English Catholics in exile. Every year, English priests from Douai were smuggled back into the kingdom to minister to Catholics in secret. For all she knew, they could be plotting rebellion, for the bull *Regnans in Excelsis* had encouraged English Catholics to regard Elizabeth as deposed and resist her authority. There was also the thorny issue of the queen of Scots, who had a strong claim to the English throne, imprisoned for the past few years in an English castle and forever the object of wild-eyed Catholic plots.

Yes, we can see why Elizabeth was uneasy about her Catholic subjects. This fear was ultimately misplaced. Very few of them entertained violent designs against the crown or would have participated in a general Catholic revolution, should one have occurred. English Catholics, like most good people of any age, simply wanted to be left alone. But to Elizabeth, they were all potential traitors, and the flurry of legislation that followed 1570 made that abundantly clear.

The so-called "Penal Laws" were meant to protect the formal establishment of the Anglican Church and prevent the practice of the Catholic faith in England. From the time Elizabeth took the throne in 1558, the Act of Supremacy was reinstituted. Under this act, no ecclesiastical prelate might maintain the authority of a foreign prince (a reference to the pope); the punishment for doing so would be forfeiture of goods and lands, and death by hanging, drawing, and quartering on the third offense. Any lay Englishman who refused to attend the services of the Church of England was fined twelve pence per omission. Following the papal bull of 1570, Elizabeth made it high treason to state that the queen ought not to enjoy the crown, to call her a heretic or schismatic, to receive any converts into the Catholic Church, to convert to the Catholic Church oneself, or to possess or publish any papal bull whatsoever. All these crimes carried the punishment of death by hanging, drawing, and quartering.

In order to stop Catholics from leaving the kingdom to study abroad at Douai or collude with other Catholic powers, it was decreed that anyone who left the kingdom without the queen's license and failed to return within six months would forfeit all his goods and property. It was later made a crime to attend Mass (punishable by a hefty fine), and priests were liable to a year's imprisonment for celebrating Mass. A law of 1585 aimed against Jesuits made it a capital crime for a Jesuit to be in the country at all. Laws were passed prohibiting known Catholics from moving more than five miles from their homes—this was to crack down on the activities of clandestine priests, who roamed about the countryside ministering to Catholics on a sort of circuit.

Laws were even stricter in Ireland where Catholics constituted a majority and were doubly repressed, for the penal system there was grounded not only in religious motives but in the contempt of the English for a conquered race; it was not solely about maintaining a religious establishment, but an imperialist occupation. They were enforced with a savage rigidity that included the wholesale murder of entire clans, the ethnic cleansing of the vast region of Munster (in which thirty thousand Irish Catholics died by sword or famine), and the brutal torture of Catholic clerics, such as Archbishop Dermot O'Hurley, who had his legs boiled before being hanged in 1584.[21]

The difficulties of English Catholics during the Elizabethan period are exemplified by the history of St. Edmund Campion. Campion was the son of a London bookseller

---

[21]   Dermot O'Hurley was canonized by Pope St. John Paul II in 1992 and is regarded as a martyr.

born during the latter years of Henry VIII. Though not of noble birth, his familiarity with books from a young age opened his mind to literature, and his father allowed him to attend grammar school and study Latin at Christ Church Hospital. Young Edmund Campion so excelled at Latin that he was chosen as the representative of the school to deliver the school's salutation to Mary Tudor upon her first entry into London as queen.

His reputation as a scholar would only grow. Campion was accepted to the newly established St. John's College at Oxford and became a junior fellow at only seventeen years of age. He spent the next twelve years at Oxford, becoming one of the most renowned scholars and orators of the age. Now twenty-six years old, he again welcomed a queen when he delivered a greeting to Queen Elizabeth upon her visit to Oxford in 1566. Elizabeth was deeply impressed with the eloquence and bearing of Campion and regarded him very highly. He also earned the respect of William Cecil. Cecil was secretary of state to Elizabeth and would be the most powerful man in the kingdom for the duration of Elizabeth's reign. Campion was also admired by Robert Dudley, Earl of Leicester and a favorite of Elizabeth. Campion's oratory and wit had brought him into the circle of the most powerful people in the kingdom.

Success in Elizabethan England meant acceptance of the prevailing Anglican establishment. Like most Englishmen who wanted to get a leg up in society, Campion was an Anglican. He was no deep theologian or mystic, but he had a sort of natural affinity for liturgy and ceremonial that drew him to moderate Anglicanism. For the puritanical element in late sixteenth-century English Christianity, he had very little use. The Puritan sect was growing in strength throughout Elizabeth's reign. Learned men throughout England, men such as Campion, were engaging in scholarly debates over questions such as the merits of episcopacy, the wearing of vestments, and the true nature of Christian worship. Campion took part in this great conversation as well, defending the more traditional or "catholic" elements within the Anglican establishment.

Like Newman centuries later, however, Campion's defense of the "catholic" aspects of Anglicanism led him back to Catholicism itself. It was clear that the popular religious mood in England was moving toward a kind of minimalist Puritanism, while Campion was coming to the conclusion that the true faith of Christ may have been preserved in the Church of Rome. He entered a period of uncertainty, seeing the force of Rome's arguments but not yet ready to abandon the Church of England, and hoping for some middle path or compromise within the Anglican fold that would allow his soul to find rest. One of his patrons, Bishop Richard Cheney of Gloucester, smoothed over some of Edmund Campion's doubts and convinced him to take Holy Orders in the Church of England; Campion subsequently swore the Oath of Supremacy and was ordained an Anglican deacon in 1564. However, like many Christians pulled by Rome but hoping to find a third way in Anglicanism, Campion's heart would remain restless.

By 1569, Campion's views were becoming a scandal. He had not openly converted to Catholicism, but his opinions were already skirting dangerously close to Romish waters.

Campion left Oxford that year to travel to Ireland. It appears the aim of his Irish sojourn was to disappear from public life, immersing himself in research and personal reflection. He obtained a tutoring position in the household of the powerful Protestant Stanyhurst family of Dublin. The Stanyhursts were formal Protestants but retained a sort of sympathy for Catholics. Campion became a sincere friend of the family and opened up to them about his Catholic convictions.

Things were not safe in Dublin, however. The presence of such a famous crypto-Catholic within the Stonyhurst house aroused the indignation of Dublin's Protestants. Campion was forced to flee and travel under an assumed name in order to escape certain death at the hands of the Dublin Protestants, who tried for three months to track him down. He eventually settled in as tutor in another household at Turvey in east Ireland, but he realized that in order to sound fully the depths of his heart in security, he would have to leave the British Isles altogether. He would have to live and breathe Catholic air before he could set his heart and his soul at rest.

He subsequently set out for the English College at Douai, traveling by way of England. While passing through London, he was witness to a grim reminder of the potential consequences of the spiritual journey upon which he had embarked. Dr. John Story, a Catholic and former member of Parliament who had fled from England to take up service with the Spanish, had been apprehended in Antwerp and dragged back to England in chains. He was tried for high treason for vocally supporting the northern rebellion against Elizabeth. Dr. Story had been tortured severely in the Tower during the duration of his trial. Campion was present at Tyburn on June 1, 1571, when Dr. Story was hanged, drawn, and quartered. The spectacle profoundly moved Campion. The groans of the elderly man suffering all the tortures the English crown could muster against him led Campion to consider his own situation. If he truly held to the Catholic faith in heart, what excuse could he possibly have for remaining outside the Church? He wanted to possess that same faith that Dr. Story had so boldly evidenced in his sufferings.

Campion hastened to leave London and, crossing the Channel, arrived at the English College at Douai in France where he was formally received into the Catholic Church. At Douai, Edmund Campion was a renowned scholar, a kind of mid-grade celebrity. News of his conversion spread quickly. William Cecil, the secretary of state, lamented that England had lost one of her diamonds. This was neither here nor there to Campion; safe in Catholic France, he took courses in theology at Douai and began to drink from the pure streams of Catholic tradition. His year-and-a-half at Douai were like a foretaste of paradise for Edmund Campion. Studying Catholic doctrine securely among brethren of the same Faith was a balm to his weary soul. As in heaven, he was reunited with old friends—acquaintances from his days at Oxford who had similarly yielded to the authority of the ancient Faith and come to Douai to study. It was a season of joy and refreshment for a man who had suffered with uncertainty for so long. He took minor orders and was ordained a sub-deacon.

Following the completion of his lesser degree in 1573, Campion set out barefoot for Rome. The great St. Pius V had only died a year earlier and the papacy was now in the hands of Gregory XIII, a reformer of blameless life who had dedicated himself to reorganizing the Roman Curia. Edmund Campion had already resolved to present himself as a candidate to the Society of Jesus and was accepted as a novice by them in April 1573. As the Jesuits had not yet established an English province due to conditions in England, Campion was sent to Brünn, Moravia, in the Austrian province to complete his two-year novitiate. He was ordained deacon and priest by the archbishop of Prague and said his first Mass on September 8, 1578.

Campion spent his time in Brünn teaching rhetoric and philosophy at the Jesuit college there. Meanwhile, the Society of Jesus was busy preparing the English mission. Things were very dangerous in England; as noted above, simply being a Jesuit priest within the realm was a capital offense. The Society took great care in formulating its strategy for ministering to English Catholics—the sorts of activities its priests should engage in, their manner of dress and travel, the fabrication of credible aliases, the establishment of logistics for getting priests in and out of the country. The Society knew that Elizabeth's government viewed Catholic priests essentially as political revolutionaries. Although the Society knew Elizabeth's government would not let go of this misconception, the Jesuits were insistent that they themselves give no occasion for misunderstanding. Consequently, all priests sent to the English mission were strictly forbidden from dealing with any matters of state policy whatsoever. It was to be clear that their mission was purely spiritual.

The Jesuit mission began in 1580. Edmund Campion was chosen, along with a superior, Fr. Robert Persons. The two were given detailed instructions on how to conduct themselves in England. They were to pass themselves off as jewel merchants. Campion was initially worried; the memory of Dr. John Story's brutal torture and execution were still fresh in his mind. Edmund wondered whether he possessed the constitutional fortitude to endure the trials that might beset him should he be captured. But before he left Brünn, he had a mystical experience that both gave him a foreshadowing of his fate as well as strengthened him with the necessary grace to go forward. He was sitting in the garden of the Jesuit college one day when he saw an apparition of Our Lady. She told him to prepare for martyrdom. Campion made the vision known to his superiors, and word soon got out. His comrades in the diocese of Prague were moved to paint a garland of roses within his cell. Campion was profoundly touched by these gestures, but also apprehensive about what lay ahead.

The trip from Brünn to England was a long one, with many detours. Campion and Fr. Persons visited Milan where they spent a week in the company of St. Charles Borromeo. In 1580, Borromeo was only forty-two years old, but he was nearing the end of his life. The eminent cardinal had a special concern for the plight of English Catholics. He kept images of St. Thomas More and St. John Fisher on his person and retained several English Catholics in his personal service. While in the company of the illustrious Borromeo, Edmund

Campion made the acquaintance of another English priest, Fr. Ralph Sherwin. Sherwin had been studying at the Jesuit college in Rome and was also preparing for the English mission. Campion and Fr. Persons went their own way, stopping in Geneva and having other side adventures, but Campion and Sherwin would meet again.

Upon arriving in France, it was discovered that letters to English Catholics announcing the arrival of Campion and Persons had been intercepted and the English authorities were on the lookout for them. They also learned that Irish Catholic adventurer James Fitzmaurice Fitzgerald had landed a sizable band of a thousand mercenaries in Ireland with the aim of provoking a general rebellion against English authority. The timing could not have been worse; the English authorities knew the Jesuits were coming, and the recent Catholic tumults in Ireland meant they would be in a foul mood.

Nevertheless, Campion and Fr. Persons successfully landed in Dover on June 16, 1580, posing as jewel merchants. Campion's mission was to administer the sacraments to Catholics and edify those who might be wavering in their commitment due to the pressure imposed upon them by Elizabeth's tyranny. It must have been a strange feeling to be back in his native land but knowing he was viewed as an unwanted agent of a foreign power. How odd it must have been to traverse the countryside in which he had grown up, recognizing the familiarity of this road, that river, this town—places he knew intimately—but yet, with the sense of being profoundly unwelcome due to the policy of a government that considered his mere presence within the kingdom a crime meriting death.

At some point in 1580, Campion composed a document that has become known as "Campion's Brag." The purpose of the Brag was to lay out his reasons for entering the country, profess his innocence of any sort of treasonous behavior, and challenge the Protestant divines of the kingdom to contest against him in a public disputation. We present here the full text of Campion's Brag:

> To the Right Honorable, the Lords of Her Majesty's Privy Council:
>
> Whereas I have come out of Germany and Bohemia, being sent by my superiors, and adventured myself into this noble realm, my dear country, for the glory of God and benefit of souls, I thought it like enough that, in this busy, watchful, and suspicious world, I should either sooner or later be intercepted and stopped of my course.
>
> Wherefore, providing for all events, and uncertain what may become of me, when God shall haply deliver my body into durance, I supposed it needful to put this in writing in a readiness, desiring your good lordships to give it your reading, for to know my cause. This doing, I trust I shall ease you of some labor. For that which otherwise you must have sought for by practice of wit, I do now lay into your hands by plain confession. And to the intent that the whole matter may be conceived in order, and so the better both understood and remembered, I make thereof these nine points or

articles, directly, truly and resolutely opening my full enterprise and purpose.

i. I confess that I am (albeit unworthy) a priest of the Catholic Church, and through the great mercy of God vowed now these eight years into the religion [religious order] of the Society of Jesus. Hereby I have taken upon me a special kind of warfare under the banner of obedience, and also resigned all my interest or possibility of wealth, honor, pleasure, and other worldly felicity.

ii. At the voice of our General, which is to me a warrant from heaven and oracle of Christ, I took my voyage from Prague to Rome (where our General Father is always resident) and from Rome to England, as I might and would have done joyously into any part of Christendom or Heatheness, had I been thereto assigned.

iii. My charge is, of free cost to preach the Gospel, to minister the Sacraments, to instruct the simple, to reform sinners, to confute errors—in brief, to cry alarm spiritual against foul vice and proud ignorance, wherewith many of my dear countrymen are abused.

iv. I never had mind, and am strictly forbidden by our Father that sent me, to deal in any respect with matter of state or policy of this realm, as things which appertain not to my vocation, and from which I gladly restrain and sequester my thoughts.

v. I do ask, to the glory of God, with all humility, and under your correction, three sorts of indifferent and quiet audiences: the first, before your Honors, wherein I will discourse of religion, so far as it touches the common weal and your nobilities: the second, whereof I make more account, before the Doctors and Masters and chosen men of both universities, wherein I undertake to avow the faith of our Catholic Church by proofs innumerable—Scriptures, councils, Fathers, history, natural and moral reasons: the third, before the lawyers, spiritual and temporal, wherein I will justify the said faith by the common wisdom of the laws standing yet in force and practice.

vi. I would be loath to speak anything that might sound of any insolent brag or challenge, especially being now as a dead man to this world and willing to put my head under every man's foot, and to kiss the ground they tread upon. Yet I have such courage in avouching the majesty of Jesus my King, and such affiance in his gracious favor, and such assurance in my quarrel, and my evidence so impregnable, and because I know perfectly that no one Protestant, nor all the Protestants living, nor any sect of our adversaries (howsoever they face men down in pulpits, and overrule us in their kingdom of grammarians and unlearned ears) can maintain their doctrine in disputation. I am to sue most humbly and instantly for combat with all and every of them, and the most principal that may be found: protesting that in this trial the better furnished they come, the better welcome they shall be.

vii. And because it hath pleased God to enrich the Queen my Sovereign Lady with notable gifts of nature, learning, and princely education, I do verily trust that if her Highness would vouchsafe her royal person and good attention to such a conference as, in the second part of my fifth article I have motioned, or to a few sermons, which in her or your hearing I am to utter such manifest and fair light by good method and plain dealing may be cast upon these controversies, that possibly her zeal of truth and love of her people shall incline her noble Grace to disfavor some proceedings hurtful to the realm, and procure towards us oppressed more equity.

viii. Moreover I doubt not but you, her Highness' Council, being of such wisdom and discreet in cases most important, when you shall have heard these questions of religion opened faithfully, which many times by our adversaries are huddled up and confounded, will see upon what substantial grounds our Catholic Faith is builded, how feeble that side is which by sway of the time prevails against us, and so at last for your own souls, and for many thousand souls that depend upon your government, will discountenance error when it is revealed, and hearken to those who would spend the best blood in their bodies for your salvation. Many innocent hands are lifted up to heaven for you daily by those English students, whose posterity shall never die, which beyond seas, gathering virtue and sufficient knowledge for the purpose, are determined never to give you over, but either to win you heaven, or to die upon your pikes. And touching our Society, be it known to you that we have made a league—all the Jesuits in the world, whose succession and multitude must overreach all the practice of England—cheerfully to carry the cross you shall lay upon us, and never to despair your recovery, while we have a man left to enjoy your Tyburn, or to be racked with your torments, or consumed with your prisons. The expense is reckoned, the enterprise is begun; it is of God; it cannot be withstood. So the faith was planted: So it must be restored.

ix. If these my offers be refused, and my endeavors can take no place, and I, having run thousands of miles to do you good, shall be rewarded with rigor. I have no more to say but to recommend your case and mine to Almighty God, the Searcher of Hearts, who send us his grace, and see us at accord before the day of payment, to the end we may at last be friends in heaven, when all injuries shall be forgotten.

The Brag was originally meant to be found only in the event of his capture; he presumes at some point he will be apprehended and addresses the document to the queen's Privy Council. An overenthusiastic supporter, however, obtained a copy of the Brag and published it prematurely. Rightly or wrongly, the document made Campion look like a reckless trumpeter just daring the authorities to catch him and torture him. And for their part, the authorities were salivating at the opportunity of dragging this insolent braggart before their courts, racking him, and watching him whimper while his limbs were mutilated and his organs ripped out and burned before his eyes.

At any rate, if the authorities were not onto Campion yet, they certainly were eager for him after the publication of the *Brag*. He spent the better part of a year circulating about the homes of Catholics in Berkshire, Oxfordshire, Northamptonshire, and Lancashire, but he was by no means safe. He was always on the move, perpetually looking over his shoulder for the royal spies who certainly knew of his existence and were already on his trail. Incentives were offered for anyone who betrayed a Catholic priest, meaning Campion had to worry not only about government spies but wavering, cash-strapped Catholics who might turn him for money.

At one point, the authorities seemed to be closing in on him and he had to flee north. While in flight, he composed the *Decem Rationes*, or *Ten Reasons*. This was a document that set forth ten arguments against the validity of the Anglican Church and proposed a debate between Anglican theologians and Catholic apologists that would proceed along the ten points. The ten points can be summarized as follows:

1. Protestants interpret Scriptures selectively, rejecting what does not support their doctrines.

2. Similarly, they distort other parts of Scripture in order to support their doctrines.

3. Protestants have a defective concept of the Church.

4. Protestants should accept Catholic teaching on the Mass, the communion of saints, and the authority of the pope as Vicar of Christ in his Church.

5. Protestant beliefs about the Church, the Eucharist, the communion of saints, and the authority

of the pope are not supported by the Church Fathers.

6. Protestants have tended to ignore the testimony of the Church Fathers, since the Fathers do not support their doctrines.

7. Protestant beliefs are not supported by the Church's history.

8. A critique of certain Protestant mottos that are misleading, like "faith alone," or "good works are as mortal sins."

9. General weakness of Protestant arguments.

10. Conclusion, namely, that Catholicism is the authentic Faith of Jesus Christ, and that this was universally believed for fifteen hundred years, meaning Protestantism is a historical anomaly.

The *Decem Rationes* were spirited off to an underground printer and soon hundreds of copies were being circulated around Oxford. The pamphlets caused quite a ruckus and made Campion the most celebrated outlaw in England. The authorities doubled down on their efforts to find the haughty Jesuit.

In his Brag, Campion said he assumed he would be captured sooner or later. It ended up being sooner. He had not even been in England for a full year when he was discovered by a government spy while preaching at a manor house called Lyford Grange. The story of Edmund Campion's arrest and discovery is one full of tragic missteps and avoidable errors. When he had finished preaching and left the estate, a delegation came to fetch him on the road and persuaded him to return, despite Campion's conviction he had already tarried too long. Once he returned, a blabbering woman told a government spy lingering around at the gates of the manor house that the famed Edmund Campion was preaching and hearing confessions inside. When this spy ran off hastily to fetch the authorities, Campion wanted to flee, but was persuaded instead to hide himself within Lyford Grange's many secret passages. The authorities searched the house once and left, only to return again with directions to break down walls if need be. After this second search failed to uncover Campion's hiding place, he allowed himself to be lured out by the hostess of the home, who asked him to preach at her bedside to her and some guests while the government guards were sleeping just a few feet outside the chambers.

In the end, Campion and two associates were discovered in hiding after a full day of searching—with so many preventable mistakes, it seems evident that his arrest was part of God's providence for the glorification of the faith in England, as the Blessed Virgin had told him. Campion was paraded to London amid great fanfare, his hands and feet bound, riding backwards with a hat labeling him a seditious Jesuit. He was thrown into the Tower, but before long was dragged forth again and conveyed to the house of Robert Dudley, the Earl of Leicester, an old admirer of Campion from his Oxford days. But things had changed since those days, and Campion was not welcomed as a friend but a prisoner.

Dudley conducted him into the hall where none other than Queen Elizabeth herself was awaiting Campion's arrival. The audience between Campion and Elizabeth is reminiscent of the old contests between the martyrs and the

Roman emperors who tempted them with all manner of gifts to deny the faith. Elizabeth called to mind Campion's erudition and former reputation as one of the greatest minds in England. She offered him liberty and advancement at court if he would but renounce the Catholic faith. Campion had once wondered if he had the fortitude to remain faithful in such an hour of temptation. The grace imparted to him by Our Lady's apparition in the garden at Brünn did not fail him; he refused Elizabeth's offers of prestige, even though he knew it meant certain death.

The subsequent treatment of Fr. Edmund Campion by his captors combined the best elements of the medieval university system with the worst aspects of the medieval torture chamber in a bizarre spectacle that was meant to humiliate Campion intellectually while breaking him physically. He was racked in the Tower multiple times, stretched on the cruel machine until his sinews were torn and his sockets displaced. But he was sometimes dragged from his torture to go stand before an assemblage of Anglican divines in the Tower's chapel of St. John to argue the points laid out in his *Decem Rationes*. Despite the exhaustion brought on by torture, despite being allowed no time to prepare, and despite being allowed only to answer questions posed to him and not ask any of his own, Campion defended his ten points with such skill that the sessions were called off prematurely. These disputations were of great merit to those who heard them; one notable peer, the Earl of Arundel Philip Howard, was convinced to return to the Catholic faith. He himself would go on to be martyred fourteen years after Campion.

And martyred Campion was. Despite his protestations that he was not a political revolutionary, Elizabeth was not about to let Campion go free after all that had passed. The crown would make an example of this Jesuit braggart. On November 20, 1581, he was dragged to Westminster to be tried. He certainly did not look the part of a dangerous traitor; his right arm was so mangled from torture that he could scarcely lift it to take the oath at the trial. Campion was not alone—two other priests who had been captured elsewhere in the kingdom stood with him, one Alexander Briant, and the other Ralph Sherwin, the same amiable man Campion had met in the residence of Charles Borromeo the previous year. How things had changed in a single year! Back then, they were all laughing together in the presence of the great cardinal-saint of Milan; today, they stood accused of treason.

Campion, Sherwin, and Briant were found guilty after only an hour of deliberation. In response to the verdict, Campion famously said, "In condemning us, you condemn all your own ancestors, all our ancient bishops and kings, all that was once the glory of England—the island of saints, and the most devoted child of the See of Peter." Lord Chief Justice Christopher Wray was not impressed; the sentence for the three was proclaimed: "You must go to the place from whence you came, there to remain until ye shall be drawn through the open city of London upon hurdles to the place of execution, and there be hanged and let down alive, and your privy parts cut off, and your entrails taken out and burnt in your sight; then your heads to be cut off and your bodies divided into four parts, to be disposed of at Her Majesty's pleasure. And God have mercy on your souls." On hearing the death sentence, Campion and his companions sang the *Te Deum*. The sentence was scheduled to be carried out in ten days. Campion was returned to his cell and spent his last days on this earth in prayer for the ordeal to come.

Edmund Campion had once wondered whether he had the constitutional fortitude to endure such a trial. Perhaps the most troubling thing about such a torturous death is that the question is really moot. It does not matter if one can or cannot take it—it is happening nonetheless, and there is not a thing that can be done about it. On the morning of December 1, 1581, Father Edmund Campion was taken from his cell and tied to a rough wooden hurdle in an uncomfortable straddling position. The hurdle was dragged through the streets of London to the dreaded Tyburn, the place of execution. It was a grueling trek of almost five miles. Once at Tyburn, Campion had a noose tied about his neck and was slowly elevated off the ground. The noose constricted and crushed his windpipe until he was almost, but not quite, unconscious. Then he was let down, had his genitals hacked off, his body sliced open and his entrails torn from him to be burned before his eyes. Finally, he had his head lopped off and his body chopped into four pieces. Fathers Briant and Sherwin suffered the same fate.

And the same thing happened to 127 other Catholic priests during the reign of Elizabeth.

Chapter 15

El Rey Prudente: King Philip II

The outrages suffered by St. Edmund Campion and other priests in Elizabethan England were only possible because Catholics there were a despised minority at the mercy of a powerful monarch. Of course, in other places the power dynamic was reversed.

During the first generation of the Protestant revolt, the political bulwark behind the Catholic cause was Emperor Charles V. Though perhaps one of the most gifted Europeans to reign in a century, Charles's attention was hopelessly diverted by a host of troubles at home and abroad. With the Lutheran alliance resisting his rule within the Empire and the Turks and French harassing his borders, Charles never realized the potential he had to preside peacefully over a powerful, efficiently managed Catholic kingdom.

That is, with the exception of Spain, although few would call early modern Spain efficiently managed. As a Hapsburg, Charles was, of course, heir to the imperial throne of Germany. But as grandson of Ferdinand and Isabella through his mother, he was also king of Spain. In Spain alone did

Charles find his ideal Catholic state, and though himself not a Spaniard, he preferred to staff his council with Spaniards, whom he found the most trustworthy. It was to the Spanish monastery of Yuste that Charles retired, exhausted from three decades of strife, in 1556 and where he died two years later.

In many ways, Charles V was the last of his kind. He was the last Holy Roman emperor to be crowned by the pope, the last Hapsburg to rule over a united Spain and Germany, and the last European monarch who had a living memory of reigning before the disorders introduced by Protestantism—and that was only for one single year, 1516–1517, when Charles ruled as king of Spain prior to ascending the imperial throne. When he retired to the monastery in 1556, the Hapsburg dominions were divided up: Germany, Bohemia, and traditional imperial lands went to Charles's younger brother, Ferdinand, while the kingdom of Spain and the provinces of the Netherlands were inherited by Charles's son, Philip II.

Philip II was the only son of Emperor Charles—or we should say, only legitimate son, for Don John, the hero of Lepanto, was the bastard son of Charles and a singing girl. When Philip II took the Spanish throne in 1556, his kingdom was probably the most powerful in Europe, for two reasons. First, the tremendous wealth then flowing into Spanish coffers from its conquests in the New World made Philip's government flush with cash and ushered in an era known as the *Siglo de oro*, the Golden Century. Second, Spain was the only western European kingdom that had not suffered political upheavals related to Protestantism. As noted in chapter 11, the Church in Spain had been thoroughly reformed prior to Luther; Catholic identity there was too firmly rooted to be overthrown by preachers of Protestantism. It thus had possessed the single-mindedness to become a great continental power and the funds to realize its ambitions.

Philip's ambitions were like those of his father—to make his kingdom the political and religious bulwark of Christendom against the revolutionary spirit of Protestantism. Due to the power and relative geographic isolation of Spain (surrounded by water on three sides and bordered by mountains on the fourth), Spain had a chance to succeed where Charles's Holy Roman Empire had not.

What kind of man was this Philip, this sovereign who would put the power of Spain at the defense of Christendom? Like many characters of the period, Philip fares better or worse depending on one's point of view. All authorities agree that he was quite serious in the practice of his faith. Catholics would call him devout; Protestants called him fanatical. His commitment to the Catholic faith was absolute, his personal devotion unquestionable. He heard Mass daily, and his court, which was staffed heavily with monks, was sometimes referred to as a monastery. He was ruthless in his suppression of Lutheranism, such that the German heresy had barely sprung up in Spain before the great king trampled it under foot. He was noted for his wise judgment; the Spaniards called him *el rey prudente*, the prudent king. Stoic and courageous, he was perhaps the hardest working monarch of the age, spending hours attending to the affairs of the kingdom. Though he was unfortunate enough to have three wives predecease him—one of them being Queen Mary of England—he found true love with his fourth wife, Anna of Austria. Though she was twenty-two years his junior, the two loved each other deeply and Anna bore him his long coveted sons. Though Pope Pius V had opposed the marriage due to consanguinity (Anna was Philip's niece), Philip's marriage with her was happy. He was a faithful husband and dutiful father.

Not to say he was perfect or saintly, by any means. His stoicism could make him cold, and he was prone to suspicion and scrupulosity. His prudence sometimes became excessive and slid into indecision or procrastination. Though a devoted Catholic, his religious practice was austere and somber, bordering on the puritanical. He seldom forgot a wrong, and his good opinion, once lost, was almost impossible to recover. Though he was extremely competent, his policies were often very reactive, which—in the dynamic political situation of the sixteenth century—meant he was often slow in perceiving the real nature of things on the ground. In short, he was a sinner trying his best.

Philip was embroiled in two wars from the very outset of his reign, both related to clashes of his interests with those of the French. In Italy, Pope Paul IV had allied himself with the French House of Guise against the Spanish interests in Naples, which were being governed by the Duke of Alva. In the Low Countries, which Philip had inherited after Charles V's abdication, Philip found himself fighting to keep the French from detaching the Netherlands from Hapsburg control. Though not an auspicious beginning for his reign, Philip obtained victory against France on both fronts. In Italy, the Duke of Alva defeated the Guises and was able to obtain reconciliation with Pope Paul. In the Low Countries, Philip himself went north to take charge of the offensive there. Two stunning victories at Saint-Quentin and Gravelines cemented his control over the region, which was formally recognized by treaty in 1559. Having made peace, Philip returned to Spain, never to leave again.

During the battle of Saint-Quentin, Philip had made a vow to erect a splendid building to commemorate his victory should God grant it. Victory having been obtained, Philip hired famed Renaissance architect Juan Bautista de Toledo, assisted by Lucas de Escalante and Pedro de Tolosa, in constructing the edifice that would become known as the Escorial.

The Escorial is a structure unique in all of Christendom. Following the pious character of Philip, it was constructed to serve as both a monastery and a seat of royal power. Bautista laid the massive complex out in the shape of a gridiron, in commemoration of St. Lawrence to whose patronage the building was committed. The style was Doric, evoking Greek motifs in its colonnaded facades. Its stately granite towers topped with domes in the highest style of the Renaissance communicated the power and solidity of the Spanish Empire. Funded with the seemingly inexhaustible supply of gold from the New World, Philip spared no expense in the construction of his new capital. Libraries as far away as Arabia and Palestine were scoured for precious books to stock the Escorial's palatial library, the finest in Europe for many years. Similar collections of exquisite tapestries and paintings would also be collected. The palace chapel and monastery, staffed by the Hieronymite monks, were decorated with elaborate metal sculptures and ornamentation cast by renowned Italian sculptor Pompeo Leoni, who had also served Charles V. Philip II donated his personal collection of over 7,500 priceless relics to the monastery. Thus, in its splendid demonstration of the convergence of royal and spiritual powers in the service of God, the Escorial palace-monastery perfectly exemplified the worldview of Philip II, that most Catholic king of Spain.

Once moved into the Escorial, Philip divided his time between the palace and Madrid, which was only a few miles distant and which he made the royal capital. From the Escorial he administered his vast kingdom. Over the years, he spent more time at the Escorial and became more reclusive in nature. He would ultimately die there in 1598.

Philip was a king who strove for uniformity in all matters. This goal was sometimes frustrated by the hodge-podge, medieval governing framework he headed. Administration of the government in sixteenth-century Spain was a haphazard, inefficient affair. Philip had to meet these inefficiencies by his personal attention to a thousand little details that rulers of a later age would have delegated to other committees or departments. Such bureaucratic machinery was only in its infancy in Philip's age, however, and we cannot fault him for the slow, stumbling pace of his government. Such was the nature of royal government of the time.

One area in which he was able to achieve uniformity was religion. We have already mentioned the reforms of the Church in Spain. Philip was successfully able to capitalize on this reform to extirpate Protestantism from his realms. Partially, this was done by example; with many priests and religious orders in Philip's time living in admirable states of discipline, would-be agitators had little to complain about. Both St. John of the Cross and St. Teresa of Avila lived and labored during the reign of Philip II, spending their energy on the reform of the Carmelite order to bring it into closer conformity with the vision of Trent. With such notable examples of religious piety—and St. John and St. Teresa were far from the only ones—the sorts of lurid attacks on clerical worldliness that Luther used successfully in Germany failed to gain traction in Spain.

Where such threats did surface, Philip was also ready to combat them with the sword of the state. The few pockets of Lutherans around Valladolid and Seville were uprooted and many were condemned to death. But a more potent religious threat came from the Moriscos. Granada, the last Muslim Spanish kingdom, had fallen to the Spaniards in 1492. After the conquest, the Spanish government agreed to allow the Moors to practice their religion in peace so long as they did so privately. The Moors rebelled, however, prompting King Ferdinand and Queen Isabella to call for Moors to choose conversion to Christianity or exile.

Most of Granada's Muslims chose the former and became known as Moriscos. The degree to which the Moriscos truly accepted Christianity is a subject of debate. Many Spaniards viewed the Moriscos as Christians in name only, men whose profession of Christianity was only skin-deep because it was coerced. That very well may have been the case. The Moriscos certainly maintained all the cultural trappings of Islam, including celebration of Islamic festivals and other more crypto-Islamic practices. They continued to speak Arabic and wear Islamic dress and were to all appearances

Muslim, save for the thin veneer of minimum Christianity necessary to comply with the law.

The Spaniards had never been happy with this situation, and the Moriscos were only tolerated, never accepted. Charles V, in his capacity as king of Spain, ordered them to cease speaking Arabic and wearing Islamic dress. The Moriscos successfully petitioned to have this decree reversed, but only after coughing up a significant fee. In all other things external, Islamic culture was suppressed. Mosques were converted into churches, all children were obliged to receive baptism, and all marriages had to be officiated by a Catholic priest. The great tragedy of all this, however, was that there appears to have been little effort to follow up on these decrees with sound catechesis. The Spanish authorities were concerned with outward conformity, not whether the Moors truly cherished the Faith of Christ.

Such a policy as a means of conversion was bound to fail. By the time of King Philip, it was clear that the Moriscos had no intention of truly embracing Christianity. Their adherence to the Faith was only superficial; but then again, the policies of church and state had essentially perpetuated that state of affairs by insisting on regulating superficialities such as dress and language. A synod of bishops met in Granada in 1565 and decided on drastic measures: all Moorish dress was to be outlawed, Morisco homes were to be inspected on Friday and Saturday to ensure they were not observing Islamic prayer times, and the sons of prominent Moriscos were to be relocated to Castile in the Spanish heartland to be brought up with Christian customs and hopefully forget those of their people. King Philip affixed his signature to these declarations in 1567 and they became law.

The Moriscos understandably found these new measures intolerable. Unlike Charles V, Philip II was implacable and would accept no payment in lieu of conformity. The Moriscos took to arms in 1568, hoping to detach Granada forcibly from Philip's kingdom. A man named Abén Humeya, a descendant of the old caliphs of Cordoba, was proclaimed king of Granada. Once war was declared, all pretense of Christianity was thrown off and Islam was proclaimed. The Moriscos destroyed churches and tortured priests who were unfortunate enough to fall into their hands. A surge of anti-Catholic violence swept through Granada. In order to get weapons, Moriscos dragged Christians from their homes and sold them to Muslim slavers in North Africa.

Though the Moriscos fought furiously, the armies of Philip were simply larger and better equipped. By spring of 1571, Don John (who would leave Spain immediately after the rebellion to lead the Holy League at Lepanto) had reduced the Morisco army to desperation. Don John exploited every advantage, pursued the Morisco troops relentlessly, and left a trail of destruction behind him to prevent them from living off the land. Abén Humeya was murdered by his own troops, who had taken to hiding in caves. The war was effectively over by that summer. But Philip would not forget the Morisco's treachery. The king decreed that the bulk of Granada's Morisco population of Granada would be expelled. As many as eighty thousand were rounded up and dispersed to disparate parts of the kingdom. Granada was repopulated with Spanish settlers.

Though Philip had many successes, he is mainly remembered for his one great failure, and that concerns his grandiose but unsuccessful attempt to invade England, depose Queen Elizabeth, and forcibly return England to the Catholic fold.

At the beginning of the sixteenth century, Spain was an ally of England. Henry VIII's wife, Catherine of Aragon, was the daughter of Ferdinand and Isabella. Philip had briefly been married to Henry's daughter, Mary, as we saw in chapter 9. The marriage was never popular in England, and by the time of Elizabeth, relations between the two kingdoms had soured considerably. When Elizabeth first took the throne, Philip briefly entertained notions of marriage with her, but this idea withered as her anti-Catholic savagery became known.

Following Elizabeth's excommunication by Pope St. Pius V, the Protestant queen struck back against the Catholic powers of Europe by declaring herself special patroness and protector of all Protestant interests throughout Europe. Elizabeth contemplated a sort of Protestant version of the Catholic Holy League, a broad union of Protestant interests united under the patronage of the queen of England.

The first place she sought to flex her muscle was in the Low Countries. As noted, after the abdication of Charles V, the Low Countries were inherited by Philip II and the crown of Spain. These countries were governed by Philip through a relative, Margaret of Parma, who brought with her a host of Spanish officials to staff the bureaucracy and hordes of Spanish troops to keep order. Though religiously divided between Catholics in the south and Protestants in the north, the merchant class of the Low Countries resented being cut out of their traditional places of influence by Margaret of Parma and the Spanish. Their discontent escalated, and Philip was compelled to send in the Duke of Alva to restore order. Alva behaved as if he was conquering a foreign country, with executions and marital law. The Dutch responded in kind, assassinating Spanish officials and mustering their militias for battle. Before long, Alva was bogged down with a brutal insurrection.

Queen Elizabeth sought to exacerbate the tensions in the region by offering arms and financial support to the Protestant Dutch against King Philip's forces. Philip was outraged that Elizabeth would meddle in what he considered the internal affairs of his kingdom. He contemplated ways to strike out at Elizabeth within her kingdom just as she was doing to him. He had toyed with the idea of funding plots to overthrow Elizabeth and replacing her with her cousin, the imprisoned queen of Scots. Elizabeth quickly quashed those designs by having Mary, Queen of Scots, executed on trumped up charges in 1587. By that time, Mary Stuart had been imprisoned by Elizabeth for nineteen years.

In response to Mary's execution, Philip began formulating a grand design: invasion of England, forcible overthrow of Elizabeth, and reinstitution of Catholicism there. The success of such a plan would have several practical benefits. It would cut off England's material aid to the Low Countries, as well as bring English attacks on Spanish shipping to a halt. Though Pius V's *Regnans in Excelsis* had not called for a foreign invasion of England, Philip's plan to depose forcibly the Protestant queen was faithful to the spirit of what Pius had written. Pius's successor, Pope Sixtus V, supported the planned invasion. He viewed the invasion as a crusade and allowed its participants indulgences for their undertaking on behalf of the Faith.

The invasion plan was massive, one of the most ambitious military operations of the millennium. It was to be a two-pronged attack encompassing land and sea. A great Spanish armada composed of 130 ships, eight thousand sailors, and eighteen thousand soldiers, with over 2,500 guns, was to set sail from Lisbon and rendezvous with thirty thousand Spanish soldiers stationed in the Netherlands. This land invasion force was to be conveyed to England on barges protected by the sprawling armada. Philip anticipated the smaller English ships would be overwhelmed by the superior size and fire-power of his fleet. Plymouth was chosen as the site of the amphibious landing and subsequent invasion.

The preparation for the invasion was reminiscent of the preparations prior to the Battle of Lepanto, complete with the blessing of the armada's banner on April 25, 1588. Philip hoped that his own invincible armada would be blessed even as God had granted favor to the fleet of the Holy League. If everything went according to plan, Elizabeth would be dethroned by the end of the year and the Catholic faith would be restored in England.

Unfortunately for Philip, it was not to be. The departure of the armada was delayed by poor weather. Several ships had to put in for repairs along the way, with the result that the fleet that arrived in the English Channel was not at full strength. Contrary winds kept the English navy bottled up in Plymouth harbor. The Spaniards wanted to take advantage of the favorable winds to destroy the English fleet, but

King Philip had directed them to rendezvous with the Spanish forces in the Netherlands before engaging the English. Thus, the armada bypassed the English on their route east, allowing fifty-five English ships to escape the harbor once the winds changed. These ships, smaller and lighter than the great galleons of the armada, were able to maneuver away from the Spanish attacks with ease.

A bigger problem for the Spaniards, however, was news that the thirty thousand troops they were supposed to pick up in the Netherlands had not yet been outfitted and were not at port. It would take them another week to prepare, but even then an army of Dutch Protestants was securely holding the position between the Spanish army and the coast, making it impossible for the armada to rendezvous with the land forces. As the Dutch Protestants had been entrenched in the area for some time, it appears this fact was clumsily overlooked by the Spanish planners of the invasion. This means that even had the Spanish armada been able to make it to the Netherlands without interference from the English, it still would have been nearly impossible to pick up the invasion force that was a key component to the plan.

Between July 20 and July 28, the English and Spanish fleets collided in the English Channel. The English had learned quickly to stay out of range of the larger Spanish guns and decimate the Spanish hulls with broadsides after they had expended their shot. The actions of July 28 in the waters off of the Flemish city of Gravelines saw victory for the English and the total disruption of the Spanish fleet. Instead of landing in England, the fleet continued up the channel, emptying out into the North Sea. The surviving ships would have to return to Spain the long way, sailing north around Scotland, then south along the west coast of Ireland.

The journey home was harrowing. With no reliable way to measure longitude, the ships needed to hug the coast to maintain their positions. But the Gulf Stream pushed the Spaniards further north and east than they desired so that when they subsequently turned south, they had not sufficiently cleared the coasts of Scotland and found themselves sailing too near the leeward shore. Powerful westerly winds off the Atlantic drove the Spanish ships crashing into the Scottish coast, where survivors were typically slaughtered by the local populace.

Those ships who managed to struggle on down to Ireland faced a similar fate. Supplies ran low, and starvation and disease broke out among the men. Only sixty-three ships of the great armada returned to Spain, and only ten thousand men—and many of these succumbed to illness even after returning home. When King Philip heard of the disaster, he reportedly said, "I sent the armada against men, not God's winds and waves." (The victorious Elizabeth, on the other hand, had a medal struck with the words: *God blew and they were scattered.*)

Perhaps it was consoling to blame the defeat of the armada on the inscrutable will of God, but there were also human elements at fault. The planning and execution of the invasion had been plagued by mismanagement and poor communication. The Spanish leaders, right up to Philip himself, were appallingly daft about what a logistical nightmare such an enterprise would become. Modern excavations on the ruined ships of the armada show that most of the Spanish ships went down without having spent their supply of powder. This is because the Spanish strategy was to close with enemy ships and board them, not destroy them with broadsides. This approach had worked at Lepanto, but the English were familiar with the strategy and kept their distance. Spanish commanders were not decisive enough to change tactics mid-battle and exposed themselves to merciless bombardments from the English ships, which were generally smaller and more maneuverable. In short, Philip may have taken solace in the defeat as God's will, but the Spaniards themselves certainly bore much of the responsibility.

Philip would continue engaging the English navy throughout the 1590s, but with little success. England continued to send aid to the rebels in the Low Countries and continued to harass Spanish shipping on the high seas. But if Philip's invasion was not successful, neither did its failure mean a total triumph for England. Spain was still wealthier than England and maintained dominance on the seas for a long time to come. But Philip's dreams of realizing Pius V's call for Elizabeth's overthrow evaporated in the storms that destroyed his glorious armada. The botched invasion of 1588 was the last attempt to forcibly restore the Catholic faith in England. For Protestants, it was a sign of God's favor to the Protestant cause.

Philip spent his last decade harassing the English and antagonizing the French, who were just concluding their own religious war. While many Spaniards blamed the commanders of the armada for the disaster, Philip was more forgiving. He made sure the veterans of the battle were cared for and gave them all generous pensions, as well as paying out vast sums of money in compensation to families of those who lost loved ones in the conflict. As the 1590s wore on, Philip grew ill, most likely from cancer. He passed away in the solitude of the Escorial on September 13, 1598.

Philip II had reigned over the most powerful kingdom in Europe for forty-two years. His legacy is, again, colored by one's perspective. For Catholics, he was a powerful and resolute monarch in the spirit of the old kings of Christendom, one who reigned with prudence, putting the influence of the crown at the service of the Church for the building up of the Faith and the extirpation of heresy. For Protestants, he was a devious tyrant, the chief of all the dark forces of papism who sought to suppress Protestant liberties by ravaging their countries with fire, sword, and inquisition. The truth is more nuanced, of course, and while it is beyond the scope of this chapter to delve fully into the opposing schools of thought on the reign of King Philip, it would not be inaccurate to say he was a man of deep faith, flawed like each and every one of us, simply trying to do what he thought was right.

The same year Spain was losing its king, France was settling its religious troubles. It is to this kingdom that we must now turn as we prepare to close our study of the Reformation and the tumultuous sixteenth century.

CHAPTER 16

Catherine de' Medici

Throughout the long medieval period, the kingdom of
France had always held a sort of pride of place among
the nations of Christendom. France was known as the
"Eldest Daughter of the Church," for in the wake of the
Roman Empire's collapse, the kingdom of the Franks had
been the first of the Germanic barbarian nations to accept
the Catholic faith. The baptism of the Frankish king Clovis
I in 496 ushered in the beginnings of Christian France, a
region whose culture and politics would dominate the affairs
of Western Europe for a millennium. In the ninth century,
the French Carolingian Empire extended its dominion over
most of Europe and was the vehicle through which the
evangelization of Germany and the standardization of the
Roman rite were facilitated. Throughout the High Middle
Ages, the language, culture, and styles of the civilized world
were those of the French. True, France's relations with the
Holy See had often been rocky, but France's fundamental
Catholic identity had never wavered. To be French was to be
Catholic—or so it seemed.

When the tempests of the Reformation initially burst forth upon Christendom, the French monarchy was content to sit back and rest comfortably upon its thousand years of tradition and assume Protestantism was a German problem. As we have seen in chapter 7, the French king Francis I, though a Catholic himself, was even willing to dally with Protestantism as a means of weakening his enemy, Charles V. Francis encouraged Lutherans within Germany and gave refuge to Protestants fleeing the religious troubles of the Holy Roman Empire. Francis certainly knew he was playing with fire, but he assumed it was a relatively small, stable fire that could be controlled and manipulated to serve French policy.

He was rudely awakened from that dream in 1534 when Protestants began a propaganda attack against the Mass and the Catholic faith throughout Paris; as we have seen, some unknown soul was even so bold as to penetrate the royal palace and affix an anti-Catholic placard to the door of the king's private chambers. Francis's former enthusiasm for Protestantism soured, and a wave of persecution swept the French capital. Recall that it was this affair that caused the young John Calvin to flee France.

Despite France's ancient Catholic pedigree and its position as the most populous and powerful kingdom of continental Europe, Francis learned that Protestantism was not merely a German problem, nor could it be safely contained. By the 1530s, France had its own thriving Protestant minority, though it was mainly a literary movement centered on the University of Paris. Their work was academic in nature: translating the Scriptures into French, composing Protestant-leaning Bible commentaries, and quietly advocating for a

French church independent of Rome—following the theories of the pre-Reformation "Gallican" theologians, who advocated for churches organized along more nationalist lines.

The crack-down subsequent to the 1534 affair of the placards squashed any chances of an organized Protestant movement in France for some time. But even though the Reform could gain little political traction, its ideas slowly began to influence the French upper classes. English merchants, newly converted to the hybrid church of Henry VIII, brought Protestant doctrines to their French counterparts. Lutheran exiles from the Holy Roman Empire continued to stream into the kingdom. A constant flow of French Protestant intellectuals made the journey to and from the Swiss Protestant centers of Basel and Geneva. This latter class in particular would end up defining the contours of French Protestantism, which was imbued with the ideas of Calvin.

These French Calvinists would eventually become known as Huguenots. The precise origin of the term is lost, though it appears to have originally been a pejorative name. The Huguenots referred to themselves as the Reformed. Like the Calvinists of Scotland, the Huguenots were fanatic iconoclasts. Places under their power saw altars and images destroyed, stained glass smashed, and in some cases entire buildings pulled down. Priests and monks were harassed and attacked. The Catholic Church was viewed as wholly corrupt and in need of radical cleansing.

We need not dwell too long on the religious ideals of the Huguenots, as we have already treated Calvinism as an ideology and a social force in chapter 7. Like the Calvinists of

Scotland, the French Calvinists coalesced into a political movement. Unlike the Scotch Calvinists, whose political aims were universal and almost utopian in scope, the political aims of French Calvinists were narrowly particular to the situation on the ground in France. They advocated for a repeal of the anti-Protestant laws that had been instituted under Francis I, as well as protested the power of the influential House of Guise. As in England, it was not the rural yeoman or the poor but the merchant class and a cross section of the nobility who embraced the new faith. As in Scotland, adherence to Calvinism became a way of expressing opposition to royal policy.

Calvinists remained a persecuted, powerless minority throughout the reign of Francis. His 1540 Edict of Fontainbleau labeled Protestantism high treason both "human and divine" and decreed torture, loss of property, public humiliation, and death as the penalties. In 1545, over twenty villages were destroyed by French troops. The destroyed towns were centers of Calvinism, Lutheranism, and Waldensianism, a proto-Protestant heresy dating from the late Middle Ages. As many as two thousand people were put to death and others sentenced to slave labor in the French galleys.

Francis I died in 1547. The throne fell to Francis's second son, Henri II. It was not Henri who would be the central character in the religious turmoil of France but his wife, Catherine de' Medici. Catherine had been betrothed to Henri at the tender age of thirteen. Francis was then attempting to curry favor with the papacy, and Clement VII was Catherine's uncle. Soon after the betrothal, Clement VII died, and Catherine's political value dissipated. Infertile for the first decade of marriage, she was relegated to the

background while her husband openly lavished his attention on a mistress. Even when Henri's elder brother died and
it became clear that Catherine would soon become queen
of France, she was kept at arm's length by her disinterested
husband.

Catherine did eventually bear King Henri three sons, and
though not allowed to participate in the affairs of the realm,
she was by no means politically inexperienced. Catherine
was a woman of penetrating intelligence and an inscrutable
judge of character. She was possessed of an intuitive shrewd-
ness that allowed her to assess a situation quickly and exploit
it to her own benefit. As she matured, she became adept
at manipulating those less intelligent and less assertive than
herself. Part of this no doubt came from her upbringing as a
Medici, a Florentine family whose very name is synonymous
with intrigue. A large part of her character probably came
also from her pitiful circumstances: an unloved, unvalued
queen continually disgraced by her husband's public infidel-
ities. Her shrewd, calculating mind was sharpened against
the nature of her circumstance. Though royalty, she existed
on the margin, and like many women in difficult straits, she
learned to do what she needed to in order to get by. And she
became quite good at it.

Despite the Edict of Fontainbleau, the Huguenots continued to grow throughout the 1530s and 40s and had become
entrenched by the time Henri II became king. The growing
Protestant presence prompted Henri to issue his own decree,
the Edict of Chateaubriand, in 1551. This edict strengthened the provisions of the Edict of Fontainbleau by creating
a special court to try cases of heresy. It also imposed strict

censorship on printing presses and forbade French subjects from sending money to Geneva. The stakes were raised again in 1557 with the Edict of Compiegne, which mandated the death penalty for all convictions for heresy. Also, recognizing Geneva as the heart of the Calvinist world, it made travel to Geneva a capital crime and also proscribed the death penalty for Frenchmen abroad who published books in Geneva.

This had little to do with Catherine; as mentioned, King Henri allowed her almost no part in managing the affairs of the kingdom. For the time being, she confined herself to her quarters and attended to the upbringing of her three sons. Her eldest, the future King Francis II, had been betrothed to Mary, Queen of Scots, then a very young girl. Their first meeting occurred at the nursery at Carrières. Queen Catherine entered the room to watch the princess and the other royal children playing. Not knowing who she was, six-year-old Mary said to Catherine, "Are you aware that you are in the presence of the queen of Scotland?" Catherine glowered at the young girl and imperiously responded, "And are you aware that you are in the presence of the queen of France?" Mary would be popular with the French court, but Catherine would despise her. Perhaps her disposition to young Mary was one of envy; when Mary arrived, she was universally lauded for her beauty, talent, and intelligence, and made to feel welcome at the court of King Henri. How different was this from Catherine's own cold reception at the French court!

Catherine's early reign as queen was full of resentments. As mentioned, she had to endure the indignity of watching the king sit on his mistress's lap and fondle her breasts while Catherine sat by idly. She resented the praise heaped upon young Mary Stuart. Another source of anxiety were the Guises, who were related to Princess Mary through her mother, Mary of Guise, whom we met in chapter 10. The Guises were heirs to the medieval House of Lorraine and had risen to prominence in the reign of Francis I. In Catherine's time, the house was governed by the brothers Charles and Francis. Charles entered the service of the Church and was the cardinal of Lorraine, while Francis headed the family's political fortunes as the Duke of Guise. The Guises harbored royal ambitions, as they were loosely related to the royal family (though another family, the Protestant House of Bourbon, had a stronger claim). Catherine bitterly resented the political intriguing of the Guises, rightly viewing their ambitions as dangerous to the security of her own sons.

The Guises would soon realize their ambitions. In June 1559, King Henri was killed in a jousting accident. An opponent's lance had pierced the visor, puncturing his face with massive shards of wood. Five shards were removed from his head, one of which had gouged out his eye and pierced his brain. The king struggled for ten days but finally expired on July 10. Catherine donned the black widow's garb and from that day forward took the sign of the broken lance as her emblem.

Henri's untimely death meant the crown devolved upon Catherine's son, Francis II, then only thirteen years old, and his young bride Mary, Queen of Scots. The Guises seized the opportunity to assert their power. Mary's uncles, Cardinal Charles and Francis, Duke of Guise, both moved themselves into the Louvre Palace and became effective regents for the young couple. Catherine once again found herself excluded, but also learned that the Guises were willing enough to tolerate her presence so long as she yielded to them, which she did out of necessity.

Even so, Catherine found in the new arrangement a means of growing her own influence. Her son King Francis was only a youth and depended upon his mother for counsel. If the Guises sought to exploit their relation to Queen Mary, Catherine succeeded no less in utilizing her bond with her son, such that Francis seldom acted without consulting his mother. Royal decrees were often issued in the name of Francis and Catherine jointly. Hence, a strange dynamic of necessity arose in the French court between the Guises, Catherine de' Medici, and the inexperienced king and queen of France.

The Guises advocated a continuation of the harsh policies of Francis I and Henri II against French Huguenots. The Guises as a whole were faithful to Rome, but their opposition to the Huguenots had a political motive as well, for as mentioned above, the Huguenot House of Bourbon had a strong claim to the French throne. The Guises thus sought to secure their own position of power by obliterating the threat posed by the Bourbons and their Huguenot allies.

Catherine's own religious opinions were more muted. She found the edicts of her late husband to be too harsh and urged the Guises to proceed with moderation against the Huguenots. This was not because of any inherent sympathy with Protestantism; in 1560, she would look on with approval while the Guises strung up the corpses of Huguenot rebels from the walls of Chateau Amboise. She was essentially a pragmatist, believing there were too many Huguenots in the kingdom to ever effectually stamp them out. Her one goal was to secure her dynasty, and to this end, she sometimes supported the Catholic party, sometimes the Huguenots, as when she made the Huguenot Anthony of Bourbon lieutenant general of the kingdom, effectively creating a check against the political power of the Guises. She intrigued with Catholic Spain against the Huguenot Bourbons, as well as with Protestant England against the Catholic Guises.

In personal religious matters, Catherine proceeded as she did in everything, seeking that which would most strengthen her own position. As an Italian and queen of France, she obviously preferred Catholicism, but her own personal tastes were more arcane. She cultivated a deep interest in astrology and retained a court astrologer (which was honestly not that uncommon); though she has never been tied directly to the black arts herself, she kept company with those who practiced them, something that has sullied her reputation over time.

By 1560, France was in a state of crisis. The Huguenots wearied of royal persecution, which they correctly identified as emanating from the policy of the Guises. Furthermore, the Protestant Bourbons were amassing men and resources for a showdown with the Guises, whom they regarded as usurpers of the Bourbon royal claim. Things deteriorated further when King Francis suddenly took ill and died in September. Huguenot forces had already begun pillaging in southern France; the interregnum only emboldened them. The sudden death of Francis II was a deep blow to Catherine, but it also gave her an excuse to send Mary Stuart back to Scotland.

Francis was succeeded by Catherine's second son, the nine-year-old Charles IX. Catherine managed his affairs directly and wielded more legal authority than ever before. But all the authority in the kingdom could not forestall the anarchy that was spreading throughout the realm as nobles and commoners alike spurned royal decrees and prepared for war. Catherine attempted to summon a meeting of religious leaders from both sides in hopes of hammering out their differences, but to no avail. Again, her actions here were very practical and aimed at protecting her family. She knew that an open war between the Protestant Bourbons and Catholic Guises would inevitably endanger her sons, as each party sought to subjugate them at best and murder them at worst. Catherine's ability to assess a situation and exploit it to her own gain was sometimes a weakness: it led her to assume that all problems were essentially matters of posturing and compromise—that there was no problem that was not ultimately political. Religiously tepid herself, she drastically misunderstood the depth of religious conviction in others. Her 1562 Edict of Saint-Germain, which called for religious tolerance, was a dead letter.

Violence broke out in March 1562 when the Duke of Guise and a band of armed followers interrupted a Huguenot service in the village of Vassay. Guise's men attempted to force their way into a barn where services were being held. In the ensuing melee the duke was struck with a rock, causing his men to fire several volleys into the crowd, killing dozens.

Though Guise was initially repentant for the slaughter, which was clearly not premeditated, it prompted the Huguenots to arm themselves for retaliation. Led by Louis

Bourbon, Prince of Condé, and Admiral Gaspar de Coligny, the Huguenots mustered a small but determined army of eighteen hundred men and began seizing towns throughout the French countryside. Catholic churches in the towns taken by the Huguenots were subject to the now ubiquitous iconoclastic vandalism: destruction of stained glass, pulling down of images, desecration of altars, and more. Catherine made one more attempt to parley with the Huguenots, even meeting Coligny personally to beg them to lay down their arms. But when Coligny refused, Catherine and the Guises mobilized the royal Catholic forces and began striking back. The wars of religion had finally come to France, though religion was subsumed under political and dynastic considerations.

The affair was not a conventional war, but more of a series of intermittent blood feuds and assassinations by partisans of both sides. Within a year of the violence at Vassay, the Duke of Guise had been assassinated, as was the Huguenot Antoine de Bourbon, the head of the House of Bourbon. The death of Guise secured peace for a time, and Catherine was willing to grant the Huguenots a certain number of limited freedoms. Her tour of the kingdom in 1564–65 was meant to build bridges with Protestants and restore unity.

This peace was shattered on September 27, 1567, when Louis Bourbon attempted to kidnap King Charles and Catherine. They escaped, but the escapade reignited the violence. Though a treaty would be reached ending the fighting in 1568, Catherine would not forget this Huguenot treachery.

By 1570, the Huguenots had won several important concessions from the crown. Catherine and King Charles had not wanted to extend further liberties to the Huguenots but were compelled by lack of funds to discontinue the war. One generous concession allowed the Huguenots to retain possession of the towns they had already seized, including fortified cities like La Rochelle on the Bay of Biscay. This effectively allowed the creation of an armed and fortified state within a state. La Rochelle became the capital of Huguenot France. The head of the Bourbons, Henry Bourbon, son of the slain Antoine and nephew of Louis, also resided in La Rochelle, presiding over an unofficial Huguenot court. Catherine again tried to ease tensions with the Huguenots by wedding her daughter Margaret to this Henry, though the match was unpopular and would amount to nothing. Indeed, the wedding of Henry and Margaret is mainly remembered for the events that occurred immediately after its solemnization.

Three days after the wedding, which all the important Huguenots of the kingdom had come to Paris to attend, the Huguenot leader Admiral de Coligny was shot in the hand by an unknown assailant. Catherine was beside herself. She understandably feared the botched assassination attempt would lead to reprisals from the Huguenots and reignite the wars she had worked so hard to end. She sent the royal physician to attend to Coligny; she even visited him and tearfully promised to punish whoever was responsible.

The capital was on edge. Despite Catherine's attempts at conciliation, she and King Charles feared retaliation from the Huguenots. Coligny's brother-in-law was encamped with an army of four thousand, just outside the capital. Protestants angrily interrupted Catherine's dinner, demanding justice for the attempt on Coligny's life. Everything was tense, with each side apparently waiting to see if the other would move. After much deliberation, Catherine and Charles agreed that there should be a preemptive strike to decapitate the leadership of the Huguenots before they had time to organize their forces for reprisals.

The exact chronology of what happened next is uncertain. The gates of the city were shut; Charles's personal guards were given a list of leading Protestants to kill. The signal to begin the action seems to have been the ringing of bells at Saint-Germain l'Auxerrois for Matins. A band of armed men led by the Guises burst into the quarters of Coligny. He was stabbed to death and his body flung from a window. Other leading Protestant nobles were hunted down and assassinated.

At this point, something happened which Catherine and the king had not anticipated. A wave of popular violence erupted throughout the city of Paris as the common people began attacking Protestants. Perhaps the people thought the king intended a general massacre of all Protestants; perhaps it was an outburst of popular rage due to deeply entrenched religious tensions that had little to do with what the king willed or did not will. Such collective mob actions are often difficult to explain.

The violence was soon out of control. Regular men and women were being targeted well beyond the scope of what Catherine and Charles had envisioned. Many Catholics were horrified by the killings and sheltered Protestants in their homes. Charles issued decrees urging an end to the violence, but it continued unabated throughout the following day. Even worse, it spread to the provinces. Twelve major

French cities exploded in violence, despite Charles swiftly dispatching his messengers to prevent any further bloodshed. It was simply out of his hands. Charles and Catherine watched with stunned futility as the kingdom descended into an orgy of killing.

The massacres finally concluded after three days, though in some places they dragged on for a month. This explosion of murder in August 1572 has gone down in history as the St. Bartholomew's Day Massacre, as it commenced on August 23, the eve of the feast of St. Bartholomew. An accurate death toll for the killings is very hard to come by. Protestant propagandists in later centuries alleged absurd amounts of people killed, upwards of two to four million, which would amount to almost one-twentieth of the entire kingdom. More reasonable estimates based on contemporary accounts and modern scholarship place the death toll somewhere between ten to fifteen thousand, with most of the deaths occurring within the city of Paris itself.

Initial news of what happened was confused. Catholics throughout Europe believed the act had been carried out in reaction to an imminent Huguenot coup and celebrated the action as deliverance from Protestant tyranny. Pope Gregory XIII also seemed to have believed the massacre was a counter-coup and initially commissioned works of art in celebration of what the pope perceived to be a victorious battle.

As months went by, the true nature of the events of August became known. The attitude of Pope Gregory chilled considerably; he refused to grant an audience to Charles de Maurevert, the killer of Coligny, on the grounds that he was a murderer. The Catholic Holy Roman emperor,

Maximilian, was appalled by the massacre. News of the killings had spread as far away as Russia, where none other than Ivan the Terrible condemned them.

All of this outrage fell squarely upon the head of Catherine de' Medici. Though neither Catherine nor Charles intended the fearful massacres, it was their plot to decapitate the Huguenot leadership that had made the killings possible. Regardless of whatever nuance Catherine could appeal to, the popular opinion of Europe laid responsibility for the killings directly at her door. The Protestant courts of Europe were disgusted with her, such that it was all she could do to keep diplomatic relations with other kingdoms from collapsing entirely.

King Charles IX died prematurely two years later. He was succeeded by Catherine's third son, Henry III. Henry III did not allow himself to be as influenced by Catherine as his two elder brothers, and under his reign, royal policy began to drift out of Catherine's control. War between the Huguenot Bourbons and the Catholic Guises continued intermittently, but Catherine found herself with increasingly less relevance. Her last son, Hercule François, Duke of Anjou, died of a fever in 1584 without heir. With King Henry III himself also without heir, Catherine resigned herself to watching the extinction of her house and the imminent rise of the Protestant House of Bourbon, who stood next in line to inherit the throne upon the death of King Henry.

If Henry resented Catherine's counsel, that does not mean he was free of all influence. In the latter years of his reign, he allowed himself to be dominated by the Duke of Guise. But by the 1580s, Henry and Guise were at odds over how

much conciliation to show the Protestants. Perhaps knowing that, eventually, the Huguenot Henry of Navarre, head
of the Bourbons, would succeed him upon his death, King
Henry III began moderating his policies toward the Huguenot party. This perturbed Henri, Duke of Guise, who was
still posturing for the succession for his family and who
could only view any show of conciliation to the Huguenots
as a blow to his own influence. In 1588, Paris again erupted
into violence, this time directed against King Henry. The
Catholic populace of Paris rioted, barricaded the streets, and
demanded that Henry cease placating the Huguenots and
bring royal policy more in line with those advocated by the
Duke of Guise. Guise, of course, was behind the tumults.

In the end, Catherine went to Guise in person to negotiate
for Henry. Guise received her as a conquered foe, extract-
ing from her a concession that preserved Henry's throne but
deprived him of significant powers. By an agreement signed
at Rouen on July 21, 1588—as the Spanish Armada was
preparing to launch—King Henry promised never to conclude peace with the Huguenots, to forbid public office to
non-Catholics, never to leave the throne to a non-Catholic,
and to pardon all members of Guise's faction for any crimes
they may have committed. Guise was also made lieutenant
general of the kingdom. He was effectively dictator. King
Henry stormed out of Rouen, plotting his vengeance.

Catherine left Rouen downcast. This old widow, now
nearly seventy years old, had witnessed the entire collapse
of her house. How she must have pondered the course of
her life in those last days! Originally forced to the margins
of the court, tragedy had dogged her and consistently forced

her to take initiative on behalf of weak or incompetent men. Honing her political skills through the reigns of her three youthful sons, she had been an axis of balance, a pivot point, between the forces of Guise and Bourbon that threatened to tear the kingdom asunder. All her subtlety, all her craft and posturing, all the dark wisdom, if any, bestowed upon her by court astrologers scrutinizing the stars for arcane knowledge that could give her advantage over her foes—what had they gained for her? A moribund house bereft of heirs. The king who was a pawn in the struggles of great men. A reputation as the cruelest woman in Christendom.

For most of her life, Catherine had viewed the religious conflict of Europe as a political problem, as something that could be solved by mere compromise without understanding or sincere conversion. She consistently underestimated the intensity of religious conviction. Late, perhaps too late, Catherine came to value authentic conciliation over political scheming.

Her son, Henry, frothing in anger at the humiliating terms imposed upon him by Guise, summoned the Duke of Guise to a meeting and had Guise stabbed to death by his body guards while he looked on. The following day, Guise's brother was also assassinated. Elated, Henry told his mother of his deeds, expecting her approbation. Instead, Catherine was mortified. She had been through enough to know that such killings would only lead to more bloody reprisals. Her response was stoic. "You have cut out, my son, but you must sew together," she told King Henry. It is easy to destroy and to tear down, but much more important to build up. Victory could not be attained by mere destruction. Henry no doubt believed his actions justified, but Catherine fretted that her son's bloody deed would only lead to his own doom.

Very soon after this last meeting, Catherine took ill. The danger to which her son had exposed himself had plunged her into despair. Her breathing became strained and her body shook. She expired on January 5, 1589, thirteen days after her final meeting with Henry III. She died in anxiety for his future and the fate of the kingdom.

It is perhaps better that Catherine died not knowing what would become of her son. Her fears were justified. Henry III outlived his mother by only eight months. The murder of Guise was incomprehensible to the Catholic populace of Paris. Henry was reproached as a murderer; the Parlement of Paris called for criminal charges against the king. The situation became so bad that King Henry was compelled to flee to his enemy, Henry Bourbon, for aid. Henry Bourbon, though Huguenot, welcomed the assistance of King Henry against the forces loyal to the House of Guise. The combined armies of King Henry and Henry Bourbon, royalist and Huguenot, marched to Paris to retake the city. The siege would come to nothing, however, as on August 1, Catherine's fears were realized when a crazed Dominican friar assassinated King Henry while feigning to bring a message. With the death of the king, the royal forces evaporated and Henry Bourbon raised the siege.

With King Henry and the heads of the House of Guise dead, and Catherine, too, safely in her grave, there was no further obstacle to the ascent of the Huguenot Henry Bourbon to the throne of France—save for the population of Paris, who vehemently refused to accept a heretic as king.

Neither the Catholic league of the Guises nor the nobles faithful to Henry III would support Henry Bourbon's claim. Henry settled the contest by force of arms, winning several major victories against the Catholic forces over the next two years. He soon realized, however, that he would never reign securely unless he had the support of France's majority Catholic populace.

On July 25, 1593, Henry Bourbon removed that obstacle by renouncing Protestantism and embracing the Catholic faith. According to legend, when told that the people of Paris would never accept a Protestant king, he shrugged and said, "Paris is well worth a Mass." The veracity of this story is uncertain. Whatever his motivations for conversion, his public renunciation of Protestantism seemed to satisfy the Catholic party, and Henry was crowned king of France at Chartres Cathedral on February 27, 1594, taking the regnal name King Henry IV. Historians have tended to portray Henry's conversion as purely political; that may be the case, but in the years following his conversion, he expressed a sincere interest in theological questions and followed the debates between Protestants and Catholics with great attention. If he was not a sincere Catholic at the time of his conversion, he certainly became one afterward.

He did not forget about the Huguenots, however, and in 1598, he issued the Edict of Nantes. The Edict of Nantes formally ended the French religious wars by granting Huguenots freedom of worship, association, and gave them the very generous right to defend themselves by maintaining fortified cities. Essentially, the Edict of Nantes settled the religious wars by allowing the Huguenots to form a state within a state.

These decisions would all have ramifications leading into the next century, but that is far beyond the scope of this chapter. By 1598, both the first and second Reformation generations had mostly passed. St. Peter Canisius had died the year before. There was scarce a man alive in 1598 who had any living memory of a unified Christendom or of the dramatic events of 1517. The rending of Christendom had become an established fact that Europeans had been born with, grown accustomed to, and were more or less content to live with. It was this mindset, more than any other historical event, which brought the Reformation era to a close.

Commitment to Truth

In the first chapter of this book, we introduced the figure of St. Peter Canisius, one of the many outstanding Jesuit saints of the Counter-Reformation. We had noted that St. Peter's life was contemporaneous with all the great events of the age—born the year Luther was excommunicated, he lived through the events in Germany, the rise of Calvin, the English break with Rome, the Council of Trent, the founding of the Jesuits, the overthrow of Mary, Queen of Scots, the reign of Philip II, the Battle of Lepanto, the Spanish Armada, and the French Wars of Religion. He was present at the 1555 gathering that ended the religious wars in Germany and died only five months before Henry IV's Edict of Nantes, which brought the struggles of the Reformation to a close in France. St. Peter was close to many of the most important personalities of the age, from emperors to popes to saints. His life and work exemplify the character of the era.

Catherine de' Medici also lived a life roughly contemporary with all the pivotal moments of the sixteenth century.

She was born in 1519, the year Luther debated with Eck in Leipzig. She, too, was close to all the great movers of the age—daughter-in-law of King Francis I and mother-in-law of Mary, Queen of Scots, niece of Pope Clement VII, wife of one king and mother of three. She died in 1589, the year the assassination of her son King Henry III practically brought the French Wars of Religion to a close.

Yet how different were the lives and deeds of these two individuals! St. Peter was born among the common working folk of the Netherlands and, through interior conversion, grew in sanctity. He labored for the Church of Christ against the theological and social disorders of the age, winning renown from kings and popes. He died a living legend, surrounded by old friends and well-wishers looking back with joy on a life lived in the service of Christ the King. Catherine was born to great power into one of the most politically conniving families of the day; her life consisted almost entirely of either being used as a political pawn or else using others as such. Sanctity meant little to her, only power. She, too, mingled with the powerful, but at the end of her life, all she had to look back on was a kingdom torn apart, a mountain of dead bodies, and the imminent prospect of the extinction of her house. She died heartbroken.

The ancient Greeks and Romans believed that one of the primary reasons for studying history is to receive moral instruction, to be edified by the actions of the good and horrified by the deeds of the wicked. The parallel but divergent lives of St. Peter Canisius and Catherine de' Medici exemplify that the Reformation, like any other event, was what the actors involved made of it. It was certainly a tragedy one way or another; from a Catholic point of view, it signifies the rending of the seamless garment of Christ, the destruction of the integral Catholic culture that characterized the Middle Ages and made Christendom possible. Such divisions in Christian unity are offensive to God as a departure from that oneness he wills for the Church, his Bride. From a Protestant perspective, events like the St. Bartholomew's Day Massacre and the failed Spanish attempt to overthrow Queen Elizabeth sowed in the Protestant ethos a fundamental distrust of Catholics that has only begun to dissipate in the modern day. These events seem to justify, in the Protestant mind, the belief that separation from the Catholic Church was the right course of action.

But even though the age had more than its share of tragedy, it was also one which made possible great sanctity. One can either overcome the evils of the age or be overcome by them. St. Peter Canisius used the disorders of the age as a means to find the truth, become a saint, and work for the reconciliation of Protestants to and the building up of the Church. Catherine, spurning truth in the interests of political posturing, fell victim to the disorders of the age and only in her last extremity began to recognize her errors.

For many people studying the Reformation from a perspective five centuries removed, there is a tendency to scratch our heads and wonder how religion could cause so much disorder. Ultimately, we moderns can understand differing opinions, but we struggle to understand how religious opinion could possibly justify violence. We often wonder what on earth our ancestors must have been thinking.

The answer to this quandary is revealed in the way the problem is posed. "Why fight over religious opinions?" If the faith of the Church is nothing other than mere opinion or hypothetical conjecture, then it makes as little sense to argue about how a man is saved as to argue whether the snow in Boston is preferable to the rain in Seattle, or whether pink Starburst are better than red. If religion is only a matter of personal preference, it is little more than a question of taste.

This is a fundamentally mistaken way of considering religious truth, although one unfortunately ubiquitous in modernity. To modern ears, saying something is an article of faith is akin to saying it is totally uncertain; one places his faith and hope in religious truth the same way one hopes to win the lottery. It is not a form of knowledge at all; rather, it is a belief in spite of empirical evidence—something essentially irrational.

Of course, this is not what faith means at all. Faith is not belief in the absence of evidence, but belief based on a certain kind of evidence. To believe on faith means to believe on the authority of somebody else. It is grounded not on the inherent believability of the propositions, but in the authority of the one who relates them. Imagine a grandfather telling his grandson about his experiences in World War II. The stories the child is being told are outside his realm of experience. He believes them not because he has personally experienced World War II, nor because he has empirically verified his grandfather's tale, but because he finds his grandfather implicitly trustworthy. He has faith in his grandfather—not in his grandfather's story, but in his grandfather as a person.

The Catholic faith is faith of this sort. It is not belief in lieu of certainty, but rather another type of certainty, a certainty grounded in the authority of someone else. Religious faith is a kind of certainty that is based on the absolute trustworthiness of God. Protestants affirmed this view of faith as well, although for a Protestant this certainty could only be grounded in the written revelation of God, whereas for the Catholic this extended to the teaching of the Church as well, which authoritatively interprets God's revelation.

The point is that for the people of the Reformation, disputes about faith were not arguments about mere opinion. They were arguments about the nature of truth itself, something that struck at the very core of what it means to be a human being in the world. They were hardly irrelevant and never considered a matter of simple conjecture. This argument about what constituted the faith could be said to be the philosophical crux of the Reformation era controversies.

We could also consider the social aspect of the question, "Why fight over religion?" To overturn the accepted religious arrangement in Europe was no mere theological endeavor; it was a socio-political one as well. This becomes clear when we recognize that the men of the sixteenth century, as countless generations before them, did not view religion as a private thing. If faith was a form of truth, then it had its rightful place at the table of civilization beside politics, culture, and economics. In fact, if it claimed to be the highest truth, then faith must be a kind of ordering principle to all the affairs of men's lives, whether personal or social. The concepts of religion as a private affair or "separation of church and state" were entirely foreign to premodern men.

Rather, religion was integrated into public life. Catholic canon law stood shoulder to shoulder with civil law. Political rulers were expected to assent to the principles of Christian living personally (even if they observed them often in the breach) and govern in accord with them publicly. The Church, with her universities, hospitals, poor houses, and countless parishes and monasteries, was a vibrant and socially significant institution whose impact on society was profound. Economic laws, cultural norms, and even international relations were all in some way under the aegis of Christian polity. The pope was not a mere religious icon but a ruler of immense power who spoke in paternal terms to the kings and queens of Christendom.

In other words, Christian civil society was the creation of the Catholic Church. If we ask why the Reformation period was so full of evils, it is because in Christendom the religious Reformation also meant social revolution; it could never be about merely changing men's opinions, but was rather about upending an entire way of living. Sometimes this truth was clearest in the most extreme examples. For example, in 1534 the revolutionary Dutch "prophets" Jan Bockelson and Jan Matthys seized control of the German city of Münster with a band of fanatical followers. Bockelson and Matthys were Anabaptists, members of a fringe Protestant sect that rejected infant baptism. Like Thomas Müntzer, the Münster Anabaptists were filled with fiery apocalypticism and anticipated the imminent return of Christ. Once in charge of Münster, Bockelson and Matthys expelled all Catholics and inaugurated a system that can best be described as communism, which included the redistribution of wealth and the sharing of all property. Polygamy was adopted, and Bockelson took sixteen wives. All who had been baptized as children were forced to undergo rebaptism on pain of death. After six months, a Catholic army succeeded in retaking the city and killing the leaders of the rebellion. Matthys was fortunate enough to die in battle. Bockleson was taken alive and tortured with red-hot tongs before having his tongue pulled out and a burning dagger thrust into his heart. His body was hung to rot inside a cage suspended from the steeple of the city's cathedral. The gruesome death of Bockleson is not so much an example of cruel, premodern capital punishment as much as a testimony of the deep, visceral hostility people felt to such revolutionary notions.

The revolutionary aspects of Protestantism are easy to see when considering characters such as Jan Bockelson or Thomas Müntzer, but even the teachings of Luther and Calvin implied social revolution. Luther's teaching on the secularization of Church property meant in practice the forcible expropriation and transfer of millions of acres of property from the Catholic Church to the petty princes of the Holy Roman Empire. The tirades of Calvin and Knox against episcopacy meant the abolition of a very ancient form of local government that in many cases predated the secular government. For example, the bishops of Fulda in Germany had been governing the Church there since the eighth century, when many Germans were still practicing human sacrifice and worshiping Thor. The wholesale overthrow of episcopal government in Scotland and other regions influenced by Calvinism signified not just a change in religious opinion but the destruction of a social institution that had been the backbone of Christian culture for a thousand years. The same can be said of Henry VIII's dissolution of the monasteries in England, an event that some consider the largest land grab in history.

To the original question of why religion was such a matter for conflict at the time, we see that it was never merely a religious question. It was a social question. The modern may scoff and say, "Perfect example of why religion should only be a private matter." To be sure, the intertwining of religion and culture had certain drawbacks, but so has the subsequent vacuuming of religion out of the public sphere. Is society better with a public institution that points men toward truth, or is this matter too personal to be the subject of public policy? Christian tradition has unanimously affirmed the former—that *everybody* is obligated to give worship to God, not only individuals, but also societies, organizations, and even governments.

Needless to say, the forcible dissolution of Christendom in the tempests of the sixteenth century has left a lot of ill feeling on both sides. Things like the St. Bartholomew's Day Massacre or the systematic hunting down and execution of priests in Elizabethan England are not easily forgotten. Mutual antagonism characterized the Catholic and Protestant divide in the centuries following the Reformation. Europe fought one more conflict, the bitter Thirty Years War (1618–1648), to try to settle the religious balance of the continent, but by the end, the war was purely political and had lost any real semblance of religious motive, if it even existed to begin with.

Religious violence was largely extinct in Europe by 1700, though Catholics remained legally oppressed in the dominions of England, where they suffered legal and social discrimination into the nineteenth century. This was true in the North American colonies as well, where anti-Catholic laws were ubiquitous in the colonies; the first fighting among Europeans in the future United States was the 1655 Battle of the Severn near modern day Annapolis, Maryland, where Puritan and Catholic militias fought for control of the Maryland colony. Catholics did not win the universal right to vote in the United States until 1790, and the right to hold public office in some states came even later. In the 1928 presidential election, Catholic presidential candidate Al Smith was vilified for his religion, with Protestant detractors dusting off the old Elizabethan era accusation that a Catholic's loyalty to the pope was a hindrance to patriotism and made him implicitly suspect of treason.

By the twentieth century, however, the nature of the Protestant-Catholic divide would be fundamentally altered in the face of growing religious skepticism. As educated westerners increasingly rejected the concept of revealed religion in favor of atheistic philosophies, Protestants and Catholics continually found themselves on the same side of a global battle, not about the content of faith, but between religious faith and total unbelief. Protestants and Catholics suffered together under the Nazi regime in Germany as well as the various Communist dictatorships established across Europe throughout the century.

This common battle of Catholics and Protestants understandably led some to conclude that the differences separating the two were not as important as once thought. The early 1900s saw the rise of the "ecumenical movement," which sought to unify the various sects of Christianity based on the things held in common by all. This led to interdenominational worship, ecumenical prayer meetings, and more spirited cooperation between Catholics and Protestants on social and charitable works.

The popes were rightfully wary of the excesses of such endeavors, seeing in them the seeds of religious indifferentism, the idea that it did not fundamentally matter what religion one professed. Pope St. Pius X in 1910 warned French Catholics against participating in interdenominational charitable organizations whose work was based on the premise that religious differences were superficial. A more severe rebuke came in 1928 with Pope Pius XI's encyclical *Mortalium Animos*, which reaffirmed the traditional Catholic position that Catholics may not worship or pray in common with Protestants and prohibited Catholics from participating in pan-Christian ecumenical movements. Pius wrote, "It is clear why this Apostolic See has never allowed its subjects to take part in the assemblies of non-Catholics: for the union of Christians can only be promoted by promoting the return to the one true Church of Christ of those who are separated from it, for in the past they have unhappily left it."[22] If the Catholic Church holds the true faith, then there can be no basis of reunion other than a full and formal return to the Church in union with the successor

---

[22]   Pius XI, *Mortalium Animos*, 10 (1928).

of St. Peter. Thus was the teaching of *Mortalium Animos*, a document that has never been revoked.

The Catholic's first commitment should be to the truth, and insofar as ecumenical activity relativizes the truth or promotes religious indifferentism, he is right to shun it. But the fathers of the Second Vatican Council (1962–1965) realized that it was possible to construct a more unified Christian witness in the world without necessarily adopting an attitude of religious indifference. While not denying the admonitions of St. Pius X and Pius XI, the contemporary posture of the Church is that Catholics and Protestants can come together in areas in which we agree while continuing a charitable dialogue on matters that divide us. To be sure, the ever-present push for "dialogue" can, at times, become an idol by making dialogue the end instead of the means, but this should not cause Catholics to refuse to engage Protestants in charity. Thus, the contemporary position of the Church does not deny the fact that real and substantial divisions exist between Catholics and Protestants; rather, it seeks to build bonds between them by focusing on places where bridges already exist.

That is why the Second Vatican Council advocated dropping the term "heretic" in reference to Protestants, opting instead to call them "Separated Brethren." Some, confused by this change, have assumed the Church no longer believes Protestantism is heresy. This is untrue; the errant doctrines of Protestantism remain heretical in the formal sense, but the heresies themselves are distinct from those who profess them. A key aspect of heresy is "obstinacy"—that is, the heretic cannot be sincerely mistaken or merely ignorant, he must be intentionally persevering in his errors despite admonishments to the contrary from authoritative sources. While no one can judge the level of obstinacy in any particular Protestant, the Second Vatican Council recognized that contemporary individuals born into Protestant communities that are now going on five centuries old cannot be subjectively culpable of the same degree of obstinacy that characterized the revolts of Luther, Knox, and others.

One thing remains for consideration: how to view the Reformation today, five hundred years later, from the vantage point of modernity. Here the line is much clearer. For a Catholic who believes God's will is the formal unity of all Christians around the successor of St. Peter, it is difficult to see the events of the sixteenth century as anything but a catastrophe. If Christ really taught that the Church should be one (see Jn 17:21), then we cannot be indifferent to the sundering of that unity. It was a tragedy, a tragedy the consequences of which we still live with to this day.

Of course, this is not to say we must become hyperpartisan and affirm everything Catholics did during the Reformation, much less assert that true reform was not needed. We certainly need feel no compunction to defend the Duke of Guise, nor agree that the hanging of Calvinist placards should merit burning at the stake, as King Francis I decreed. Still less must we defend pre-Lutheran Catholicism as the apogee of Christianity. Many of the best Catholics of the age were in fundamental agreement that the Church was crying for reform. The Council of Trent was summoned not only to counter the claims of the Protestants but also to implement the disciplinary reforms that the holiest men agreed were long overdue.

Ultimately, the Catholic Church is an extended family, the family of God, as the Second Vatican Council taught. Like any family, it has its advantages and drawbacks. Like any family, or even like any individual, the good and the evil are often mixed together. The wheat and the tares grow in the same field. We cannot be afraid of our own family history; we ought to take pride in the accomplishments of our family—and we are right to regret the departure from and pray for the return of our separated brethren to the bosom of Holy Mother Church.

Sources and Suggestions
for Further Reading

Anderson, Robert. *Saint Pius V*. Charlotte: TAN Books, 2009.

Brecht, Martin. *Martin Luther*. Translated by James L. Schaaf. Philadelphia: Fortress Press, 1985–93.

Belloc, Hilaire. *Characters of the Reformation*. San Francisco: Ignatius Press, 2017.

———. *How the Reformation Happened*. Charlotte: TAN Books, 2009.

Campbell, Phillip. *The Rending of Christendom Sourcebook*. Howell, MI: Cruachan Hill Press, 2015.

Chesterton, G. K. *Lepanto*. Edited by Dale Ahlquist. San Francisco: Ignatius Press, 2004.

Cobbett, William. *A History of the Protestant Reformation in England and Ireland*. Charlotte: TAN Books, 2009.

Fraser, Antonia. *Mary Queen of Scots*. New York: Delacorte Press, 1970.

Frieda, Leonie. *Catherine de Medici: Renaissance Queen of France*. New York: Harper Perennial, 2006.

Genelli, Christoph. *Life of St. Ignatius of Loyola*. Rockford, IL: TAN Books and Publishers, 1988.

Hope, Anne. *Life of St. Philip Neri, Apostle of Rome*. Post Falls, ID: Mediatrix Press, 2015.

McHugh, John, and Charles Callan, trans. *Catechism of the Council of Trent*. Rockford, IL: TAN Books and Publishers, 1982.

McNabb, Vincent. *St. John Fisher*. Post Falls, ID: Mediatrix Press, 2015.

Rao, John C. *Luther and His Progeny*. Kettering, OH: Angelico Press, 2017.

Reanny, Walter. *A Champion of the Church: The Life of St. Peter Canisius*. Post Falls, ID: Mediatrix Press, 2015.

Reynolds, E. E. *St. John Fisher: Reformer, Humanist, Martyr*. Post Falls, ID: Mediatrix Press, 2015.

Spaeth, Adolph, L.D. Reed, Henry Eyster Jacobs, et al., eds. and trans. *The Works of Martin Luther*. Philadelphia: A. J. Holman Company, 1915.

Wace, Henry, and C. A. Buchheim. *First Principles of the Reformation*. London: John Murray, 1883.

Waugh, Evelyn. *Edmund Campion: A Life*. San Francisco: Ignatius Press, 2012.

Online Sources Consulted

In addition to those sources cited in the notes, every modern writer is greatly aided in his work through the various outstanding online repositories of public domain, primary source material. I would like to acknowledge specifically the Internet Medieval History Sourcebook (https://sourcebooks. fordham.edu/sbook.asp) for making publicly available certain of Luther's writings as well as some papal documents and correspondence. Papalencyclicals.net is also an outstanding resource for researchers. Of course, any Catholic writer today benefits from the website www.newadvent. org, the host of which, Kevin Knight, has for many years maintained online the invaluable 1913 edition of *The Catholic Encyclopedia*. Special thanks also to EWTN, the global Catholic network, for making *Campion's Brag* readily available, as well as the Liberty Fund's Online Library of Liberty for Erasmus's *Manual of a Christian Knight*.

TAN·BOOKS

TAN Books is the Publisher You Can Trust With Your Faith.

TAN Books was founded in 1967 to preserve the spiritual, intellectual, and liturgical traditions of the Catholic Church. At a critical moment in history TAN kept alive the great classics of the Faith and drew many to the Church. In 2008 TAN was acquired by Saint Benedict Press. Today TAN continues to teach and defend the Faith to a new generation of readers.

TAN publishes more than 600 booklets, Bibles, and books. Popular subject areas include theology and doctrine, prayer and the supernatural, history, biography, and the lives of the saints. TAN's line of educational and homeschooling resources is featured at TANHomeschool.com.

TAN publishes under several imprints, including TAN, Neumann Press, ACS Books, and the Confraternity of the Precious Blood. Sister imprints include Saint Benedict Press, Catholic Courses, and Catholic Scripture Study.

For more information about TAN,
or to request a free catalog, visit
TANBooks.com

Or call us toll-free at
(800) 437-5876